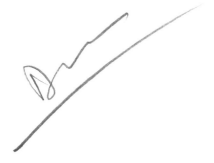

Mind Rules

Mind Rules

Who's in Control - You or Your Mind?

DAVID ZIERK, PSYD

Copyright © 2023 David Zierk, PsyD.

All rights reserved. No part of this book may be used or reproduced by any means, graphic, electronic, or mechanical, including photocopying, recording, taping or by any information storage retrieval system without the written permission of the author except in the case of brief quotations embodied in critical articles and reviews.

Archway Publishing books may be ordered through booksellers or by contacting:

Archway Publishing
1663 Liberty Drive
Bloomington, IN 47403
www.archwaypublishing.com
844-669-3957

Because of the dynamic nature of the Internet, any web addresses or links contained in this book may have changed since publication and may no longer be valid. The views expressed in this work are solely those of the author and do not necessarily reflect the views of the publisher, and the publisher hereby disclaims any responsibility for them.

Any people depicted in stock imagery provided by Getty Images are models, and such images are being used for illustrative purposes only. Certain stock imagery © Getty Images.

ISBN: 978-1-6657-4441-6 (sc)
ISBN: 978-1-6657-4442-3 (hc)
ISBN: 978-1-6657-4440-9 (e)

Library of Congress Control Number: 2023909574

Print information available on the last page.

Archway Publishing rev. date: 08/25/2023

CONTENTS

Acknowledgement vii
Preface xi
Introducing Mind Rules xiii

Chapter 1   The Mind Is Not Relational............................. 1
Chapter 2   The Mind Is Self-Serving 9
Chapter 3   Avoidance Is the Mind's Natural Reflex 17
Chapter 4   The Mind Only Remembers What It Can't Forget 24
Chapter 5   The Mind Can't Forget What It Doesn't Want to Remember 31
Chapter 6   The Mind Is Designed to Resolve Uncertainty 38
Chapter 7   The Mind's Favorite Number Is One........................ 46
Chapter 8   Once the Mind Makes Up Its Mind, It Believes Itself to Be Correct.. 55
Chapter 9   The Mind Doesn't Know When It Might Be Wrong... 64
Chapter 10 The Mind Organizes and Prioritizes What It Knows to Be True 68
Chapter 11 The Mind Is Time Blind.. 75
Chapter 12 The Mind Expands by Learning 82
Chapter 13 The Mind Is a Pattern Detector 88
Chapter 14 The Mind Is Hypersensitive and Struggles with Empathy 96
Chapter 15 The Mind's Favorite Color Is Black 104
Chapter 16 The Mind Self-Regulates 113
Chapter 17 The Mind Is Directly Connected to the Past............ 120

Chapter 18   The Mind Is Designed to Reduce Pain 126
Chapter 19   Under Times of Duress, the Mind Imagines the
             Worst.. 133
Chapter 20   The Mind Has a Blind Spot...................................... 139
Chapter 21   The Mind Struggles with an Attention Deficit
             Disorder 146
Chapter 22   The Mind Prefers Repetition 152
Chapter 23   The Mind Believes It's Constantly Being Judged...... 159
Chapter 24   The Mind Resolves Conflict by Repeating the Past 167
Chapter 25   The Mind Is Often Approximately Correct and
             Absolutely Wrong.. 176
Chapter 26   The Mind Has a Low Pain Threshold.......................182
Chapter 27   The Mind Never Lies, but It Doesn't Always
             Tell the Truth.. 195
Chapter 28   The Mind Struggles with Facial Recognition........... 203
Chapter 29   The Last Thing on the Mind Is to Be Vulnerable......211
Chapter 30   Becoming a Mastermind 224

Epilogue 259

ACKNOWLEDGEMENT

The idea of writing a book is ubiquitous. If asked to dig deep, everyone has something worth saying. Taking the next step and putting thoughts on paper, however, is a uniquely formidable, intensely personal and, let me add, well worth pursuing if you are inclined to be humbled, amazed, and interested in having an only-know-it-when-you-feel-it emotion. By writing a book, you will learn much about yourself, your values, your perspective of the world, your relationship to commitment, the gray area between reason and emotion, and, most important, you will discover something amazing - your voice.

At least, these thoughts reflect my journey into the world of becoming an author.

The process of writing a book is straightforward. Sit down, adjust your seat, scratch your head as you contemplate your subject matter, put pen to paper, and let your thoughts fly. Simple enough, but the method behind having something worthy to say and the confidence to say it is another matter. This is where having a supportive cast and an enduring fan base become essential to reaching the finish line.

For this author, without having key people in place, insecurities too often would push, elbow, and bully into the mental ether and disrupt the writing process.

Infected by intermittent bouts of intense self-doubt and misplaced vision, it was the steadfast encouragement and unshaken belief in my capacities from my wife, Carol, who reminded me of the option to succeed. The quality of having this exceptional person by my side who never doubts my ability and always glorifies my gifts gives rise to a level of self-assurance never previously imagined. She's the one person, the only one, who gives me the feedback I need to hear but not always prepared to receive. Thank you for making me a better version of myself. Thank you for over three decades of support, kindness, commitment, and, most important, having the will and perseverance to get to know me better than I know myself. You are the amazing gift in my life that makes life worth living.

If Carol is the wind in my sail, then Dave Herrera is unquestionably the rudder who shaped and directed the compositional structure and integrity of Mind Rules. After I wrote the first draft, Dave came into my life, serendipitously, by way of another person, Mike Mitchell, whose strength of character, directness with truth, and creative intensity always impressed me. When I met Dave, our comfortable connectedness was pure and effortlessly inspirational. Not only did Dave energize my determination and shake my imagination, but he, quite literally, showed me, kindly and gracefully, always patiently, how to write. He may not have told me what to write, but Dave is directly responsible for the pieces of the Mind Rules puzzle fitting together so seamlessly. He is an elite wordsmith and amazingly crafty at putting words together in ways that left this author breathless and regularly thinking "How does he know so well how to say what my words are trying so hard to reveal." In a word, Dave is a magician with his pen. Crossing paths and getting to know him has been a magical gift that was given to me for which I will always treasure and never forget.

Andrew Fields, thank you for constantly humoring my spontaneity and being the resolute sounding board to my ideas that ranged from off-the-wall to insanely useful. The common sense and creative twists you brought to my thinking taught me to polish and sharpen my ideas before introducing them to the world. Also, thank you for your constant encouragement to take my concepts to the next level.

Finally, my children, all four of them, deserve acknowledgement for reminding me that I'm worthy of being looked up to and respected for being myself, just myself, not what I do or fail to do. Especially to

Michelle, thank you for your creative gift that made Mind Rules visually pop. For me, having children shuffled the existential deck. Upon their arrival, my youthful sense of endlessness and purposefulness transferred to their souls. They have all proven worthy of my choice to make them more important than life itself.

PREFACE

> There are three things human beings are afraid of:
> death, other people, and their own minds.
> —R.D. Laing

Brace yourself. The things we're about to say about the mind may, well, blow your mind. For starters, did you know that your mind is not relational? That's right. It hates vulnerability. It can't tell time. It has a low pain threshold. It has ADHD with a weird nostalgia for the past. In fact, it often won't let go of the past no matter how much you want it to. What's more, paradoxically, your mind only remembers what it can't forget. In the same token, it can't forget what it doesn't want to remember—especially when things go off course. Your mind also specializes in being approximately correct and absolutely wrong.

The mind is constantly formulating thoughts and processing emotions. It's as powerful as it is vulnerable, as amazing as it is befuddling. And while it constantly craves and seeks knowledge, it brashly refuses to be fully known. It fiercely adheres to truth, while also filtering out the things that are unlikely, unpleasant, or even uproarious, and then synthesizing what's preferred and possible, in that order.

The mind, as they say, indeed has a mind of its own; a frightening notion if you think about it. R.D. Laing, the famously contrarian Scottish psychiatrist who wrote extensively about mental illness, once mused that human beings have good reason to be afraid of their own mind, and he was absolutely right. Thing is, though, your mind doesn't have to rule you. You can take control and learn to master your mind.

How, exactly? Ah, yes, glad you asked.

Allow us to introduce you to *mind rules*, a set of notions and tenets about the mind—more specifically, your mind—that can help you make sense of the complicated engine that drives your being and defines your essence. As *Mind Rules* examines the enigma that is the mind, an exploration that endeavors to both enlighten and equip you to tackle the complexities of life, you'll find answers to an array of intriguing questions.

When somebody asks you what's on your mind, for instance, does your answer reflect your truth, your deepest truth, the one that matters most? Or, like a stone skipping across a pond, does your reply more often reveal what's on the surface, limited to thoughts most easily accessed and openly shared? If so, is your mind forever vulnerable to deflection and self-deception? Do all minds operate the same? Is mind control something that can be learned? What's going on when your mind goes one direction and your partner's mind goes another? Does your mind predetermine your fate, or simply predispose you to move toward certain possibilities?

How about these questions?

Is the mind made of matter? Is the body a prisoner of the mind? Does the body sway the mind one way or the other? How do the mind and body interact? Do they communicate down a one-way or two-way street? What happens when the mind and the body disagree? Perhaps most intriguing, can a mind understand itself, completely or even adequately? In essence, the question comes down to who's in control, you, or your mind?

Mind Rules takes a deep dive into all these explicable inquiries. To put it most simply, *Mind Rules* is like a cheat code to the mind games we all play. The truth about the mind is tricky, though. As you learn the rules, you'll quickly discover that it takes practice to see beyond your blind spots, increase your pain threshold, manage your ADHD, and get out of your mind so you can move in the direction of becoming the person you were always meant to be.

INTRODUCING MIND RULES

Great Minds Think Alike

Learn the rules like a pro, so you can break them like an artist.
—Pablo Picasso

Imagine a world without rules. Consider the chaos this would create. When planes aren't colliding in midair, they would take off and land at will. Driving a car would be like entering a demolition derby. Schools would be a symphony of ear-shattering noise with students indulging in an unending surge of impulsive inclinations. Not to mention everyday acts like crossing the street, riding a bike, and going into a bank would involve taking your life in your hands. Summing up and moving on, a world without rules would lead to mayhem.

By contrast, then, a world with rules decreases the madness and prevents you from plunging into chaos. Rules maintain order, guide your choices, and keep you safe and out of harm's way. Rules help define purpose, provide structure and boundaries, and offer direction. Think of the simple game of tic-tac-toe. The rules dictate where the players add their Xs and Os and where they must be placed consecutively within the boxes to win. Because the rules are explicit and unambiguous, they provide an even playing field for all participants, which remains true even when games become decidedly more complex and not readily solvable. In this way, rules ensure fairness and promote purposeful action. They keep people on track and in line and moving in the direction of anticipated success and, yes, toward mutual benefit. Even more, particularly relevant to the endeavor of this book, what applies to the outside world likewise applies to your inner world, your private domain and most precious reality—your mind.

What Are Mind Rules?

The mind operates on a set of unspoken yet extremely persuasive rules. Understanding how these *mind rules* operate provides you a remarkable advantage for improving your present state of being, navigating the world around you, creating a sustainable perspective, and becoming the person you've always wanted to be. Equipped with a better understanding as to how your mind is designed allows you to be more in control of your mind, as opposed to your mind controlling you.

Knowing how the mind works helps you examine how you think, feel, and perceive and even imagine yourself in the world. And that awareness gives you greater control over how you choose to live. Interestingly, when the mind persistently acts on its own and without your direct input, your personal growth stalls and you feel stuck. Suspended between the life that's gathered around you across time and circumstance and your preferred world, the one you dream about and hunger for, the sense of not being able to move forward with focused intent becomes unsustainable.

Innately, your mind is designed to keep you safe and out of harm's way—an essential process that happens rapidly, continuously, and largely unnoticed. This drive is based on two impulses, self-preservation and self-concern, which is a good thing. However, the mind's preference for safety and serenity can prevent you from living life to its fullest. Consequently, seeking uncertainty and discomfort requires intentionality and deliberate action, and taking such risks can often be rewarded with the satisfaction of the empowerment of being your best self regardless of the outcome.

Think of mind rules as a type of playbook that is built into your brain. Becoming increasingly familiar with its contents greatly improves the odds of you moving forward in the direction of becoming the person you were always meant to be. When studied and comprehended, this playbook becomes the advantage you've been seeking.

But there's a catch.

While the playbook teaches you how the mind works, you will need to discern which mind rules are most applicable to your life situation and desired future. In addition, you are responsible for keeping such mind rules in mind and implementing pertinent life skills until they become so well practiced you can forget about them because they've been deeply wired into the infrastructure of your mind's way of operating.

Based on your genetics and lived experiences, a constellation of traits, temperaments, aptitudes, abilities, interests, and quirks have been collected and synthesized. While substantially relevant to knowing your place in this world, this collection of inherited material (eye color, straight or curly hair, skin color, height, body type) and learned knowledge (the sky is blue, a watched pot never boils, blonds have more fun, and doughnuts are yummy) does not go anywhere without instruction and leadership.

Mind rules form the crucial blueprint from which plays are called. Without knowing it, these mind rules affect, impact, influence, control, and hold power over your inside world. Your thoughts, emotions, beliefs, perceptions, and desires are impacted by what your mind does behind the scenes. By becoming knowledgeable about mind rules, you become a purposeful survivor of your life's journey, one instilled with a spirit of appreciating and admiring what's possible not just around you but, more evocatively, what's meant to come out of you, from you, through you, by you and only you. You gain greater influence over the chances you take and the choices you make. You become an active agent of your personal growth and ascendancy.

Mind: A Brief and Biased History

Before implementing these mind rules, you must first gain a surface-level understanding of how the mind works. This basic knowledge is essentially like a compass that provides direction. Delving deeper with mind rules, you'll obtain discernment, which serves more like a GPS to guide you safely and confidently as you navigate the internal and external worlds that compete for power and persuasion.

Although each journey is different for every individual, the tenets are essentially the same. While we all have a great deal in common as human beings, your temperaments and life experiences make you distinctive and uniquely shape how you view yourself, make sense of the world, and elect to interact with other people, and they affect whether you step toward or away from opportunities that challenge the present version of selfhood that you esteem, protect, and promote.

When scholars are asked about the mind, they generally agree on the characteristics but rarely define it in the same way. Viewed as an inner, subjective state of consciousness, the mind governs our awareness of internal and external circumstances; it shapes our thoughts, feelings, and understanding of how the outside world works and synthesizes our internal experience with our perception of the external world.

The notion of the *mind* was long believed to be unknowable and even untouchable by mortal men, as it was historically considered to be a product of the divine. Then, this mysterious and intimidating doctrine began to be intellectually disentangled by the advent of philosophical investigation and the introduction of modern neuropsychiatry.

In the seventeenth century, when renowned philosopher Rene Descartes (*Day-CART*) stated, "I think therefore I am"—perhaps the most celebrated declaration in the history of philosophy—he summarily and convincingly separated the mind from the physical body. The Cartesian mind was a self-enclosed mental apparatus containing world experiences yet radically separated from its surroundings. The esteemed Cartesian split set the stage for society to accept the notion that it was proper for scientific inquiry to explore the body separately from the mind. In doing so, he opened the doors to modern biological medicine.

Fast-forward a few hundred years. Perhaps you've heard the phrase "ghost in the machine." This expression was conceived by Gilbert Ryle in his compelling 1949 book, *The Concept of the Mind*. Ryle postulated that Descartes's distinction between the mind and body was a "category mistake," meaning that it was absurd to believe that mental and physical activity were separate from each other and that the mind is not physical. According to Ryle's philosophical thinking, mental and physical activity are interdependent and occur simultaneously but separately. Following Ryle's line of thinking, the mind—the ghost—is really just an intelligent behavior of the body. That is, instead of the mind being conceived as nonphysical, as Cartesian dualism led the world to believe for centuries, the mind should be viewed as the form or organizing principle of the body.

In the modern era, the esteemed neuroscientist Antonio Damasio offered an illuminating opinion that further spliced the mind and body back together. In his remarkable 1994 book, *Descartes' Error*, Damasio described how the mind and its operation are contingent upon its interactions with social and cultural factors. He also formulated the "somatic marker hypothesis" that promoted the idea that emotions that originate in the body (*soma* is Greek for the word *body*) guide behavior. Even further, Damasio's groundbreaking work holds that emotions play a central role in human's highest order reasoning—what we do in social situations and how an array of decision-making gets executed.

Furthering our contemporary understanding of the mind, Canadian American experimental psychologist Steven Pinker makes the central point that "the mind is what the brain does," in his best-selling book from 1997, *How the Mind Works*. This means that the mind, engineered by evolution, is the activity of the brain and that our mental life is a computational reflection of how information is processed and meaning is established. Brilliant idea from a brilliant mind.

Offering a more detailed and functional perspective, top-selling author Dan Siegel—a wildly popular speaker in the field of attachment psychology and clinical professor of psychiatry at the UCLA School of Medicine—defines the mind as "an embodied and relational process that regulates the flow of energy and information." This is a powerful and dynamic definition, as it spotlights the mind as a self-organizing process that emerges within the self and between the self and others in patterns of communication and connections. In one fell swoop of definitional wisdom, Dr. Siegel cleverly and empirically joins together the brain, relationships, and mind to help explain the human experience.

Sounds heavy. When whittled down, Dr. Siegel's dazzling research and resplendence of interdisciplinary dialogue informs us that being human involves the mind processing two things, just two things, energy and information flow, and doing so stunningly within the body and across the interactive and bewildering space that separates self from others.

Yet another way of pondering the answer to the age-old question "What is the mind?" is to understand its function by way of an acronym. When the word is broken down by its letters, M-I-N-D, it can be conceptualized as a Mutually Influencing Narrative Device. Like yin and yang, for every up, there's a down; for every left, there's a right; and for every dark cloud, there's a silver lining, or at least it's hoped. Similarly, how you define reality, how you view yourself and deal with different situations, is a choice, a flip of a coin, but it requires a willingness and capacity to shift your mind.

While the mind can hold two opposing ideas, due to its inherent dislike of complexities and uncertainties, it rapidly decides what's best based on what it knows to be true and exerts influence as to what to do next. In this way, because your mind tends to operate as a weighted coin, you are likely to repeat what's happened to you in the past. To make things fairer, to distance yourself from your past and to break away from your cherished habits and old legacies depends on whether your mind is influencing you or, like finding the right key to the lock, if you have learned how to influence your mind. Remember, a fair coin has two sides.

As a cursory summary, the mind is more than an inspired

metaphor, and it works at a conscious and unconscious level. On the one hand, the mind consists of experiences learned explicitly, clearly and in detail, leaving no room for confusion and doubt. You will always remember your ABCs and that one plus one equals two. Referencing the other hand, the mind also learns implicitly or silently, behind the scenes, when what you learned emerged from moments when you didn't know you were being taught. Influenced by the rhythmic inducement of yin and yang, the mind is mutually persuasive in instructing you what to do and what not to do. Some minds, for example, see a snake and rapidly think, *Run—now, fast!* while other minds say, *Cool. Let me pick it up and see how it behaves.* Do you see the mutually influencing nature of the mind? One snake, two different mindsets.

By resplendent design, the mind is amazing. When you get to know how your mind operates, well, that's just spectacular!

Putting Pieces Together

Fundamentally, your mind is an entangled composite of nature and nurture. An examination of the entanglement of these two competing forces essentially weighs the hand that you were dealt (nature, what you inherited by genetic serendipity) against the luck you've had along the way (nurture, what you learned and didn't learn from what happened and didn't happen to you).

Nature is composed and controlled by genetics, reflexes, instincts, hormones—not to mention an incredibly complex and highly interconnected bundle of billions of neural pathways in your nervous system, all of which take only milliseconds to activate and connect prodigiously and spectacularly. Together, this brilliant interplay of human biology functions as an internal message and self-regulating system that becomes highly active during different states of arousal. There's even a large-scale network of interacting brain regions, referred to as the default mode network, that gets quiet when you're actively engaged in an attention-demanding task and, here's the kicker, whose activity increases when you're not focused on the outside world and your attention turns toward such mind wandering activities as daydreaming, summoning back memories, and imagining what might happen in the future.

Quite luckily, during stressful times, your internal message system works on its own and without input from your conscious brain. The essential purpose of this private message system is to restore and maintain homeostasis, a fancy word for physiological stability and feeling balanced.

Nurture, meanwhile, is a term that describes the notion of how the mind is composed of and guided by learned behaviors. Your learning is a mishmash of facts and fears acquired throughout your upbringing and relationship history. Your sense of self is filtered through a lens made up of the richness and restrictiveness of your relationship experiences. It also reflects the availability of diverse experiences of personal development, the extent to which you've lived up to your potential, along with your experiences of fortune and misfortune, and the luck you've had along the way.

Of course, some of us were luckier than others. For some, our luck happened early in life. The earliest memories of those folks involve feeling safe and supported. They were raised in an environment that was generally healthy and attentive. As babies, they were probably held and touched, their cries were heard, and their needs were met. As a busy toddler learning about the world, their stumbles and frustrations were responded to with patience and caring. When they fell, someone was there to pick them up. When they cried, someone kept them. When they did something amazing, someone celebrated alongside them.

For others, luck happened a little later. In their early school years, for instance, someone showed great interest and nurtured their growth, promoted their efforts, and taught them the power of contributing. Perhaps they felt valued and validated during the ups and downs of adolescence, when they were given the opportunity for more independence while still having a valuable safety net to catch them when they fell.

For each of the folks described above, their early relationships likely taught them that other people will understand them, that their needs matter, and that it is safe to rely on others to meet their needs.

Another group of people may have encountered luck outside of relationships. They were gifted with natural talent and opportunities for performance that were met with unconditional admiration and inspiring applause. It was as if, at times, people couldn't get enough of them.

On the positive side, if the spotlight continues to shine on them, they feel uplifted or larger than life. However, when the spotlight fades, as it inevitably does, so does their capacity to remain self-assured, optimistic, and hopeful. In these cases, it's as though their sense of self is directly connected to the admiration, recognition, and accolades of others.

For those with substantially less obvious luck—those raised in a family filled with broken promises, inconsistent nurturing, physical or emotional abuse, or being given everything except what was needed—their luck comes in the form of resilience.

These folks have learned how to bounce back. In the face of emotional dishonesty, they've developed self-sufficiency. They've learned how to stay focused amidst mounting fears and turn away from dissenters. They've been able to outpace self-destructive patterns and beat the odds by facing reality, pushing past barriers, finding direction and drive, and learning how to discern life lessons that encourage success.

Being confronted with an absence of nurturing and unrealistic expectations, they've learned to somehow trust themselves and invest deeply in their future. Amidst a backdrop of impoverished parenting and limited resources, they've persevered and risen above their circumstances, proving everyone wrong and showing them that they do matter.

There are others, still, who haven't quite thrived amidst the noise, fear, and chaos of their upbringing. Perhaps they've been burdened with addiction potential and were never taught how to manage the disappointments, discouragements, and distress of everyday life. For those folks who've never received enough of what they needed, wanted, desired, and deserved, their survival skills allowed them to push through it all, but just barely.

Regardless of the life that was given to you and the luck you've had along the way, coming to understand how mind rules operate provides you a remarkable advantage for improving your present state of being and becoming the person you've always wanted to be. Equipped with a better understanding as to how your mind is designed, you can begin the journey of mastering your mind by learning how to control your mind as opposed to allowing your mind to control you.

Moving Forward

This book has two lofty ambitions. First, we intend to help you better understand how *the mind* works. Knowing the basic operating principles of the mind is essential for guiding you safely and confidently through your life travels. In this way, *Mind Rules* provides a mental road map for better understanding one of our greatest mysteries—the mind.

The second aim of this book is for you to appreciate how *your mind* is prone or prefers to operate. While we all have a great deal in common as human beings, the alchemy of your temperaments, life experiences, and personality make you distinctive and uniquely shape the psychology of your self-direction—how you view yourself, how you make sense of your world, and how you elect to interact with other people and handle those tricky moments when life doesn't go according to plan.

When you come to understand the workings of your mind, it's a bit like learning how to read and trust a compass. While you're still likely to experience moments that are persistently pesky and have feelings of being unsteady and a bit lost, by knowing how to operate the compass associated with learning mind rules, you'll increase the odds of finding a way forward that aligns with your preferences, values, and desired life goals. Together, this road map and compass can dramatically help you negotiate and enjoy this great adventure called life.

While each mind rule speaks to a specific feature as to how your mind operates, the best way to understand mind rules is that, in practice, they overlap and play off one another. Indeed, it is this playful movement between and among the various mind rules that best explains how your mind, the mysterious ascending ramp of your beingness, works.

One last consideration. To jumpstart your learning of mind rules, at the end of each chapter you will find a *mind rule life lesson*. These lessons consist of takeaway thoughts about the importance of each mind rule along with ways to challenge yourself and strategies to integrate each mind rule into your daily walk of life. As you read about mind rules, contemplate how some, more than others, shed light on how you navigate the turbulence of everyday life. The hope is that by identifying specific mind rules that speak to the secret of who you were always meant to be, you will have a mind-bending tour de force experience.

CHAPTER 1

The Mind Is Not Relational
The Mind Is Not Designed to Bring People Together

Imperceptible to the naked eye, hidden deep within the inner machinery of your essence, your mind hums with lonely persistence and tenacious spirit. It's you, it's only you, that your mind seeks to protect and impress. Across time, knitted together by chance and choice, and shaped by challenges and ordeals, your mind became a master of improvisation with a single vision—your security.

Your mind is driven by a dominant impulse to self-protect. With its clear and unmistakable focus on distancing you from adversity, the inner voice of your mind walks you away from relationships, not toward. At face value, this assertion may sound counterintuitive, even ridiculous. To explain, let's explore what happens in your mind when people come into your life.

If the world were whittled down to absolutes—all or nothing, good or bad, right or wrong—life would seem a whole bunch easier. If every predicament you encountered came down to just two choices, the decision-making process would be clear-cut and relatively stress-free, like picking between chocolate or vanilla ice cream, for instance.

But life, as you know, is more complicated than merely choosing between two flavors of frozen dessert. Instead of being presented with merely a pair of options, there are many variations from which to consider—strawberry, rocky road, buttered pecan, mint chocolate chip, banana nut fudge, cookies and cream—all made from blending together different ingredients.

In life, that sort of variety comes from your interactions. Without this relational dynamic, the mind simply sees everything in black and white and processes everything factually, as designed. The primary duty of the mind is to reduce noise to a minimum and keep you safe and sound. As the mind focuses on keeping you out of harm's way, it maximizes your chances of enjoying another tomorrow. But your job is to learn how to master your mind by making today better than yesterday so your tomorrows are better than ever.

A One-Track Mind

If you think about it, the fact that the mind is singularly focused on survival makes sense from an evolutionary perspective. Darwin's theory of natural selection informs us that life adapts to progress in response to prevailing conditions. In this way, the human mind evolved to maintain a faithful commitment to keeping us alive. Besides evolving into bigger and upright bodies, humans developed larger and staggeringly more complex brains.

By nature, the mind is inherently selfish. Consistent with Darwin's theory, reason dictates that the mind is forced to choose between keeping you from plunging headfirst into danger or moving you in the direction of happiness. To your mind, there is no choice at all. Your mind is hardwired to adapt rapidly, often eschewing reason and emotion, programmed by following the axiom that happiness is optional but survival is mandatory.

The mind's self-centered disposition of life at all costs is counterintuitive to the human desire for community and the exciting expectation of connection with others. Since the mind naturally focuses on survival, this directive for protecting life and limb at all costs makes relationships, by default, a lower priority. The mind is simply not relational; it doesn't care if you're happy or popular or the latest big thing. If the girl asks you to dance, your book gets picked up by a publisher, or even if you win the lottery, the mind isn't moved.

That's the job of your conscience, that inner feeling or voice that guides you toward facing the music, your sense of self that shows up when you learn how to get out of your mind.

Beyond the momentous pull of evolution, there's another reason the mind deprioritized relationships. Relationships are messy, unpredictable, and complex. To the mind, these descriptors are synonymous with hazardous. Because of this, the mind chooses to focus on more vital matters than social affairs. To the mind, as it responds instinctively and aims decisively toward self-preservation, matters of social interest—such as who likes you and who doesn't, where you fit in, and what makes you stand out—are trivial and distracting, chickens not worth counting, if you will.

All the same, relationships are vitally important to your quality of life. A person's basic sense of self is derived directly from the countless social experiences collected throughout their upbringing and relationship history. Your mother, your father, and the outside world shape you. You gather these formative experiences throughout your life's journey as you interact with meaningful others and compete against them, looking up to some people, while envying others.

Because the mind is attracted to things with childlike devotion that sustain life and avoids things that involve risk, the mind is not relational. Being relational involves taking a chance. If you let your mind guide you, it's likely you'll never learn how to dance. If you choose to learn how to dance, however, you're bound to have your toes stepped on now and again. The choice is yours; just don't let your mind know you may be taking over. The mind is cautious and, by design, guides you to be safe rather than sorry. Counting chickens before they hatch is not something that interests the mind. To the mind, relationships are a knotty problem with no clear upside.

The Ups and Downs of Relationships

For better or worse, across time and situation, you become a reflection of what your relationships have told you about yourself. When things are good and people are clearly on your side, as reflected by moments of comfort, support, and praise, your sense of self swells. Uplifted by positive feedback and assurance, you feel good about yourself. On the other hand, when things tilt and people seem to be against you, when you're rejected, excluded, or devalued, your personal stock drops. Being pulled down by unfriendly feedback degrades your self-worth, leaving you feeling downgraded and confused.

While relationships can build you up or tear you down, ultimately giving color and texture to your life, the mind would rather refrain from such matters until it is assured you are confidently and consistently safe. Without feeling safe, fear takes over, and anxiety causes the mind to become cluttered with intense emotions, unwanted thoughts, and disagreeable images, the ingredients of upheaval.

Often, feeling puzzled and afraid, such circumstances cause you to fall victim to miscalculating life situations. You make errors, get lost, and suffer lasting consequences. Without safety and security, life can become perplexing. Because of the blend of intense emotions and accumulated stress, you lose that vital balance that is needed to move forward, tackle challenges, and strive to reach the next level.

If the mind were relational, if it made connecting with others its top priority, humans would likely have perished as a species long ago. Instead of foraging for food, the mind would have directed humans toward fellowship and flirting. A relational mind would have persuaded humans to say yes to every social opportunity, distracting them from tilling the fields and harvesting the crops. "It was fun while it lasted," the last person on planet Earth would mutter as their relational mind became extinct.

If being relational was job one, humans would have little use for such words in the English language as self-discipline, restraint, control, tenacity, and willpower. Humans would also have been deprived of such idioms as *keep your nose to the grindstone, go the extra mile, leave no stone unturned, burn the candle at both ends*, and *pull yourself up by your bootstraps*. To be sure, these expressions are the groundwork for the best stories of all time.

The Telling Tale of Todd and Rachel

Knowing that the mind has a split identity and pronounced proclivities, the story that follows illustrates how mind rules can be applied to real-world situations and facilitate eye-opening results.

Having been married for eight years and both holding steady jobs, a couple named Todd and Rachel decided to throw caution to the wind and move to a new country. Setting the stage for this life transition was a promising job opportunity for Todd, one that made the game-changing risk of making the move abroad worth pursuing.

By leaving the United States, the couple left behind nearly everything and everyone they held dearly. They were incredibly excited to begin this new adventure and couldn't wait for their next chapter together to begin.

Once settled, Todd and Rachel set about exploring their surroundings and making new memories. Everything was going great. Todd's new job was an amazing fit. He enjoyed his new colleagues and the challenges that came along with his new position. He even began picking up the local language and took great pride in being conversational with the native speakers.

For Rachel's part, she found joy in making new friends and taking on interesting hobbies. She became especially interested in the local cuisine and gradually became an accomplished cook, gaining renown for her creative use of spices.

Life could not have been much better for Todd and Rachel. Their love for each other grew alongside their new life experiences. It's as if moving woke up their senses. They both agreed that they were happier than ever before.

In early spring, Samantha, one of Rachel's new friends, asked her to babysit her eight-month-old daughter. Since Rachel was medically trained, she felt reasonably confident she could handle any emergency or unforeseen event. At the same time, since she and Todd did not have children of their own, Rachel was slightly unnerved at the prospect of looking after a young child. Nonetheless, she stepped up, and the experience ended up being life changing.

Upon reflection, after Rachel watched Sam's child, a night filled with snuggles and watching the child sleep peacefully, she acknowledged the experience was rather uneventful—except for one thing. As Rachel was walking home from Sam's apartment, she stopped at a local café. Ordering herself a latte, she sat down at a small table on the cafe's outdoor patio. This is when something shifted inside her.

Rachel had been born into a rather large family, which was much closer on paper than in person. Both of Rachel's parents worked outside the house, and she was raised by more babysitters than she can remember. Her three sisters were quite a bit older than her, and she became the only child at home after her youngest sister moved out when Rachel was twelve. If asked who raised her, Rachel's most honest answer would be "Myself."

For Todd's part, he was adopted at an early age into a family that never seemed like a family. He was the middle of three children, an older sister and a younger brother who had also been adopted. Todd's parents were professionals. His father was a successful engineer, and his mother was a big shot in the finance world. If asked to describe his childhood in a single word, being extremely polite by nature, Todd would say, "Unmemorable." When pressed further than he was used to, Todd describes his father as an extreme disciplinarian, "Beyond firm," he says. His mother, meanwhile, always seemed to be active, engaged, and regularly involved in everything except her children. Like Rachel, Todd developed his independence at a young age and learned to trust himself but not much else around him.

Together, Todd and Rachel found an incredible partnership. They fell in love quickly and easily. One thing they had in common that gave them that we-were-made-for-each-other feeling was a shared sense of always searching for something they knew was missing but couldn't quite put their finger on it—until they met. They had discovered togetherness and agreed never to tempt fate by bringing a child into their relationship.

As Rachel sat sipping her coffee in a daze, the late-morning sun warming her skin, she began experiencing uncommon feelings. Then it came to her. The unfamiliar feeling that had come over her was something she had never felt before. She barely was able to bring her thoughts to the surface. Then it happened; she whispered her new truth to herself—she wanted a child of her own.

Now that Rachel has connected with her new vision, she worries about how Todd will feel about this. Should she tell him or keep it to herself? If she chooses to share, how should she bring up this desire in conversation? Will Rachel's private epiphany create a permanent rift in her relationship with Todd? Will Todd and Rachel live happily ever after?

As you read further, the story of Todd and Rachel will be brought up now and again. You will learn how they wrestle with this life-challenging dilemma and how, with the assistance of mind rules, they eventually discover a resolution that works for both.

Mind Rule Life Lesson
The Mind Is Not Relational

In the meantime, the takeaway from this first mind rule is the realization that because the mind is not relational—and is, instead, infinitely welded to safety, security, and survival—your chances for living a long life are vastly increased. However, without relationships, without forging meaningful connections with others, long life may not be all that fulfilling.

At their best, relationships bring us joy and inspiration, expanding our lives and making us feel better than ever before. At their worst, they bring us shame, guilt, and disappointment, contracting our lives and leaving us feeling inadequate, detached, and puzzled. Just as challenging, the unexpectedness of relationships makes things exciting, sometimes thrilling beyond belief, while also creating utter chaos and bringing out an ugliness better reserved for rainy days never to arrive.

One of the greatest paradoxes as a human is that by inviting people into our lives, life becomes harder than it needs to be, as our interactions with others often become a source of frustration and exasperation. Yet, without surrounding ourselves with people who can offer support and validation, life can end up being harder than it needs to be and feel incredibly empty. Separated from others, left behind or cast aside, we can even end up wondering if there is any purpose to life, our life, at all.

Ultimately, since the mind is not relational, it's your choice to reach out to others, to connect meaningfully and memorably, and to discern how the opinions of others impact your self-worth and shape your sense of permanence. Just remember, you're taking a big chance with the essence of who you are, your identity, when you reach out to others to connect. Without exaggeration, the outcome could be complete and amazingly empowering or, just as easily, patchy and dreadful. Consequently, take your time, search in places often omitted, and don't look for someone to get rid of the pain. Your private pain is a signal that deserves to be listened to, not ignored or avoided.

Here are a few other notes to consider along your relational journey. Relationships don't come with warning signs, but look for them anyway. It's amazingly sad when others don't understand; seek to understand yourself and let others catch up. Allow yourself to be choosy with the people who come into your life, bearing in mind you can always choose to let them go. Don't mistake chance for choice. Both will affect your life, but one demands deliberate thought, discernment, and calculation; just a flip of a coin will do for the other. Chasing happiness instead of pursuing meaning and savoring what others may never know about you demands tremendous emotional currency. In simplest terms, choices come at a cost. Keep in mind what and how much you can afford.

Given that we come into relationships with an innate focus on self, there is much to learn about what it takes to be in a relationship. That said, if you wait for your mind to tell you when and how to navigate an uncertain or tricky interpersonal situation, you'll likely be left waiting a very long time. Because your mind is not relational, it's up to you to make good choices by understanding how you are constantly forming and being formed by relationships.

CHAPTER 2

The Mind Is Self-Serving
Self-Preservation Is the Mind's Top Priority

On guard around the clock, your mind remains steadfastly focused on keeping you from harm, without any conscious effort on your part. With self-preservation as its top priority, the mind constantly looks out for any signs of looming danger, remaining ever vigilant to your welfare. It's your most powerful instinctual drive. Nothing else comes close.

It is this ingenuity and toughness of your mind's core directive that guides and explains much of human behavior. What you do without thinking is heavily influenced by your mind doing exactly what it's supposed to do, following its evolved assignment of keeping you from getting hurt by activating its preservation instinct.

Of course, though, there is much more to life than merely staying safe and sound, a reality the mind doesn't always accommodate. To truly understand what makes life worth living, you must examine what makes folks happy in the first place. For some, it equates to being promoted or getting a raise at work or buying a new car or moving into a bigger house. Others, meanwhile, may find joy in more fundamental things, basking in being healthy or enjoying the freedom to do what they want to do when they want to do it.

Although the source of happiness and fulfillment is different for everybody, social science suggests that our happiness ultimately hinges on having something positive happen to us, after which we return to a baseline level of contentment. This phenomenon, known as a "hedonic treadmill," is based on the notion that our general happiness as humans is not permanently altered by the ups and downs we experience.

In this way, your contentment is cyclical, a sentiment embodied by the expression *what goes up, must come down*. While you certainly experience a boost of happiness when your dreams, big or small, come true, after the thrill of your good fortune wears off, you go back to feeling whatever you were feeling before you sampled the sweet taste of victory. Discerning this distinction represents the difference between living and living well.

Beyond Just Living

The human survival instinct and our visceral responses—fight, flight, or freeze—are intended to improve the odds of having another tomorrow. This built-in automatic response system generates behavior that increases our chances of survival but does nothing to elevate the level of our happiness. The mind's hardwired instinct to protect serves as a primal measure to assure our existence. We survive, but at what cost?

Fact is that humans in the twenty-first century have come to expect much more from life than merely outliving the prior generation's life expectancy. Yet, while much more is desired, perhaps believing it is deserved, this generational commitment to obtain greater substance from life is greatly stymied by the mind's long-established preference for continuity and predictability.

What's the force that opposes your aspirational pursuit of being championed as being better than your predecessors? Simply stated, the mind rule involving your self-preserving nature can stall your ambition of realizing your dreams and living happily ever after. That is, your mind prefers to get in your way because of its strong and unshakable mission to persist and not be diverted from its course of keeping you safe and secure. The phrase *better safe than sorry* depicts your mind's default mode of operation.

If it is true that *a rising tide lifts all boats*, as they say, then why does your mind seem to swim against the tide? Have you been seduced by modern society and the allure of having your dreams come true? Is your illusion of living happily ever after so overpowering that you no longer understand how flamboyantly optimistic and self-congratulatory you've become? Have you long since passed the time of understanding the whispered truths associated with your humanity and come full circle to believing in your invincibility?

Against this backdrop, the short answer invites you to fight against strange amnesia—a disconnect between your fashionable arrogance, fueled by privileged consumption, and a deeper dive for meaning and purpose. Hence, as a human, you are confronted with a dilemma: do you remain selfish and self-protected, or do you learn how to get out of your mind, break from tradition, and strive toward realizing an improved balance between surviving and thriving?

Revisiting a Basic Truth

While the mind is an exceptional guardian for signs of danger, threats, and other forms of potential harm, sometimes your mind's intense focus causes you to lose sight of other needs that provide meaning to life.

Beyond the vital need to feel safe and secure, there is a deeply felt desire for support, validation, connection, and inspiration to become a better version of ourselves. When such needs are chronically deprived, you tend to fall back into a trance and end up feeling imbalanced and confused, perhaps even questioning the meaning of life.

By remaining securely attached to living inside your comfort zone in the service of self-preservation, not being disappointed, distressed, or injured, you bypass the experience of excitement that comes with adventure seeking and stepping into what's possible. Consequently, the act of being spontaneous, taking risks, and moving toward the mysteries that life can offer requires you to make a conscious and deliberate effort of freeing yourself from your mind's innate grip on keeping you safe and well preserved.

Traumatized by Hope

Charlotte had everything going for her until that day. In middle school, living a full life and enjoying every minute, she was a gifted student and approached her studies with intense focus and eagerness. Her talents in athletics were natural, and she excelled in everything she did.

It didn't matter if she was kicking a ball, swinging a bat, or swimming laps, Charlotte always seemed to finish on top. She was well liked by everyone and was always smiling. Her parents were inordinately impressed with Charlotte—not for what she did but how she did it. Charlotte was the real deal from everyone's perspective, her teachers, her coaches, her fellow students, and friends.

Then, it happened.

During a soccer scrimmage on a day that had been raining on and off, Charlotte was running down the field and positioning herself to make yet another goal. When she went to kick the ball, she slipped on the damp turf and fell awkwardly. Since falling and scraping a knee or bruising a shoulder was part of the game, no one thought much about Charlotte's mishap. But when she didn't get up right away, her coach knew something was wrong.

Racing over to Charlotte, her coach saw that she was in trouble. She had suffered a compound fracture to her right lower leg; she was white as a ghost. Something about Charlotte's breathing wasn't right. Her coach worried that she wasn't breathing at all. Emergency medical responders were called, and Charlotte was taken to the hospital by ambulance for urgent treatment.

After being examined, doctors delivered news to Charlotte and her parents that was jarring. The neurosurgeon said that while her leg was severely injured, Charlotte had also suffered a highly unusual and complex compression fracture in her upper spine and may have experienced a loss of oxygen, causing possible brain trauma. She needed to be hospitalized for an extended period to monitor her recovery and facilitate the best outcome. Charlotte's parents were told to hope for the best and prepare for the worst—and then the worst happened.

While Charlotte was not technically paralyzed, her spine would never be the same. She was left immobilized by severe and incapacitating pain. She wasn't able to return to school, her days of being an athlete were long gone, and she was forced to be isolated in her room.

Over the years, Charlotte and her greatest fan, her father, researched every medical treatment possible. Charlotte had surgeries. She was prescribed countless medications. She even was identified as being a candidate for stem cell injections and underwent a variety of state-of-the-art medical procedures. Yet, year and after year went by with no change. Charlotte's existence, which was bigger than life at one time, had shrunk to being barely noticeable. She was left in survival mode.

Because of Charlotte's inborn resilience, optimism, and drive, she never gave up. While her reality was terrible and beyond imaginable—rarely did she get a full night's sleep because of her pain, and except for her father, her family and friends gradually distancing themselves from her and being left in an unsteady state of unremitting loneliness and anonymity—somehow, Charlotte reached deep within herself and found hope.

She was the epitome of grit. Whenever a doctor identified a new treatment option, Charlotte's spirit would rise. Quite sadly, every single time, the promising treatment failed to offer her any measure of improved functioning. Consequently, Charlotte was forced to adapt again and again to the possibility of never getting better.

Trapped by her unsolvable medical condition, Charlotte remained virtually housebound for decades. When asked about the worst part of her life situation, guided by painstakingly examined deep truth and unrelenting courage, Charlotte shared that the hardest part of her heartbreaking journey had been having expectations.

Providing further explanation, Charlotte reported that she would become filled with hope when a medical procedure was identified. Then, when the treatment did not pan out, she would psychologically crash. It was the crashing back down to reality, not her insufferable pain, that was her greatest struggle. In this way, Charlotte would say that her life's journey could be summed up by the phrase *traumatized by hope*.

The story of Charlotte illustrates how the mind's top priority is self-preservation. Had Charlotte never challenged her mind by daring herself to hope, she may not have experienced the unrelenting despair associated with her disheartening reality.

If, instead, she had accepted her life's solitary confinement and lowered her expectations, perhaps Charlotte would have remained content and less psychologically tortured. However, as Charlotte's story attests, she knows something about living and about how the mind operates that we often fail to remember.

Mind Rule Life Lesson
The Mind Is Self-Serving

Because of the standoff between your choice for living longer or living well, you may find yourself at the proverbial fork in the road. If you go down the first path, you tend to live following a familiar road map that was drawn from your past life lessons, family traditions, your relationship history, and, let's not forget, your parents' principles and famous platitudes, such as "Better safe than sorry," "Money doesn't grow on trees," "Your face is going to freeze that way," "Don't burn the candle at both ends," "Don't go to bed angry," and "Can't never did."

By following this road map, for better or worse, oftentimes a bit of both, you end up blindly following in the footprints of those who vastly influenced you during your upbringing. In other words, secretly, what you've been told and what you've been shown deeply sways what you believe and how you act, react, and, sometimes, overreact. This information is securely placed within the vault of your mind and, without clear-cut permission, is accessed by the mind to keep you on the path of least resistance—the path guided by your old learning and well-worn habits.

To underscore the potency of how modeling deeply influences both your belief system and your sense of self, in our clinic, clients are often told, "We are nothing like our parents, but we resemble them now and again, often when it's least expected."

When the second path is chosen, when you choose to expand your horizons and focus on living well, you are giving yourself an allowance to break free from your upbringing in a way that loosens your grip on your overlearned habits and old ways of living. This second path is like pressing a reset button.

Stepping into new life experiences broadens your perspective and breaks the cycle of doing what you typically do. This process can provide you a unique insight into your long-held but rarely examined life lessons. Walking down this alternate path sheds light on what is being done to you, so you can regain mastery of becoming the person you've always wanted to be.

Instead of reacting, you adapt. In place of doing what's "right," you do what matters. Rather than always looking for a solution, you focus on patterns. As an alternative to being safe rather than sorry, you elect to do things intentionally with curiosity and flexibility. By being inclined to stick your neck out, you're creating opportunities to see what life is like on the other side of your upbringing.

While the mind, by nature and design, is assuredly self-preserving, to live the life you need, want, desire, and deserve requires a special kind of conscious and deliberate effort. To create lasting memories, to feel alive, and to reach your peak potential necessitates that you consider the benefits of getting out of your mind, which infers you actively consider the benefits that are derived from doing something other than what you typically do.

An expression attributed to Jackie "Moms" Mabley—and frequently but inaccurately credited to Henry Ford, and regularly repeated by Tony Robbins—charmingly makes the point associated with this mind rule: *"If you always do what you've always done, you always get what you've always got."*

The lesson here is that by staying the course and allowing the mind to be your primary guide, you are being sidetracked and mugged in a sense. If you don't want to be mishandled by your mind, then it's time for you to consider taking steps that bend the rules and rock the boat. This is accomplished by asking yourself, "Are you in control of your mind or is your mind controlling you?"

Knowing that the mind is self-serving and hyper-focused on survival, you are now placed in the driver's seat for selecting whether you would like to continue down the well-worn path of your past or choose another path, one that comes with greater risk and uncertainty, one that may give you a boost of happiness. Moving forward requires a willingness to take your foot off the brake and step on the throttle.

Developing a keen understanding of the interplay among the various mind rules becomes incredibly informative and instrumental, if not life transforming. But a word of caution. When you find yourself in an extreme circumstance, of course, it makes complete sense to hand the reins over to your survival instincts. By doing so, whether you choose to fight, take flight, or freeze, you are doing what needs to be done to best handle the challenge of the moment. But what about all those other moments when your well-being is not being threatened?

So what makes us happy? It's a willingness to choose new experiences. It's a mindset that requires us to dial down our survival instincts, step out of our unconscious learning, and dial up a willingness to take new chances, make new choices, and allow ourselves the opportunity to thrive.

CHAPTER 3

Avoidance Is the Mind's Natural Reflex
Self-Preservation Is the Mind's Top Priority

By sidestepping reality, the mind protects us from repeating our worst experiences. When the going gets tough, the tough get going—that's how the saying goes. When it comes to the mind, however, *get going* has a different connotation.

Instead of doubling down and moving forward with grit and determination, your mind is more inclined to steer you away from troublesome situations, urging you to go anywhere but in the direction of discomfort or harm. The mind learned long ago to avoid things that seem unpleasant, repulsive, or painful.

The power of avoidance is highly seductive. Although the problem or obstacle doesn't go away, avoidance, in essence, makes it stop existing, like a magic trick. Close your eyes, fold your arms, nod your head, and presto! The problem is gone. Not really, of course, but as far as the mind is concerned, it is.

In the world of behavioral psychology, avoidance is known as a negative reinforcer. In negative reinforcement, a response or behavior is strengthened and, therefore, more likely to occur again by stopping, removing, or avoiding a negative outcome or aversive stimulus.

Negative reinforcement is not punishment. The best way to think of negative reinforcement is something that brings about a sense of relief. For example, Jamie does her homework to prevent or stop her mother's nagging (aversive stimulus). Subsequently, she experiences relief (lowered stress and a lot less noise). Her primary motivation here is not getting her homework done but avoiding having her mother become so annoying.

Unfortunately, without having insight into Jamie's thinking process, her mother's nagging is rewarded (positive reinforcement) based on her perception that persistent grumbling is what her daughter needs to get things done. Consequently, it is highly likely that mom's badgering will increase, not decrease. What Jamie needs to know is that her mother's bad habit of pestering will decrease if she beats her mom to the punch—she starts doing her homework *before* her mother starts her hounding.

Avoiding Everything Leads to Nothing

On the upside, the mind's natural aptitude for avoidance distances you from the unpleasantness associated with doing something you'd rather not do, like a soothing elixir that allows you to believe that things won't get worse in the short run. The downside, of course, is that things don't get better. In fact, by definition, putting things off means things don't get done. Spotlighting this phenomenon, let's reference a popular motivational line, "nothing changes if nothing changes."

Think about how often we avoid things throughout our lives, be it relationships or everyday situations. Consider a scene in which there's a special someone whom you admire from afar. Time passes, and you never make a move. Instead, you keep your feelings to yourself.

So what makes you keep your distance? Fear of rejection? Lack of confidence? Or a belief that someone like her would never want someone like you? Rather than experiencing the reality of being in a relationship with this person, regardless of its brevity or depth, you remain comfortable with holding in your imagination a romanticized notion of having a relationship. If this scenario sounds familiar, realize that this is simply your mind steering you away from what it perceives as an anticipated personal injury.

It's like being a teenager and learning how to drive. Maybe you initially avoided highways or heavy traffic conditions for fear of being overwhelmed and getting into an accident. Such avoidance likewise kept you safe from harm. Just like your instincts protected you from heartbreak, your intuition kept your vehicle from being totaled and you from being grounded the rest of your life.

With your mind being so committed to keeping you far away from possible harm, the challenge you face is revealed in the following critical question: are you in control of your mind, or is your mind controlling you? The truth is your willpower and mind power are both in play. How you choose to balance these two forces is up to you—if you know how.

Your Thinking Brain

Fortunately, beyond the mind's natural reflex to protect itself, you have a prefrontal cortex, a thinking brain. Located directly behind and above your eyes, your prefrontal cortex gives you the capacity to have conscious and deliberate thought. It's your control center and where important decisions get made.

This remarkable part of your brain also provides you the capacity to be purposeful, driven by willful action, experience self-awareness, and achieve something exceptionally human—complex decision-making. By harnessing the incredible power of your thinking brain, you can expand your mind and move deliberately in the direction of achieving goals and increasing your felt happiness.

Being amazingly complex and interconnected with other brain regions, the prefrontal cortex gives you the capacity for executive function. Executive functions are self-regulation or "step-aside-I'm-in-charge" skills that help with sustaining attention, resisting distraction, managing frustration, setting goals, assessing consequences of action, planning for the future, and dabbling with insight. The executive brain is responsible for your most advanced and complex human capacities.

Your executive capacity has a dramatic effect on how you adapt to life situations. For example, your ability to organize and design a plan of action, to follow through on a task, and to modify an approach based on changing conditions in your environment have far-reaching implications for everyday life as well as your sense of mastering your destiny.

Without a prefrontal cortex, you would be controlled completely by reflexes, instincts, and a drive to satisfy your basic needs. As a result, much of life would be shaped by avoiding potential threats, giving wide berth to prospective risky propositions, and postponing opportunities for personal growth, in favor of doing something else that keeps you safe and in control of your immediate circumstances. In other words, you'd be a lizard.

To drive home the point that avoidance is the mind's natural reflex, think about an infant who's just learning how to talk. Typically, the young child's first words are "Momma" or "Da-Da." This is both adorable and expected. However, the child's third word is much less lovable and mostly unexpected. Yet this third word reveals the substantial power of avoidance.

What is this powerful third word? To keep you pondering for just a few more moments, the answer is given at the end of this chapter. If you haven't already guessed what this third word might be, once you read the answer, you will likely say to yourself, "Of course!"

Returning to Rachel's Predicament

When we last checked in with Rachel in chapter 2, she was contemplating whether she should share her epiphany with Todd. As she attempted to absorb and process this newfound realization, her innate longing to have a child of her own, she was presented with the daunting prospect of spoiling the best relationship and best life experience she'd ever had by sharing this significant new aspiration.

As you might recall, Rachel and Todd had mutually decided to pack their bags and redefine normal by moving overseas. Their relationship only grew deeper and more meaningful with their new surroundings. Living happily ever after is exactly what Rachel was thinking she and Todd were doing before her newly awakened maternal instincts kicked in.

Contemplating the pros and cons of telling Todd, Rachel's first thought was, *Why spoil a great thing?* This thought was clear as a bell to Rachel. Never being much of a risk-taker, she feared that if she told Todd about her craving for motherhood, she would not only knock over the applecart, but the apples themselves would never be as sweet again.

Just the same, Rachel couldn't stop running through the what-if scenarios. What if she told Todd what she was thinking, and he was overjoyed about her unexpected change of heart? What if they were able to conceive and her pregnancy made her feel more beautiful and special than ever before? What if the birth of their child brought her and Todd even closer together? *What if ... what if ... what if ...* she just kept thinking.

Rachel was faced with a perplexing problem. For every positive and uplifting reason she identified for sharing her desires, an equally negative and disconcerting thought would arise that urged her to keep quiet. What to do? What to do?

Then something interesting happened. During Rachel's deeply personal ponderings, she realized that time had slipped by. For the first few days, as she weighed the ups and downs of her prospects, the proposition was preoccupying, permeating her thoughts to the point of obsessiveness.

A few weeks later, although she remained distracted by her internal debate, she noticed she was able to resume a more active engagement in her everyday life. Without knowing it, Rachael was mentally multitasking, and thoughts of having a baby would more comfortably shift between the foreground and the background.

As the notion of having a baby became more familiar, for right now, the *idea* of having a child with Todd in the future seemed to be good enough for her. So she decided to hold her tongue and keep her longings to herself. And, as you may have already guessed, by making this decision, Rachel felt a sigh of relief. Avoidance, after all, is a powerful drug.

At this moment, Rachel's self-protecting mind won out. As the mind rule that espouses that avoidance is the mind's natural reflex allows, without fully realizing her obedience to her mind, Rachel decided that avoidance is the best policy, at least for the time being. In doing so, Rachel put her mind at ease. Aah, relief.

Mind Rule Life Lesson
Avoidance Is the Mind's Natural Reflex

When well managed, your executive skills are immensely powerful. When things are relatively calm and you're being challenged in an expected and respectful fashion, your top-of-food-chain brain works amazingly well. These are conditions under which mysteries get solved, discoveries are made, and the world becomes a bit more understandable and manageable.

By strong contrast, during times of distress, fear, or unbearable uncertainty, your thinking brain shuts off, and your mind activates the cerebral infantry of raw emotions. Your heart rate rises, breathing speeds up, and sugar, lots of it in the form of glucose, is dumped into your metabolic system. In turn, your survival reflex is activated, and your choices for action are limited to fight, flight, or freeze. During times when your executive brain gets hijacked, it may seem as though you don't have a choice of what to do or how to act.

But you do.

Being aware of your mind's proclivity for avoidance, you now have a chance to go in a different direction—to live intentionally and on purpose. If the function of avoidance provides a short-term remedy to life's challenges, then opposite action, to approach, may hold the key to a longer-term solution.

Moving in a new direction is made possible when you choose to do something in a different way or elect to try something new altogether. The act of seeking novelty can be extremely exhilarating. In fact, by definition, doing something that sounds interesting that you are not yet skilled in is exciting. For instance, take the sport of white water kayaking. When you see other people paddling the rapids, making it look so easy, you might catch yourself saying, "That looks like fun. That's for me." Amped by the fuel of spontaneity, you begin researching what it takes to get started.

In this moment, you are moving forward with deliberate velocity; your mind is open to what's possible and hasn't yet happened, and your actions are approaching, not avoiding, the possibility of getting involved in this adrenaline sport. This situation reflects a mind shift in which you've decided to invest in making memories rather than sitting back and reflecting on what might have been.

Here's the point. When your friends or family members hear about your interest in white water kayaking and you inform them that you've signed up for a beginner's class, they might say, "Are you out of your mind?" Knowing what you now know about mind rules, your rapid answer needs to be "Yes, finally!"

Whatever you might choose to approach in life, have fun splashing around, respect the current, and stay safe on the river of your choice—remember, white water (a.k.a., new life experiences) can be extremely powerful, so start easy and finish strong.

By the way, as promised, here is the answer to the question "What is the child's third word?" After the young child learns to say "Momma" or "Da-Da," their third word is usually "No." This word reflects the young person learning to regulate their inner world by taking control over their outside world. Don't confuse the child's expression with negativity. This simple word actually has amazing implications. The simple utterance of the sound *no* reflects a clear choice that evokes astonishing features of courage, integrity, limit setting, and personal responsibility.

To end this section with a robust worldview of the rapidly growing child, there's another word that typically shows up, one that has deep existential implications, and it reflects something all of us, regardless of age, deeply desire, even if the word doesn't make it past our lips. That special word is *more*.

CHAPTER 4

The Mind Only Remembers What It Can't Forget

Your Best and Worst Experiences Are Stored Securely—Although Not Always Accurately

A convincing argument can be made that the purpose of life comes down to your ability to make memories. What you remember shapes the person you become. Early in life, you form indelible images of yourself and others and how the two fit together. Your inner mental map becomes further enriched by the twists and turns you encounter in the fluid, fuzzy, and fast experience associated with growing up. Thankfully, the human brain is remarkably capable of recalling moments, contemplating, cataloging, and contextualizing your fondest memories.

From retracing the steps of your upbringing to reliving your relationships, your mind can reconstruct your wildest tales with surprisingly *good enough* accuracy. While you may not be able to recall the vivid details of every life event, you'll likely be able to piece together a pleasing enough portrait of plausibility.

When something happens to you that is interesting and extremely relevant, to your mind, it feels personal. As the importance of such moments peak, the experience gets laid down and heads to becoming a memory. Then, each time this experience is replayed, often happening during sleep, the memory gets deposited deeper in the cortical tissue of your brain. This is how "I'll-never-forget-when" moments get stored permanently in your memory banks and are retrieved with relative ease and delightful distortion.

As a fascinating sidenote, you have a variety of memory banks, not just one. For instance, your deeply ingrained muscle memories, the ones used when riding a bike or playing hacky sack, are stored in the cerebellum (the "little brain" located at the back of the big brain, tucked under and partly fused to it) and putamen (a round structure located at the base of the forebrain).

Facts you commit to memory, such as reciting the state capitals and recalling who was the president of the United States at the time of the Civil War, are encoded in the temporal lobe, one of the major lobes of the cerebral cortex that sits close to ear level within the skull.

Scary memories, the ones associated with the worst days of your life, are stored in the amygdala, an almond-shaped mass of gray matter nestled in the middle of your brain, specifically designed to detect danger or threat. The amygdala has a well-earned reputation for registering fear.

Then there are your personal life experiences, commonly referred to as autobiographical memories, which are encoded by the hippocampus (Greek for *seahorse* and located deep in the temporal lobe, often referred to as the memory center of the brain) and eventually scattered around different cortical areas of your brain.

One more memory tidbit involves how you tinker with your recollections every time you recall a memory. When you bring back something from the past, the process of reexamining allows you to tweak it by adding a fact or two, or tamper with its veracity by stretching the truth, or shrink it down by forgetting pieces and parts of the story, or unabashedly embellishing the story to the point it is no longer recognizable even by those who were alongside you when it first happened. The technical name for filling in otherwise blank spaces or telling false stories is called *confabulation*. Take comfort in knowing you're not alone; we all exaggerate and take creative liberties when retelling our story.

When you think about it, your ability to look back and reflect is an amazing feat of brain activity, one that you often take for granted. More fascinating, your memories have a shaky capacity for choosing fact from fiction.

Separating Fact and Fiction

On the fact side, some memories are recalled in elaborate detail, a trait commonly referred to as a *flashbulb memory*. Such indelible and emotion-packed moments are recalled with exceptionally clear details and can be quite accurate. Memories that fall into this category include the harrowing assassination of President John F. Kennedy and the devastating travesty of 9/11. These life experiences fall under the "where-were-you-when" heading.

Flashbulb memories can also be highly personal, from experiencing the premature death of a loved one to the first time you kissed another person, like in really kissed, the kind of kiss that somehow changed everything and nothing all at once. The term *flashbulb memory* was coined in the days when flash photography required a disposable flashbulb for each picture. When the picture was taken, a flash would occur, and the photographic image was captured forever.

A less flashy form of memory is your conscious recollection of names, dates, events, people, places, and objects. Neuroscientists have termed this type of knowledge *explicit* or *declarative memory*, which is further subdivided into two categories.

The book-driven information you remember from your days in school—such as the year that Columbus sailed the ocean blue or the name of the US president during the time of the Civil War—is called semantic memory. This type of historical memory is incredibly handy when you are playing a game of trivia.

Then there is episodic memory, which categorizes your autobiographical experiences—the name of the first person you kissed, your recollection of spending summers at the beach, and the experience that is recalled when you smell freshly cut grass.

There is also implicit memory, another type of memory that is stored below your immediate awareness. This is a term to describe your recollections of what you learned during times you weren't aware that you were being taught. This type of memory, which is stored automatically and without conscious thinking, refers to things such as tying your shoes, riding a bike, brushing your teeth, or singing along with a Beatles tune. It also applies to things you learned during your upbringing, experiences with trust, truth, commitment, and intimacy that were cemented without your immediate or volitional awareness.

As you watched your parents handle their moments of conflict, for instance, whether they kissed and made up or raged on about each other's bad behaviors, watching these scenes play out taught you plenty about conflict. What's amazing about such life experiences is there can be an impressive chasm between what happened and how you interpreted what happened. Both are correct, only one really occurred.

Interestingly, since your parents' behaviors became part of the background of your life, you weren't officially notified of what they were teaching you about relationships.

Instead, witnessing their fighting and watching moments in which they made up was tucked implicitly into the relational fabric that you recognized as being *normal* in loving relationships. Take note that *normal* and *healthy* can be two strikingly different realities.

There is a critical distinction between explicit and implicit memories; the latter influences your behavior without you knowing it, while the former requires awareness and deliberate effort. If a memory affects your behavior or thinking without rising into your consciousness (think about riding a bike), it's implicit. Explicit memories, meanwhile, involve intentional work, as they are stored and retrieved (learning a foreign language, for example).

Your memory can have a relatively high error rate on the fiction side, influenced by such factors as suggestibility, misattribution, bias, fading memories, exaggeration, fabrication, and preferred beliefs. Thanks to these factors, your memory can sometimes fail you. The tricky part here is that you may never know the difference between something that is true and something you remember to be true. To your mind, fact and fiction are separated by what you decide to hold onto versus what is pushed away to avoid unnecessary clutter or confusion.

Every moment of every day, your mind does its best to focus on what's most important and sends everything else to the sidelines. By following this process, your mind is doing exactly what it's designed to do—concentrating on protecting and providing for you by remembering what it can't forget. And what it remembers best are the highest and lowest moments in your life, although the exactness of what you remember may not be as accurate as you would hope.

Running through One's Mind

Why are some memories so precise and others more flawed? Perhaps of even greater importance, is your mind able to distinguish when you are recalling a memory accurately or viewing your past through a lens of preferred truth? Further, contemplate the consequences if what you remember to have happened is only a version of what's recalled.

Consider, for instance, the popular telling of a fish story. Upon each retelling of the story, amazingly, the fish grows bigger. This is a classic example of how your mind exaggerates what really happened and how what you remember may only be a version of what took place.

As for remembering things accurately or elaborately, it helps to remember that human memory is essentially an interpretive system. As your mind takes in information, it attends to certain details while discarding others, to organize the whole of what you gathered into a meaningful pattern. Once the pattern is established, the mind locks this information into memory and relies upon it in the future under similar circumstances. If the information gathered is determined to be meaningful, then it is placed into permanent storage.

Let's put this idea of how memories are selected to the test. Of course, you believe that what you remember must be true. However, so much of what you remember is merely a version of what happened. Look at the figure below. What do you see?

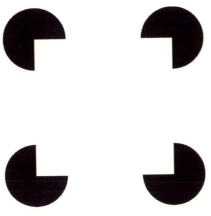

OPTICAL ILLUSION, FOUR PAC-MEN

The above figure reveals some of the mystery of how the mind works. The mind first focuses on details that seem most important, and then it seeks to verify if the details fit into a pattern. Referring back to the fact-versus-fiction model of memory, the fact associated with the figure above is that there are four black sectors, each facing inward—that's it, nothing more. Or do you see something else? The fiction you might see is the white square lying on top of the four black sectors—but is the square there, or do you just believe it's there?

The reason you see a square is due to your mind's fondness for taking mental shortcuts. Your mind responds to information in your environment and rapidly interprets its meaning against the backdrop of what you've already learned. Because memory and learning are different sides of the same coin, sometimes what you remember has a greater resemblance to what you've learned or thought you learned rather than what reality was trying to teach you.

Let's now return to our mind rules. The mind rule of *the mind only remembers what it can't forget* is an example of how we automatically encode, store, and retrieve information, even when we don't know that's what we're doing. Once something is learned of towering importance, especially when strong emotions are involved, the mind can never forget the significance of this experience. Consequently, such memories remain forever available for recall. But they're not available without the influence or bias from our perception and interpretation of what happened.

This mind rule explains why when asked, "Tell me about the best or worst day of your life," you can access an idea, emotion, or image at lightning speed. Your access to these memories occurs automatically and without permission. So when asked to recall a peak or valley that happened in your life, your mind goes to work instinctively and retrieves stored information impulsively.

Mind Rule Life Lesson
The Mind Only Remembers What It Can't Forget

What's important to remember is that while you have a tremendous ability to recall memories that are highly salient and emotion packed, you should be a bit wary when your mind goes *fishing* for your most unforgettable memories. What you recall may end up being only a version of what happened.

Here's a simple trick to avoid going over the top and stretching your story beyond recognition. When sharing a story from yesteryear, imagine yourself holding out your arms like someone telling a fish story. Then, as your story is being told, pay attention to the distance between your hands. If the gap is huge, you're likely telling a whopper. If the gap is less sizable, have fun and keep telling your story, knowing that everyone embellishes; it's what makes storytelling so captivating.

Summing up, what happened that didn't completely unhappen may not have happened in the way you remember. Your mind only soaks up pieces and parts of events and curiosities ebbing and flowing around you and within. Also, since your mind has a love affair with quick, it decides at the speed of conviction what is true. So now that you've been put on notice that your mind only remembers what it can't forget, you're in a more enlightened position to snag a trophy the next time you cast your line out into the pond of possibility.

CHAPTER 5

The Mind Can't Forget What It Doesn't Want to Remember

Memories with Intense Emotional Significance Are Remembered More Vividly and Retrieved More Easily

Life can get scary sometimes, especially when you experience something traumatic, namely an unexpected, unwanted, and undeserved event that causes emotional upheaval and leaves you feeling disoriented. Such extreme distress is difficult for the mind to interpret and manage in real time. The psychological impact felt is as deep as any possible human encounter, as the experiences send shockwaves to the nervous system and sear dreadful memories into your memory banks.

By contrast, much of what you experience in life is forgotten, and for good reason. Living our day-to-day lives is challenging enough without the burden of remembering everything. If every detail of your waking life was always available for recall, you would be flooded with information and much less efficient in recalling salient details and vital facts. What you remember, therefore, must have a distinct purpose.

Trauma is like an unsolvable puzzle. Learning how to fit the pieces together across time, making sense of what isn't easy to make sense of, helps manage the immediacy of discomfort that goes along with not being able to forget what you don't want to remember.

Forget about Forgetting

To make the point about how deeply impactful and lasting a traumatic memory can be, consider what happened to Tyler during childhood.

Tyler's father was a hardworking and extremely reserved man. When asked to describe his father in a few words, Tyler says, without hesitation, that he was strict and unflappable, a man who kept his thoughts and emotions to himself. Tyler says he couldn't recall a time when his father showed any type of empathy or concern for anyone other than himself.

When he drank, Tyler remembers, his father was mean. When he drank, his father took his frustrations out on everyone in the family. No one was excluded. Tyler says that while he endured his father's punishing nature, his mother received the brunt of his father's brutality.

Throughout his childhood, Tyler says he and his two older brothers learned masterfully to avoid their father, especially after seven in the evening when their dad was on his third or fourth drink. For Tyler's mother, meanwhile, avoidance was not possible, and escape was not an option. What's more, Tyler says, his father's ugly temperament and cruel behavior were even worse when his mother kept her distance.

Without any prompting, Tyler provides more details. His father would routinely take out his aggressions on his wife four to five times a week, and the fights, he recalls, were ill-matched and one-sided. In the aftermath, Tyler's mother always seemed to be left some remnant from the clashes; she had so many black eyes, bruises, and scrapes during that time that Tyler says he lost count. She often wore long-sleeved blouses to conceal her wounds and hidden pain.

As his brothers grew older and bigger, Tyler remembers how they would step into the fights to deflect their father's viciousness or create a distraction to quell the intensity of his assaults. While Tyler saw the efforts of his brothers as being heroic, he also notes how their involvement gave his father more targets for his outrage. "The body count only got bigger," Tyler says when his brothers intervened.

As an adult, Tyler is happily married and has four children of his own. Yet his wife has urged him to seek therapy because of his difficulty expressing his feelings. She noted his distaste in the areas of trust and vulnerability, and discomfort with intimacy. It seems that Tyler's upbringing taught him survival rather than living skills. Because his emotional depth is so limited, his wife is not only worried about him, but she also believes she deserves to have a better husband, someone she can go to in unhappy times and feel understood and validated. In therapy, Tyler's wife keeps repeating the same refrain: "You're present but unavailable."

Knowing that memories shape and define us, Tyler decided to seek help to better understand how his early life experiences, which collectively represented the worst days of his life, had stifled his capacity for a loving and close relationship with the one person with whom he truly loved and adored the most.

In Tyler's case, it becomes increasingly obvious how witnessing the physical and emotional abuse of his father across time took its toll, especially as the abuse was handed out by a person he was supposed to love and respect, and primarily leveled against the one person, his mother, who loved him no matter what.

Since old memories cannot be erased, Tyler's therapeutic journey needs to focus on helping him learn how to tone down and soften the effects of his developmental trauma. As he progresses, Tyler will learn how to examine the life lessons he learned during times that he wasn't aware he was being taught. He will gain insight into the conclusions he reached related to critical aspects of how to be connected to others.

By doing so, then and only then, Tyler will be able to come to understand that healthy, intimate relationships are based on honesty, vulnerability, and compassionate confrontation with one's past, and he will gain skills to share his private world with key individuals in his present life.

In our daily lives, curiously, and with varying degrees of discomfort and disruption, the worst days of our lives are easily recalled, often rapidly, and with vivid and bothersome detail.

Once a memory becomes permanent, especially those firmly

established by an intensely negative life experience, the old memory cannot be forgotten. Since the mind can't forget what it doesn't want to remember, it is wise to forget about forgetting. Further, the focus needs to shift toward altering the meaning attached to old memories and bravely investing in making new memories, ones that provide healing and opportunity to learn that emotions are not dangerous and that they shouldn't be divided into good and bad. When Tyler's conspiracy of silence is broken, he will come to embrace the understanding that relationships are opportunities to learn to trust, love, give, and receive in a balanced and healthy way.

In Tyler's case, if therapy goes well, if he really digs in and allows himself to explore the hidden trauma of his past and learn the lesson that conflict has been trying to teach him, he will be able to live by the philosophical expression of *a bad start but a beautiful ending*. Perhaps most ambitious of all, Tyler can develop the ability to engage in close relationships with compassion and openness without losing himself in the shadow of his upbringing. Unscrambling the themes of early childhood, finding new ways to piece together the puzzle of who Tyler is and can be in relationships, and learning how to turn conflict into connection will allow him to become the person he was always meant to be. Indeed, a beautiful ending.

Sensing Your Past

If you don't want to remember something, why do troublesome memories stay so clear and present? Why can't you let go of your most dreadful life experiences? The answer to this question is embedded in the phrase *worst first*.

Because the central function of the mind is to protect you, it makes complete sense that, first and foremost, you are being sheltered from your worst life experiences happening again.

If, like Tyler, you harbor terrible memories of witnessing hostile and unfair interactions between your parents during your formative years, then, quite sensibly, your mind would keep such unbearable observances in the forefront, so it can quickly detect any similar rumblings happening in your present.

Once detected in real time, your brain sends a clear and unmistakable signal to the body in the form of powerful stress hormones, which increases your heart rate, blood pressure, and breathing rate, along with other changes that increase your alertness. This process happens in a split second and outside of your conscious awareness, as a way of preparing you to take immediate action—to fight back, run away, or freeze in your tracks.

The quickest way for the mind to do its job is to store your most dreadful, egregious, frightful, and offensive memories in a *worst first* position. By doing so, such mental images, strong emotions, and bodily sensations can be activated without pause. The mind's capacity to take swift and resolute action during times of danger prevents you from experiencing the painful consequences of hesitation.

Another example of how your mind can't forget what it doesn't want to remember involves your olfactory (smell) system. Your sense of smell is unique and different from all other senses, as it is the only sense directly linked to your limbic system or emotional brain. Your limbic system is often referred to as being a part of your primitive brain and responsible for how you process emotions and memories.

Since scent signals bypass your consciousness and thinking brain, your detection of odors has a direct and brisk impact on your nervous system that can regulate, or dysregulate, your biochemistry. Therefore, you can be rapidly influenced by certain odors without realizing it.

Of particular interest, the power behind your olfactory system is what allows you to so effortlessly remember something buried long ago. Knowing that the olfactory system passes along information about smell directly to the part of the brain that controls emotions and memories, it is not surprising that certain smells can trigger specific memories or evoke certain mood states.

Think about how a specific smell can instantly remind you of something that occurred long ago. Perhaps the smell of watermelon or fresh corn, for instance, sends you back to your earlier days when life was easy and carefree. Because these smells are closely linked with memory, such scents can remind you of some of your better days while also causing you to wear an unsuspecting smile on your face.

Of course, what works for positive memories also works for unpleasant ones. If one of your teachers in grade school was especially unkind and wore an intensely aromatic perfume, then, much later in life, when exposed to this same fragrance, your mind automatically races back to the disagreeable memory. "My gosh," you might say to yourself, "won't she ever go away and stay away?"

Your mind's predisposition for not being able to forget what it doesn't want to remember is intimately tied to its central role in protecting you from your worst days happening again. Since your mind vividly remembers your darkest days, you are more likely to respond swiftly and protectively from cues in your environment that are like your deepest and most intrusive memories.

Mind Rule Life Lesson
The Mind Can't Forget What It Doesn't Want to Remember

The moral behind this mind rule—the mind can't forget what it doesn't want to remember—boils down to this: while you may, at times, wish you didn't have such sharp recollection of your most unpleasant and crushing memories, because you do, odds are improved that you won't have as many bad days in your future.

In this way, because your mind is designed to recall memories that have strong emotional significance more vividly and easily than any other type of memory, you can rest a bit easier knowing that your mind will forewarn you when it detects dangers and feels threatened. That's the upside to your mind's sharp and narrowed focus on your deeply private and most painful lived experiences.

However, having deep-seated hypersensitivity to specific images, sounds, and nuanced flutterings can cause you to experience false alarms. While your mind follows a better-safe-than-sorry course of action and is not bothered by a faulty alarm system, in relationships, false alarms become quite taxing and wear thin on each other's tolerance and patience. If, for instance, betrayal and degradation were threaded into your upbringing by way of unspeakable abuse and violence, the raw material of such adversity and upheaval will not disappear, but it can dissolve, its potency weakened over time by bold endeavors and healing connections.

Although the jarring nature of trauma is accompanied by an irreversibility—what happened will never completely unhappen—to your mind, this is a good thing. The painful familiarity of dark times against the foreground of what is happening, or may not be happening, right in front of you, right now, is the crescendo of your mind being nonamnestic and doing exactly what its imprinted manifesto commands—remain alert to signs of malevolence amid a twenty-four-hour news cycle of mostly benign happenings.

Knowing what to do when the worst fragments of your past return, other than doing what you always have done, is the crux of pivotal and essential personal growth and development. It's at the core of so many therapy sessions. Learning that you have options during times when your mind is commanding you to duck and cover is what true freedom is all about.

CHAPTER 6

The Mind Is Designed to Resolve Uncertainty

The Mind Dislikes Confusion, So It Rapidly Problem Solves, Sometimes Correctly

When active, your brain consumes a tremendous amount of physical energy. In *The Brain Explained*, author Daniel Drubach notes that while the brain accounts for less than 2 percent of a person's weight, it consumes about 20 percent of the body's total energy supply. This fact gives clout to what is meant when someone says they are *drained* or *worn out* after sitting all day and remaining intensely engaged in challenging mental tasks.

When your mind is not needed, it shifts into a type of relative slumber referred to as a resting state, saving energy for times when it's really needed. Just the same, although it may seem as though your brain flips off based on the level and type of stimulation in your surroundings, it never stops working. Consequently, your mind is always on duty.

Intriguingly, when your brain is in neutral, the region of the brain not involved in focused attention of the external world bursts into action. When you close your eyes and place yourself in a relaxed state of mind with deliberate disengagement from your surrounding world, what happens is a specific system of connected brain areas comes alive. These interconnected brain areas are referred to as the default mode network, or DMN for short.

The DMN was discovered by neuroscientists who asked individuals to undergo specialized functional neuroimaging called positron emission tomography (commonly known as a PET scan), which measures blood flow and oxygen consumption. Surprisingly, what was discovered was that specific brain areas decreased in activity as brain activity increased in association with task engagement. Inversely, the activity of the DMN increased as task disengagement occurred, which happens when you go into autopilot or otherwise zone out. Who knew that daydreaming involved so much brain activity?

An amazing aspect of the brain is that it is highly interconnected. As noted above, specific brain areas associated with the DMN become active when you are focused on what is happening inside of you and not around you. When your attention shifts to the outside world, other brain regions jump into action.

While there are numerous well-known brain regions, two such external world networks include the salience and executive control networks. The function of the former is to alert you to what is important and where you should shift your attention. When you are feeling scared, for instance, the salience network activates and becomes intensely focused on searching for threats that may be harmful.

For example, remember Tyler, the young man highlighted in the previous chapter who grew up with an extremely abusive and alcoholic father? As a boy, when Tyler saw his father tip the bottle in the late afternoon, his salience network lit up with intense activity. His mind became laser focused on his father's addicted actions so he could be prepared to take evasive action, which brings us to the second network.

The executive control network, meanwhile, keeps track of what is happening around you. It governs the emotional parts of your brain, controls your attention when divided by competing stimuli, and is pivotal during times of problem solving and decision-making.

Throughout Tyler's upbringing, while his executive control network worked overtime for a solution to protect his mother, quite traumatically, he was placed in a powerless position that resulted in him learning to tolerate intolerable behavior with intensely negative consequences.

From the perspective of Tyler's wife, who grew up without being subjected to such emotional dishonesty and overt parental hostility, her executive control network worked quite effectively. That is why she directed Tyler to go to therapy, so he could examine his past and become more present, identify unhealthy habits, challenge unconscious beliefs, recognize and navigate difficult emotions, and develop life skills that are more relational and mutually beneficial. Tyler's therapeutic journey would focus on helping him learn the right life lessons that conflict has been trying to teach him so that he can stop avoiding conflict and, instead, discover how to turn conflict into connection.

Your Breaking Point

As you might think, your mind is most active when it is being intensely challenged either emotionally or cognitively. The dynamic relationship between the mind and the outside world causes it to rev its engine during times of complexity, uncertainty, and increasingly stressful situations.

In popular psychology, there's a lot of talk about stress. Let's break it down into some bite-sized chunks.

On the one hand, there is the concept of a stressor. Technically, a stressor is environmental. It is something that happens in your external world that causes you to experience some level of inner tension or anxiety. There are helpful and hurtful stressors.

On the helpful side, one stressor might be the expected birth of a child, obviously a joyful change that requires you to adjust or respond to life with a newborn. On the hurtful side, another stressor might be the unexpected loss of a job, a jarring event that requires you to adapt to a sudden outbreak of uncertainty, rush of insecurity, and raw feelings of rejection and devaluation.

On the other hand, there is good old-fashioned stress. Stress is biological. It is your body's natural defense to a stressor. Whether the stressor is wanted or unwanted, your body reacts to change with physical, mental, and emotional responses. While stress is natural, when it is experienced too often or for too long, the combined experience of increased blood pressure, halted digestion, heightened muscle tension, sweating, and surging chemicals puts the body into a state of high readiness, which can feel quite strange, unwanted, and, in a word, unnatural.

The experience of stress, especially when it's intense and chronic, can cause you to reach a breaking point. This is the point at which the intensity of the moment exceeds your capacity to adapt. What you do next likely reflects what you've always done. When overstimulated or overwhelmed, from a mental perspective, your past ziplines into the present and takes over. During such moments, the question becomes, are you in control or are you being controlled by what you've learned from similar situations in your past?

What the Mind Does under Stress

When you experience a situation that overwhelms you, floods your emotions, and strangles your thoughts, in this state of disarray, your mind gets busy. Busy doing what? Your mind gets about its business trying to figure out what's going on, separating the wheat from the chaff, deciphering fact from fiction, and moving rapidly toward certainty.

The figure below illustrates your mind's predisposition to cycle from uncertainty to certainty briskly and instinctively. Such instincts are motivated by a neurophysiological compulsion to experience relief, to suspend or terminate discomfort, in lay terms, attain instant gratification, and doing so as quickly as it takes for the clock to strike midnight. The key principle associated with this *mind cycle* is that once relief has been secured, like hitting the jackpot, whatever caused its appearance is reinforced, which guarantees its repetition. Hence, the term *cycle* when referring to what your mind does under conditions of distress, confusion, and volatility.

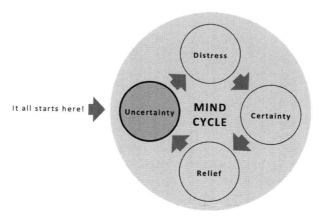

MIND CYCLE

Think of a child in middle school. She gets up in the morning, eats a healthy breakfast, packs her things, and heads to the bus stop, arriving in plenty of time to catch the bus and sit next to her best friend. Upon arrival at school, she goes to her locker, empties her backpack, and proceeds to class, pleasantly enjoying the chitchat that occurs along the way.

So far, so good. Since her day is going according to plan, she hasn't needed her mind for much of anything. Instead, she is simply enjoying the flow of her day and relying upon her authentic self. No reason for her to worry about being anyone but who she is when her walk of life is going according to plan.

Then, when she arrives at her first-period math class, out of nowhere, she's told of a pop quiz. This is when her mind gets busy. Not knowing what to expect and not feeling especially prepared, her body starts to feel the impact of cortisol, epinephrine, and norepinephrine surging through her autonomic nervous system, all of which are released in response to feeling ambushed by the unexpected moment.

If that weren't enough, her blood pressure is a bit high, her breathing is faster and shallower, her digestive system has slowed down, and her muscles have become tense. Even so, she knows she has natural skills in math, and her solid grades support this self-assessment. This girl is experiencing uncertainty. She is having a stress reaction. She is overwhelmed by her circumstances and is distressed.

Responding to this moment of perceived threat, her mind gets to work. Her thoughts are crisscrossing, her emotions are somersaulting, and she's imagining herself doing poorly on the quiz, while also believing she can achieve anything thrown her way.

This example shows how the mind gets busy during times of complexity. In this way, the mind is designed to resolve uncertainty. Although on the outside the young student does her best to maintain a calm demeanor, inside she's feeling nervous and caught off guard; she really doesn't want to ruin her track record of having straight A's. Her mind's reaction to this stressful moment is teetering between hoping for the best and preparing for the worst, while keeping her fingers tightly crossed.

If this girl had low self-confidence, her mind may be inclined to stay focused on the negative aspects of a pop quiz and end up contributing to her underperforming. In this pessimistic scenario, believing she has not lived up to her potential, her mind prepares her for the downside of doing poorly, disappointing her parents, and wondering why math comes so easily to everyone but her.

Alternatively, in a second scenario, the same girl may choose to accept the stress and mentally step into the situation by reminding herself of her natural talents, trusting her skills, and allowing her learning capacity to lead the way—likely resulting in a good enough, if not impressive, grade.

In the first scenario, while this girl's negatively saturated mind does not make things better, it prevents the situation from getting worse. Her mind, in this case, has prepared her to accept an unacceptable grade. Her mind braces for a worst-case result. By doing so, her mind has fully cycled from uncertainty to distress, which was then partially relieved by her decision to surrender to her circumstances. While she may not feel like a winner, her mind has somewhat mitigated her loss.

In the second scenario, quite differently, while the stress of the situation was tempting her to believe she may not do well, the girl short-circuited her initial mind's reaction and instead relied upon her learning history. Simply put, she thought better of the situation and factored into her life equation life experiences that fostered her to be successful. While this may not be an example of mind over matter, it does show how to focus on what matters so the mind can follow suit.

Mind Rule Life Lesson
The Mind Is Designed to Resolve Uncertainty

In times of uncertainty, when the intensity of the moment heats up, your mind becomes active and extremely focused on what's going on around you. During times of high stress, the dilemma with which you're faced is whether you want your mind to control you or if you prefer to be, at least partially, in control of your mind. Take your pick. Remember, your future is counting on you to let go of your past.

A key to being able to tilt this dilemma in your favor is knowing, really knowing, that you are caught in the crosshairs of uncertainty, ambiguity, and negotiating contradictions. This requires a heightened state of awareness, which is accomplished by turning your attention to what's going on and placing this immediate experience into your central vision. Don't ignore the significance of the moment. Don't push aside what's going on. Don't minimize the impact this situation is having on your mind and body. Instead, say to yourself, "I'm facing a tough situation right now. I need to slow down, take a breath, and let my emotions settle and thoughts come into focus." A quick mind trick is to think of five potatoes, as in one-potato, two-potato, three-potato … up to five. When you reclaim your balance, you're ready to take the next step.

Step two. Now that you've slowed things down and found a bit of calm in the storm, give yourself some extra space to make sense of the situation. A fantastic way of dealing with difficult moments is to consider the following the axiom: when in doubt, think twice. Since your first response may not be your best and, quite likely, merely an echo from days gone by, giving yourself the space to think, and then think some more, enhances your ability to better understand what's going on both inside of you and all around.

Summing up, when you give yourself time and space to think through a situation, your perspective expands, your vision becomes clearer, and you are much less likely to jump at shadows. By doing so, you are learning to release yourself from your past by embracing what's going on in real time, not remembered time. The practice of finding time and space during moments of madness teaches you how to open your mind and replace uncertainty, not with knowledge but with a willingness to accept what's in front of you and what you don't yet know. The experience of intentionally not knowing is more commonly referred to as the mindset of curiosity and the practice of creative, attentive listening.

Curiosity is a form of mental agility. It's what is needed when the a priori domination of dark moments from your past collide with the intensity of the moment. The destructive shadows of past wounds stemming from relational hiccups to times of shock and awe intensifies the moment with the fullness of unspoken letdowns, curveballs, and washouts. By remaining open-minded to or curious about what is happening as opposed to regressing with childlike devotion to the displeasure of the moment, you are gripping the inner landscape of your mental map and saying, "Let's take a chance, knowing that sometimes the chances taken don't work out, and not let our mind take over, and instead of focusing with a backward glance on the ambiguous nature of the moment, let's convert frustration and discontent into curiosity, which lends itself to creative surprises."

CHAPTER 7

The Mind's Favorite Number Is One

*Competing Truths Create Confusion and Doubt;
Preferring Certainty, the Mind Struggles to Balance Rival
Truths and Ends Up Choosing One over the Other*

How do you like your eggs?

The mind is strongly influenced by patterns and themes. It is capable of digesting incredibly complex data, cataloging competing information, deciphering what's important, and then proceeding confidently with a decision-making strategy. Once your mind has made up its mind, so to speak, it then returns to a relative state of rest, feeling proud and accomplished. Because of your mind's desire to save energy, it quickly determines what is true, regardless of the complexity of the issue, and zeroes in on a singular truth.

Consider, for example, the question that is sometimes posed by a partner struggling in a romantic relationship: "Do you still love me?" This heartfelt query seems to be suitable for a yes or no answer. Truth is, though, it's not that simple. In a committed relationship, competing perceptions and realities can arise over time and cultivate a culture of conflict.

When frustrations, annoyances, and irritations build up, disappointment and doubt can take over. Once a person reaches the end of their rope, they may request reassurance. Since neither answer adequately articulates how that person truly feels, they may be hesitant to provide an answer. Unfortunately, when they don't answer promptly, the other person assumes the answer is no. (Later in this chapter, we'll discuss how to answer this tricky question, which serves as a conversational template that works for many other difficult conversations.)

The combination of your mind relying upon different mental shortcuts and working speedily causes you to have thoughts so fast that later you might not fully remember having them. Yet, amidst an input of swirling information, your mind somehow always (or almost always) finds the answer it prefers. Your preferences, not reality, therefore, greatly influence what you believe to be true. Let's explore briefly how your mind makes up its mind.

Too Much of a Good Thing!

An abundance of choice is commonplace in modern society. Whether you're shopping for a loaf of bread, choosing a restaurant, or buying a car, you are bombarded with options, which, paradoxically, makes it harder for your mind to choose and can lead to detrimental feelings of stress and anxiety. When you are given what seems to be unlimited choices, your mind gets bogged down. Instead of just picking up a loaf of bread, for instance, you are challenged with choosing from white, whole wheat, multigrain, regular or thinly sliced, gluten-free, and so on.

In his popular book titled *The Paradox of Choice*, Barry Schwartz makes a compelling argument as to why more is less. Stated succinctly, Schwartz argues that having too much choice, too many options, too much freedom is detrimental to your mental health. Schultz contends that your psychological and emotional well-being is contingent upon having just enough but not too many choices and options.

The point is your mind becomes overwhelmed with too much information. Therefore, eliminating noise or distracting information as quickly as possible is critically important to ascertaining your truth. Further, the great enterprise of your mind eliminating unnecessary information lends itself to impulsively jumping to conclusions. By doing so, your mind achieves something extremely satisfying—it secures a sense of certainty.

To help solve problems and make decisions, your mind has devised a way of making problems less challenging by focusing on certain information and ignoring the rest. This mental shortcut (also called heuristics) comes down to a simple strategy of divide and conquer. That is, the mind takes a bundle of information, groups things together, and applies judgment and certitude.

If asked to count the number of dots in the boxes below, for instance, you'll notice that it takes less time to count the dots in the box on the left side than on the right side. Why? Because the dots have been divided and arranged in a pattern. It is the pattern of dots that allows your mind to solve the problem so easily. By contrast, the dots in the box on the right side are scattered, and, as such, your mind needs to work a bit harder.

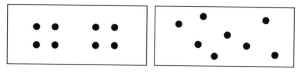

Two rectangles with dots

In everyday life, your mind is essentially performing this same process automatically and repeatedly. Your mind is designed to separate the wheat from the chaff as it determines what is true. Because it works on autopilot, your mind is making up its mind all the time, without you even realizing it. This is driven by a spirited need to reduce confusion and doubt. In this way, your mind is telling you what to do automatically. The good news is that your mind's knack for autopiloting works. The bad news is that it can also work against you.

Is Right Ever Wrong?

When your mind makes up its mind, is it always right? What's more, can you always trust the mind? To answer these questions, it is important to understand that there are various names for when your mind takes shortcuts: bias, prejudice, partisanship, favoritism, bigotry, racism, homophobia, and more. When you engage in such one-sided thinking, your mind is rapidly making sense of uncertainty or confusion by focusing on the one thing that is most relevant to your values, priorities, and preferences. Then, with the top priority selected, your mind decides the truth of the matter.

Walking into an ice-cream shop, you may become overwhelmed by the variety of flavors, which might make you opt to go back to basics. Let's say chocolate is your favorite go-to ice cream. By settling on this flavor, you've effectively eliminated a vast number of choices, making your final choice much easier. Deciding if you want cookie dough bits or fudge pieces in your ice cream is a much easier decision than contemplating the countless flavors and variations available.

The image below depicts another example of how your mind decides quickly and asserts confidence in its decision. When asked, "What do you see?" the most common answer is a young woman. When examined, the initially ambiguous picture reveals an attractive young woman turning her head away, her eyelash suggesting a state of quiet confidence and youthful beauty. Given this answer, the next question is "Can we trust this answer?"

IMAGE, MY WIFE AND MOTHER-IN-LAW
PHOTO CREDIT: WIKIMEDIA COMMONS.

Notice how your mind rapidly discerns the information above and resolves the visual challenge with little effort. However, in doing so, without knowing it, your mind may not realize there is more to the image than initially suspected. If so, then what you first see above should not be fully trusted.

Now that you understand how your mind handles complexity, we need to ask whether the mind is always right. The short answer is no. Your mind only makes up its mind based on things it believes to be true. So, if you asked your mind if it is always right, you would likely hear such replies as "absolutely," "of course," "certainly," and "without question." Yet, the deep truth is we all make mistakes. We all get ahead of ourselves. We all jump to conclusions and act with haste.

Back to the image above, when examined more closely, the young woman disappears, and in her place, a much older woman emerges. Even more amazing, now that your mind knows that two competing realities exist within this image, when you focus on the older woman, the younger one disappears, and vice versa. An interesting scientific trinket about this optical illusion is that while upon first gaze the younger woman is typically identified, it depends on your age. That is, older people tend to see the older woman first. This finding highlights how perception is directly influenced by available knowledge. Stated differently, what's on your mind is swayed by what's in your mind. Your learning, memory, emotions, and life experiences become a filter through which you see either an attractive younger woman or a much older one.

Preferring certainty, this optical illusion shows how your mind struggles to balance rival truths and, therefore, inevitably chooses one over the other.

IMAGE, MY WIFE AND MOTHER-IN-LAW
PHOTO CREDIT: WIKIMEDIA COMMONS.

Because your brain is a massive network of neural connections that requires an enormous amount of energy to keep it running, another example of how your mind employs a popular tactic to save valuable energy involves the "Is the cup half-empty or half-full?" challenge. This well-known question is based on a rapid psychological test that asks individuals to describe what they see after being shown a glass filled halfway. As is well known, some people immediately say the glass is half-full, while others just as quickly assert the same glass is half-empty.

In truth, everyone is correct.

What this simple test shows is how your mind, when faced with an obstacle, picks a side. This picking process underscores how your mind's favorite number is one. Choosing one thing, seeing the world one way, or having a preference, one way or the other, simplifies complexity while significantly reducing the energy cost associated with being befuddled.

By the way, are you more of an optimist or pessimist? Having some fun, answer the following questions to find out which way your mind tilts. Here's an important tip: your first answer is likely your truthful answer.

1. Do you tend to predict fortune (optimism bias) or misfortune (pessimism bias)?
2. Are you more positive (optimism bias) or negative (pessimism bias)?
3. If given the choice, do you typically choose to not choose (pessimism bias), or do you roll the dice and leave it to chance (optimism bias)?
4. When you don't know what to do, what do you do? Do you smirk and do the same thing over and over (cynicism bias)? Or are you more likely to smile and try something new (optimism bias)?
5. Do you engage in wishful thinking (optimism bias), or prefer not to wish at all (pessimism bias)?
6. How do you like your eggs? Sunny side up or over-hard?

To make your decision even easier, ask yourself which of the following statements sounds most like you.

"Prepare for the worst, hope for nothing better" (pessimism bias).

"Hope for the best, thinking of nothing else" (optimism bias).

When discussing the two opposing worldviews, it may appear the dichotomy is easy to distinguish and that people fall convincingly to one side or the other. In truth, on both sides, there are those who lean somewhat in one direction, while others are heavily entrenched in their state of mind. For instance, some people become cynical now and again (freethinkers and doubters), while others are deeply and endlessly cynical by nature (scoffers, sneerers, and mockers). So, too, some people regularly respond with optimism (positive thinkers), and others are extreme in their optimistic ways (dreamers, idealists, true believers). Then there are many of us who swing back and forth between the two worldviews based on different situations and experiences.

Regardless of the way your mind slants, by continuing to read this book, it is hoped you will improve your mind control to move more effectively toward personal greatness.

Do You Still Love Me?

Earlier in this chapter, the question of "Do you still love me?" was introduced. When confronted with this type of awkward moment, your mind tends to think in binary terms, such as yes or no. This preference for quick and easy processing can get you into trouble. Why? Because neither of these answers represents the complete truth of your private experience.

Consider a scenario in which two people have known each other for over a decade and have been in a life partnership for the past eight. Thanks to the length of their relationship, they have reached a place in which their differences, the things that were unique and captivating initially, have transformed into sources of frustration and aggravation.

Imagine this same couple has thrown themselves into their respective careers, developing separate circles of colleagues and acquaintances along the way, leading at least one of them to feel as though they are drifting apart. Responding to a felt sense of distance and lack of attention, one of the partners may begin to question the quality of the relationship, asking, "Do you still love me?"

This question of vulnerability deserves a quality answer. If the partner reflects meaningfully, their answer will surely contain a depth of thought beyond a one-word answer. To help this partner find their deep truth about their feelings related to the partnership, they would be wise to understand that the complexity of relationships incorporates a multitude of truths.

Knowing that deep truth is layered and interwoven, the most honest answer might sound like, "I love you now and forever, but lately it's been hard for me to find my love for you. This scares me, and I want to find my way back to us. Thanks for asking me to get real about our relationship. Let's talk about our next steps."

This answer reveals an important truth about truth: if you remain patient and search intentionally and with curiosity, you will be able to express your deepest truth. By doing so, you are at once being vulnerable, placing emphasis upon your highest values, and doing so in a way that validates your mindset as well as your partner's.

Mind Rule Life Lesson
The Mind's Favorite Number Is One

When thinking about whether you can and should always trust your mind, it's safe to say your mind is always doing its best. Remember, your mind is geared to keep you safe and secure, notify you of signs of danger, and take immediate action when feeling threatened. It's also quite adept at deciding how you like your eggs—sunny side up, over-hard, or perhaps a bit runny.

To verify if you can trust your mind, knowing that your mind's favorite number is one, it behooves you to notice that *one thing* your mind is focused on. If the answer is chocolate, then let your mind do its thing and enjoy every bite. If the answer involves judgment at another person's expense, then it's wise for you to ponder, have a second thought, and take a shot at being more open-minded. Opening your mind becomes possible when you choose to reflect instead of reacting, to be curious, to rethink the situation, to consider what's going on from another perspective, and to put your brain into learning mode so that your search for a deeper truth can be discovered.

Without opening your mind, you become decidedly vulnerable to building and believing in a one-world view of life. Because your viewpoint may be comforting, even gratifying, you become attracted to like-minded people who serve to bolster your point of view. While you may think your one-world is getting bigger, in fact, it's not expanding. Your one-world is unidimensional and leaves you susceptible to developing rigid beliefs and conventional behaviors to the point that others might say you are set in your way.

Since your mind's fondness for the number one inspires you to judge rapidly, decisions are made in a split second. For this reason, it's imperative to be mindful of what fills your mind. Then and only then can you begin to unhinge yourself from your upbringing, relationship history, and what you've learned during times you weren't aware you were being taught.

CHAPTER 8

Once the Mind Makes Up Its Mind, It Believes Itself to Be Correct

Craving Clarity and Certainty, the Mind Errs on the Side of What It Already Knows

Your mind uses an enormous amount of energy to work at an optimal level. For that reason, when it doesn't need to be active, it slows down to conserve energy after making decisions rapidly or burning the midnight oil. When a decision is made, it's as if your mind completes its decision-making duty, says to itself, "Job well done," and then leans back, places its feet on the desk, and enjoys a well-earned nap. Here's the catch, and it's a big one—once your mind's made up its mind, it believes itself to be correct.

Do you see the catch?

Learning with Our Eyes Closed

As humans, we're gifted with the amazing ability to think abstractly, contemplate options, and pick favorites among numerous options. But while you likely take considerable pride in your ability to be in control of your thinking, as opposed to your thoughts controlling you, this isn't always the case.

Learning happens both intentionally and by happenstance. If you take up skateboarding, for instance, you rapidly begin to lay down new neural pathways inside specific regions of your brain. These fresh pathways reflect your experience of doing something for the first time. Since your brain is composed of billions of neurons (brain cells) and trillions of connections among them (synapses), the creation of specific pathways provides your brain a handy way of retracing its steps.

When you then repeat the same activity over and over, the neural pathways inside your brain get wider and wider, so to speak. The wider or stronger the pathway, the more overlearned something becomes. When a pathway is wide enough, for better or worse, it can be said that what you've learned, you could do with your eyes closed. These pathways have taken you from novice to master without you even knowing.

Visualize what happens when a person walks across a lawn for the first time. What is left behind is a faint impression from this single track. But if the person walked along the same path day after day, the grass would eventually wear down, leaving behind a distinct path. Similarly, your brain's neural pathways become increasingly well-defined the steeper you get into your learning curve. This tracking system explains the process of what happens when habits develop.

While some habits are incredibly handy, such as brushing your teeth, making your bed, or saying *please* and *thank you*, other habits are less helpful. Think of the habit that develops when you have a glass of wine or two at the end of your day. While this routine may be well deserved and highly effective in terms of taking the edge off, if your habit follows the well-known neural pathway of *more is better than less*, then your pattern of increased drinking can become a habit that is counterproductive, even destructive.

For another example of how repetition shapes reality, consider the benign phrase *blonds have more fun*. Although this expression is meant to convey something lighthearted and playful, it can also be harmful socially. Upon hearing this expression repeated in television shows and movies, social media, and everyday banter, the meaning behind this turn of phrase can be rude and dismissive, even misogynistic.

The truth is that brunettes, redheads, and even people who dye their hair blue are all capable of having the same amount of fun. The color of hair has nothing to do with the person's fun-loving nature.

The point here is that when your neural pathways widen by repeated exposure, your mind is enticed to go down that same path over and over. While the expression about blonds was meant to be just a no-harm, no-foul figure of speech, when repeated enough times across enough life experiences, this innocuous expression transforms into a deep-seated belief. Once transformed, such rigidified and overgeneralized thoughts become highly formidable along your journey to stay on top of things, make sense of everything, rule the world around you, and all other mind-boggling things that lie at the heart of the human condition.

While beliefs are enormously helpful in decreasing complexity and making decisions quickly, the downside is they slow down or hinder your critical-thinking process. After all, if your belief functions as a type of factory-loaded answer, in a situation that deserves thoughtful reflection and analytical thinking, instead of slowing down and contemplating options and choosing wisely, your mind will be inclined to access your belief system, and what you say may not be well received. To your mind, blonds may really be having more fun.

If, for example, you possess a firm belief that bluegrass is the best type of music, and someone asks you about classical music, it's quite likely that your immediate response will be rather unfavorable. Guided by your belief system, your mind determines, "If it's not bluegrass, then it's not good music." In the wake of your rapid answer, the person who asked you the question may think you're unsophisticated and closed-minded. They'd be wrong about their first thought but quite correct on the second.

Knowing the mind rule *once the mind makes up its mind, it believes it's correct* helps you to know better when you should know better. Let's try an experiment. Find the pattern in the series of numbers below.

| 8 | 5 | 4 | 9 | 1 | 7 | 6 | 3 | 2 | 0 |

Numbers, eight to zero

By and large, most people struggle with this mental puzzle. They attempt all different computations. They try in vain to decipher the numerical pattern among the various numbers. What makes this puzzle so tricky is that, without knowing it, they are attempting to solve the problem with a closed mind.

That is, the visual information in the puzzle advises them to think in numbers. By doing so, the puzzle is unsolvable. This puzzle provides an example of how the mind makes up its mind and believes itself to be correct, but this isn't always true. (Refer to the end of this section to find the answer to the puzzle. Hint—open your mind.)

The Price of Being Closed-Minded

When it comes to keeping an open mind, your mind is determined, methodical, and quite resistant, and it operates with a winner-take-all mentality. While your mind does not intentionally ignore facts or walk away from wisdom, by holding on tightly to information it believes to be correct, your mind is quite stubborn, rigid, and hardheaded, so to speak.

Based on the strength of conviction, your mind is capable of rebelling and defying authority, being emotionally cold and unresponsive, feeling righteously indignant, and displaying signs of grandiosity, limited empathy, and proud arrogance. To your mind, being right feels right.

When it comes to reasoning, your mind tends to look for information it needs to verify what it already believes to be correct, as opposed to keeping an open mind and waiting for the right answer to come along. Because looking for evidence that might disprove your belief takes time and can create confusion, simply stated, your mind prefers being right over getting it right. Knowing that your mind is quite pleased with what it already knows, the question becomes, what's the cost of being closed-minded?

In a word, immense.

Closed-mindedness is a key factor that keeps your world in gridlock while promoting self-control and increases the odds of you being in opposition to other people. Because of the commonness of this state of mind, in the world of interpersonal therapy, where relationships are dissected and being relational is promoted, there is an expression that goes *you can be right or be in a relationship*.

This truism reveals the frustration of being in a relationship with a person who always needs to be right. The stumbling block in this type of situation is not that the other person may be right; it's that you'd be proven wrong. When you are told, directly or indirectly, that your opinion is misinformed, incomplete, or flat-out incorrect, the message received is that your voice does not matter and, by proxy, nor do you.

Needing to be right is a favorite pastime of controlling people. The upside to believing that everybody is wrong except you is that it simplifies reality by dividing the world into right or wrong. And if you're always right, it's easy to know where everyone else stands. Even more, the same controlling people who are doing wrong by insisting that others are wrong don't view the wrong they are doing as wrong. Why? Because in their mind, they are justified in their action and, therefore, by all measures right. It is during such times to such minds that the truth and an attractive lie fuse.

Except for sociopaths, paranoids, and pathological liars, most people avoid doing the wrong thing, at least intentionally. Yet all of us, at one time or another, are vulnerable to doing the wrong thing for the right reason (justification; robbing the rich to give to the poor, otherwise known as Robin Hood syndrome) or doing the right thing for the wrong reason (self-promotion; giving a large donation to a worthy cause and attaching one's name for public display, or self-protection: attending the hardest school in the region to prove your father's opinion that "you'll never amount to anything" is wrong).

In any case, we all slip up. Sometimes our opinions are a bit too rigid and voiced with alarming intensity. At other times, we fight the fight in submissive and emotionally dishonest ways. And there are those times when our habit of wanting to be right is simply due to a lack of considering the other person's perspective. The point being, we all are prone now and again to needing to be right. But being right all the time, insisting your opinion is absolutely correct and beyond reproach, or being mercilessly critical of others who dare to tender an opposing viewpoint, is relationally destructive. Remember, you can either be right or in a relationship. Choose which one is most important.

Here's still more. When power and control are not mutually distributed in a relationship, there is no shared understanding. Further, without understanding each other, there is no relationship. When the relationship falters, conflict escalates quickly, resentment builds, and things progress rapidly from good to ugly.

Think of such hot topics as abortion, gun control, national health care, global warming, vaccines, immigration reform, and vaccination. All these controversial topics have one thing in common—they all elicit strong and entrenched opinions, where people take sides and different states of mind collide.

When people with strong opinions interact, the process typically becomes uncomfortable and awkward, or worse, uncivilized. Such phrases as "bumping heads," "going for the jugular," "squaring off," "putting up a fight," and "crossing swords" all evoke conflict or varying degrees of irritability, animosity, and combativeness.

An interesting sidenote about closed-mindedness is that it's rather easy to disagree with and disconnect from others. It can be argued that disputing another person's opinion and clashing with their point of view comes effortlessly to many humans.

It's likely a universal truth that no couple has ever sought therapy to learn how to disconnect and make their fighting more contentious. Too many couples become exceptionally adept at picking fights, escalating conflict, and making things far worse than they need to be without any help from others. Because of this phenomenon, a common reason couples seek therapy is to stop their fighting by learning about their triggers, exploring their background, and developing improved coping responses.

The opposite of being closed-minded is open-mindedness, which is much easier said than done. Being open-minded requires a willingness to privately confess that your thoughts and beliefs may benefit from some tweaking. It involves the ability to not be fazed by the more off-putting aspects of your personality. In practical terms, becoming more open-minded by actively searching for evidence against your highly favored beliefs is where the rubber meets the road. Given that your mind grips tightly to information it believes to be correct, being open-minded goes against this grain. Because being open-minded increases the odds of proving yourself to be incorrect, it's easy to understand how hard opening your mind can be.

Hold on. There are more reasons why being open-minded may not feel natural to you. If you choose to be open-minded, others may think of you as being wishy-washy, indecisive, cowardly, capricious, and wavering. What they don't know, however, is that being open-minded requires a high degree of intentionality, curiosity, and flexibility in your commitment to learning. To assume an intentional learning stance requires a great deal of drive, watchfulness, focus, and courage.

Mind Rule Life Lesson
Once the Mind Has Made Up Its Mind, It Believes Itself to Be Correct

While the mind is a know-it-all and craves certainty, remember that wisdom has been popularly defined as *wise is he who knows that he does not know*. Therefore, if committed to expanding your mind and bolstering your knowledge base, it is vital for you to continue collecting evidence above and beyond what you already have accepted as being gospel. In this vein, it behooves you to remember that seeking the truth often involves knowing that you'll never truly know, as *truly knowing* something requires absolute knowledge, which is beyond the human grasp.

"What else might be true?" is an easy way to check out whether your mind has made up its mind and shut down for new business. If you find your response to this query to be "I don't care" or "It doesn't matter" or "Whatever," then your mind tends to brush aside new learning and holds steadfastly to what it already knows to be correct. In this way, to a closed mind, no news is good news.

Yet ask yourself what is more important, having a casual approach to the truth so that your beliefs conveniently fit into altering configurations of reality or giving allowance to reality to form your truth? Pick wisely. Challenge yourself to be more in control of your mind rather than allowing your mind and its preassembled version of truth to be controlling over you. Not only that, keep in mind that the problem with testimonials, even when self-created, is that they do not constitute evidence in the world of hard science.

Quiz Answer

Remember the puzzle presented earlier? The challenge was to find the pattern in the series of numbers below.

8 5 4 9 1 7 6 3 2 0

NUMBERS, EIGHT TO ZERO, AGAIN

The mental struggle behind this puzzle is based on your mind's determined nature (read: persistent and stubborn) to solve the problem using some type of numerical reasoning.

On the surface, this makes total sense. After all, at first glance, what you see is what you get—a series of numbers. Then, based on your extensive learning history with numbers, it is extremely logical to attempt to solve the problem using some type of mental math. However, by doing so, you get nowhere, other than being more frustrated. It seems the more you dig in, the more unsolvable the problem becomes.

After considerable effort, relying upon your mad math skills to identify the magical sequence gets you nowhere. Why? Because when you see numbers, you don't think otherwise. In this case, your mind's best guess is to *solve* the problem using a mindset based on numerical computation. However, by doing so, indeed, the problem becomes unsolvable. But it isn't. The answer to this puzzle, reflected below, is that the pattern in the series of numbers is alphabetized.

NUMBERS, SPELLED OUT

This quiz demonstrates how your mind at times gets trapped in its old ways of doing things. This mind rule reveals how once your mind makes up its mind, it believes it's correct.

CHAPTER 9

The Mind Doesn't Know When It Might Be Wrong

The Mind Is Smug and Presumptuous and Has a Quirky Blind Spot

The opposite of being right is being wrong. At times, however, the mind struggles with this kind of universally accepted sentiment. As we endeavor to reconcile competing versions of the truth, such absolutes can almost seem subjective. When we ponder what is true, we sometimes fail to consider the differences between perception and reality. Part of the experience of being human involves denying certain aspects of reality and placing special emphasis on factors that bolster what we believe to be true.

This tendency to be selective with certain truths suggests that your mind has blind spots. Being inclined to see what you prefer to see and believing in what you've come to believe is highly useful at times but not so much in others. This is your mind's way of cooking the books, so to speak, to distance you from being challenged or disputed. According to this mind rule, your mind's blind spot illustrates how it doesn't know when it might be wrong. Let's put this idea to the test.

Is Seeing Believing?

Your mind's primary aim is to accurately understand the world in which you live. At times, however, your first take on how things work isn't always valid. In fact, your perception of what is happening can be distorted without you realizing you've been fooled.

The popular Müller-Lyer illusion provides a succinct example of how your mind doesn't know when it might be wrong. The instructions for this test are simple. Look at the figure below. What do you see? Are the two vertical lines the same or different lengths?

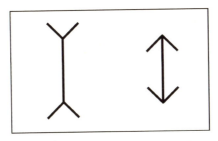

ARROWS UP AND DOWN

At first blush, all of us see the same thing—two vertical lines with arrowheads connected at each endpoint, with one set of arrowheads pointing toward inward and the other facing outward. Chances are when asked about the appearance of the vertical lines, they appear to be different. That's the illusion. Look closer. Although they appear to be different, they are the same length. That said, what you see and believe to be true is not always the same as what is right in front of you.

Knowing What We Know

The power of knowledge creates a convincing haze. To prove this point, consider the equation of 2 + 2. Without consciously thinking about it, your mind briskly answers, "Four." You're completely confident with this answer. No matter how many times you're asked, without hesitation, you'll respond with the same answer with the same level of complete confidence. Why?

The short answer is because of a phenomenon known as overlearning, the process of rehearsing or practicing a skill beyond the point of initial mastery. To overlearn something is to have mastered the material or skill to the point it has become ingrained inside of you. Just like you can jump on a bike and ride away without hesitation or doubt, you can likewise solve the equation without actively thinking.

If you're interested in playing the violin or achieving the highest possible score on the SAT, then overlearning is particularly relevant and highly effective. When your mind has mastered something, it fills you with confidence and allows you to perform at the top of your game. On the other hand, if you're negotiating world peace with an unfriendly surrounding country or discussing where you should go to dinner tonight, then overlearning may result in a type of gridlock with emotions running at a fever-pitch level.

In the end, much of what you know to be true is based on either overlearning (2 + 2 = 4) or not wanting to be bothered by a contrary opinion or unwelcomed stance (welcome to your blind spot). Of course, knowing something to be true and feeling confident about what you know is fun and rewarding. Think of how gratifying it is to participate in a trivia game and get a few answers correct. In these instances, info you attained long ago comes tumbling back.

Even if you can't immediately come up with the right answer, chances are your memory banks are triggered and you're able to vividly recall clips from a movie, along with its basic plot and perhaps how it ends. Maybe you see the protagonist's face or recall some dialogue between the main characters. As we established, however, knowing something is true does not always make it true.

Mind Rule Life Lesson
The Mind Doesn't Know When It Might Be Wrong

Let me say that again: the mind doesn't know when it might be wrong. This statement is repeated to emphasize how strikingly pivotal knowing this mind rule is in gaining improved mind control in a complex world. When you're unaware your mind may be operating on cherry-picked facts, truncated findings, or crank theories, you become more susceptible to falling victim to conspiracy thinking and micro tales weaved together from muddled statistics and gerrymandered knowledge.

The life lesson here is that without giving any attention to the possibility of being wrong, you may find yourself digging in deeply, shrugging off the opinions of others, and remaining smugly content with your belief system and preferred version of the truth.

In the quasireligious and sloganized world of truth associated with the Church of Scientology, "If it's true for you, it's true." From the outside looking in, it's not difficult to see the pseudo-scientific nature of this foundational claim. But to those who follow the comforting qualities associated with this type of belief-building process, the world rapidly makes sense. Being able to trust what *true for you* is, in fact, therapeutic. But so is skydiving, as long as your parachute opens.

While it is fantastically satisfying to believe that you're always right, when you keep in mind how your habit of being right may put off others, you might consider developing a more flexible relationship with the truth, your truth, and nothing but the truth.

In view of this, it is beneficial to keep in mind that the world is not black and white; never has been and never will be. Truth comes in a variety of shapes, sizes, textures, and colors. Surprisingly, when you combine competing facts with your working version of the truth, you may land in an amazing place called wisdom.

The near opposite of wisdom is unconscious bias. The antidote for being blinded by your mind not knowing when it might be wrong is knowing that what you don't know is far greater than what you will ever know.

CHAPTER 10

The Mind Organizes and Prioritizes What It Knows to Be True

The Mind Is Neat and Tidy with "Truths" Stacked in Order of Importance and Preference

When you learn something new, it is stored in your memory bank. Such information and experiences get logged deliberately and for good reason. Some of these moments you enjoy. Others, meanwhile, you'd rather leave behind.

When you learn something consciously that requires deliberate effort, neuroscientists call it explicit memory. Learning names and locations of different countries on a map, for instance, or recalling all the items on a shopping list, or remembering the birth dates of loved ones, or learning your ABCs—these are all examples of explicit memory and learning achieved by design.

There are two types of explicit memory. First, there are recollections that unfolded across your upbringing and relationship history. These are details like playing in the park with your best friend in middle school, for example, or vignettes of your favorite family vacation, or recalling the name of your first pet. These details are related to your life story; as such, they're also referred to as your autobiographical memory.

There is also semantic memory. This database of information involves the countless facts, formulas, and problem-solving strategies that you learned throughout your lifetime. Knowing that Austin is the capital of Texas comes from your semantic memory pool. Explicit memory is critical when you take a test or attend a class reunion. This type of learning is gathered intentionally in your everyday walk of life.

Another type of memory is implicit memory, which involves information gathered outside of your immediate awareness. This info includes everything from details for navigating a familiar area, such as your neighborhood, to remembering the words to a popular song after hearing the first few notes. It also accounts for utilitarian aspects of daily life, like remembering how to drive a car or button a shirt or tying your shoes or riding a bike. This type of memory allows you to behave without having to give it a thought.

Now that you know the mind holds two types of memories, let's explore how the mind retrieves memories and why.

How the Mind Retrieves Memories

By paying attention to something, the odds increase enormously you will remember it. To ensure that you do, however, you need to engage in an additional three-step process—encoding, storing, and retrieving. Encoding is when you mentally label or tag an experience so that it sticks in your mind. Think of when you meet someone for the first time, and they tell you their name. Knowing that you're not good at remembering names, you need an encoding trick or two up your sleeve.

It was Dale Carnegie who said, "A person's name is, to that person, the sweetest, most important sound in any language." Consequently, when you remember that person's name and say it out loud, your connection with that person grows stronger because you are striking that sweet sound.

In a sense, the process of remembering a person's name is no different from learning mathematics. In math, there's a lot going on. In fact, for many, there's too much going on, which makes math intimidating to learn. Being good at math requires having a good memory—or, more specifically, having a good *working memory*.

This type of memory allows you to retain various bits of information in your mind at the same time. When you combine your working memory with a recognition of number patterns and recall of specific math rules, viola, you become a math wizard. On the other hand, when too much information surrounds you, it is experienced as noise. What is needed to learn a person's name is the same for remembering the Pythagorean theorem—you need to learn how to separate the signal from noise.

So what are some tricks? When a person shares their name with you, try repeating it silently to yourself three times ("Elaine, Elaine, Elaine") while casually studying various features of her face. Knowing that a person's name is the centerpiece to their identity, by placing their name in the center of your focused attention, you are engaging in a process known as controlled processing.

Consequently, instead of allowing Elaine's name to go in one ear and out the other—something that happens often when you engage in multitasking or are distracted by the noise in the moment—you pay explicit attention to Elaine and consciously pair the sound of her name to your experience.

Another trick to remember Elaine's name is to use her name in conversation a few times. By threading her name into the dialogue, not only are you getting her attention by playing that sweet sound, but you are bringing her name back to your attention over and over.

By doing so, you are overriding your old habit of forgetting the names of people and replacing it with a new strategy of *learning* names. For instance, instead of saying, "Can I get you something to drink?" you would say, "Elaine, can I get you something to drink?" This trick has a powerful effect on your capacity to turn learning Elaine's name from a practice into a habit that is later, like magic, completed automatically and without thinking.

After deliberately encoding information with controlled processing in place of automatic processing, you take the information you just learned and store it away in such a manner that you don't lose track of it (more about the storage process in just a moment).

Then, if you have paid attention, tagged it, and stored it securely, you've improved the odds of retrieving it. Retrieval is what gets all the glory. When you take a test and get one of the highest grades in the class, it's your retrieval capacity that gets the gold star. Yet, truth be told, stars should also be handed out to attention and encoding because learning is a team effort.

About the storage process, to find the material most efficiently you're looking for, there must be some type of organizational system, like in a library or bookstore. In your mind, you store an incredible amount of data and information, some of which are extremely relevant and highly useful. Other stored info is more trivial and has limited lasting value.

Just the same, all the information you have stored has one thing in common—you accept it as being a version of the truth. Why is this the case? Because you only hold onto information that has passed your truth test. This makes incredible sense. Of course, you wouldn't clutter your head with incorrect, misguided, or imprecise information. Consequently, your mind quickly separates the wheat from the chaff and only holds onto the good stuff.

An essential step in your highly valuable memory storage process involves taking all the information you believe to be correct and arranging it so you can later find it as fast as possible, preferably without noticeable delay. This process involves organizing and prioritizing. For you to recall information timely and accurately, your mind stacks things in order of importance and preference, allowing you to remember what's most important to you. You can rapidly call to mind your first kiss, for instance, or the year you graduated from high school, or your mother's maiden name.

You also archive your memories in order of preference. You likely recall the name of the books written by your favorite author; you remember the name of your most adored teacher; you vividly reminisce about your youthful adventures on the beach, going camping, or playing board games with family members during Christmas break. But your memory of those dreary summer days when you didn't think it would ever stop raining have faded away and no longer clutter your mind or compete against more important and preferred memories. Ultimately, what you remember represents preferred or necessary experiences.

Why Your Mind Retrieves Memories

This question likely sounds nonsensical. To some extent, you know why your mind retrieves memories—so you don't have to relearn something over and over. While this answer is completely acceptable, a more philosophical answer is also needed. Think about this statement: the purpose of life is to make memories!

This bold sentiment reinforces the notion that by making memories, you are giving meaning to your life. With some degree of accuracy, you can recall the good, bad, and ugly events that happened to you throughout your life. By retrieving your good memories, you revisit the happiest times, and a smile appears. In this way, good memories are engaging and uplifting.

The retrieval of bad memories can have motivational value too. If you remember doing poorly on the last test, it's more likely you'll try harder, get tutoring, or apply a new learning strategy that will improve the likelihood of making your next grade more favorable.

Although it sounds peculiar, your ability to recall your most harrowing memories is one of the greatest features of human development. Bringing back those menacing moments from days gone by protects you. When you remember the worst days of your life, you are in a better position to prevent such days from repeating and better prepared to navigate similar unfavorable life experiences in the future.

Mind Rule Life Lesson
The Mind Organizes and Prioritizes What It Knows to Be True

The mind shuffles through incoming information, selecting what is deemed relevant, and arranges its findings in order of importance.

Determining what's most valuable is how your mind decides what it knows to be true.

But can you trust your truth?

We all deeply believe in our ideas and beliefs. In fact, some of our convictions reach such epic heights that we become true believers. Regardless of how fantastic a flapdoodle, such a person has determined their beliefs are true and incontrovertible. The process of becoming a true believer involves gathering preferred versions of best evidence and thematically organizing such thoughts. Of critical importance, bear in mind, is that once thoughts are formulated into a belief, thinking is no longer required.

Put differently, we are all afforded free will and given readied access to its close companion known as freethinking. Yet when you have the same thought time and again, such repetitive thinking gradually turns into a personal philosophy formed by a narrowed perspective, handpicked principles, and cherished, if not hardened, belief. This process makes sense neurologically and psychologically. Thinking things over again and again is time-consuming and requires enormous mental energy. That's why having a belief system is so handy. Your beliefs cut through the chatter of daily life by separating signals from noise. Acting like an elixir to your private world, beliefs quiet your mind as your focus shifts toward information that confirms what you already know to be true. The downside associated with this circularity is beliefs can transform into dogma, a point of view held so tightly it motivates people to plunge headlong into a situation without adequate grounds and despite obvious flaws.

The upside of holding a belief is that it resolves, for instance, the tension of Pascal's wager—the bet as to whether God exists or not, and on which side of the wager you are willing to bet your life. The downside of keeping a tight grip on an unquestioned truth is that it distances you from the benefit that accompanies the process of being open-minded, and you are no longer burdened by such things as an opposing view, objectivity, partiality, or propagandistic accusations.

At the end of the day, some of us are loyal fans of the information ecosystem that contains our opinions and beliefs, while others of us are more fanatical. In either case, it is vital to remember that your *truths* are not absolute but relative, and as such, deserve to be reviewed, reshuffled, and reexamined now and again.

CHAPTER 11

The Mind Is Time Blind

*To the Mind, the Future Is as Real as the Past;
In This Way, the Mind Often Confuses What Has Happened
with What Is Happening and What Has Yet to Happen*

The mind organizes the past, responds to the present, and prepares for the future so you can know confidently and decisively what to do next. This is an important objective of the mind, which connects and balances time with motion.

Time is ubiquitous and never ending. No matter what you do or how you do it, or choose not to do it, the passage of time advances nonstop. But what you do can alter your perception of time. In this way, time can warp.

When you do something fun, time flies. When you're bored, it drags. Under times of pressure and dealing with a looming deadline, you may feel time is working against you, as if you're running out of time. Under different circumstances, time can be on your side. Time can be fluid. When you have a déjà vu moment, it's as if you went back in time. Time can slip away from you, as expressed by the phrase "Where did the time go?" Looking back on your life, you may long for more time. Then there are those moments when you want to set aside quality time for friends, family, or just a good long soak in the tub.

It seems, therefore, Einstein got it right when he discovered that time is relative. Of course, Einstein's groundbreaking insight was highly scientific, requiring an understanding at an advanced level of relative motion or gravitational forces and oodles of complex math. By contrast, your mind's notion of relativity is subjective, fleeting, even fanciful. Further, it's put forward in this chapter that your mind is time blind.

Time and Time Again

Young children have a limited grasp of time. Perhaps they are the lucky ones. Imagine the freedom in not knowing (or caring about) the difference between tomorrow, next week, or six years ago. Think about how much less stressful it would be if you weren't bothered by designations like urgent, ASAP, imperative, immediate, or dire.

As you grow, the concept of time expands until it becomes a practical benchmark in your day-to-day life. Your grasp of time helps you navigate competing demands, keeping you on track so you can prioritize what's important. Managing time makes life easier to control, allowing you to reduce stress, increase your productivity, and waste less time. For these reasons, keeping an eye on the clock brings considerable benefits.

Just the same, time is less relevant to the mind. Why? Because the most important time to your mind is right now. Your mind does its best work in the here and now. While your mind can reference the present, time is mostly out of sight and out of mind.

Your mind's primary focus on the present is not a flaw. By keeping an eagle eye on what's going on in the current situation, your mind serves as a type of warning system that alerts you to the good and bad things that may be happening, have yet to happen, or brings to mind things that have happened time and time again. On the other hand, since the mind is time blind, your relationship with time can make life a bit messy.

Trauma and Time

To the mind, what's happening in the present can be as real as what happened in the past. For instance, a memory of an intensely harrowing experience, an incident that caused you emotional upheaval, can be easily reactivated by something similar in nature or remotely related. Once your trauma has been triggered, the distressful memory is so deeply stored and intensely recreated in your mind that you can be convinced it's happening again, even when it's not. Replaying a particularly upsetting memory can be so disagreeable and unspeakable that you psychologically disconnect from yourself and the world around you.

This condition is known as dissociation or derealization, and these terms speak volumes about your mind's capacity to travel back in time without even realizing it ever left the current time. While everyone's experience of dissociation is unique, a common thread is a feeling of detachment from your body or a feeling that the world around is unreal. During such upsetting moments, your mind struggles to reconcile what really happened from the memories that have been triggered. This is a perfect example of your mind's ability to disconnect from the present through time blindness.

In a previous chapter, we shared Charlotte's story. She was the middle schooler who sustained a freak accident while playing soccer that resulted in an unresolvable spinal condition that left her homebound for the remainder of her childhood and into adulthood.

This resulted in her being in what we described as *traumatized by hope*, an expression that nodded to Charlotte's resilient nature and determined spirit, which allowed her to never give up hope or her search for some well-deserved relief and improved quality of life. Yet, because of her resolute hopefulness, when medical treatment failed to resolve her difficulties or improve her life situation, she would crash emotionally and be left wondering whether her life was worth living.

The mind rule detailed in this chapter (the mind is time blind) sheds light on the trap that Charlotte finds herself in. To her, the past and present are blurred beyond recognition, while her future is nowhere in sight. Every day seems like yesterday, and yesterday seems so long ago. Because her daily life does not vary to any meaningful degree, her opportunities to lay down new memories are minimal.

A core issue in trauma is reality and a person's ability to discern what is happening here and now from what took place then and there. Given this knowledge, it's clear that Charlotte's mind is indeed time blind. Although she certainly knows that time is ticking and the sun is rising and setting every day, the traumatic medical event she experienced is causing her to feel stuck. Not only is she bogged down by unrelenting pain, but her social network is, at best, modest. These two things are compounded by her mind's tendency to confuse today with yesterday, which leaves her disillusioned and disheartened.

Getting Ahead but Feeling Left Behind

If trauma is about your mind confusing the past and present and twisting them together unwillingly and unpleasantly, then worrying involves your mind traveling into the future and becoming less connected with the present. Are you a worrier? Welcome to the club. To some extent, we worry about what's about to happen, and when our worry gets a bit out of control, it's called anxiety.

With anxiety, our thoughts focus on what could happen, our emotions turn toward fear, our bodies rev up with our heart beating a bit faster, our breath quickens, and we move toward a fight, flight, or freeze mode.

When our anxiety jumps to that next level, panic shows up. Panic is anxiety on steroids. If you feel like your heart is racing and you become dizzy, and then you start sweating or shaking, feel sick to your stomach, have pain in your chest or abdomen, and feel disconnected from your surroundings (remember dissociation), then you may be having a panic attack. These same symptoms are often confused with having a cardiac event.

Whether we experience worry, anxiety, or panic, these states of mind are focused steadfastly on the future and the concern about what might appear around the next corner. To see how we can get ahead of ourselves, let's return to Tyler's story.

Remember Tyler? He's the guy whose past was troubled by a stern, controlling, and alcoholic father. Despite his father's obvious shortcomings and bad habits, Tyler looked up to him. When asked whether he loved his father, Tyler answered dutifully, "Of course." When asked what he loved about him, with much greater and reflective effort, Tyler said he respected his father immensely. Coyly, Tyler did not answer the question. But to be fair, to Tyler, love and respect were intertwined. Tyler's respect for his father, who provided shelter for the family and kept everyone fed, fueled his belief that he *loved* his father.

Without knowing it, Tyler replicated many of his father's behaviors as he moved into adulthood and started raising three children of his own. Of course, Tyler loved his children inside and out. He promoted their welfare, encouraged their accomplishments, and attended nearly all their activities. Tyler was a much-advanced version of his father when it came to demonstrating his love for his children. But not so much in other ways.

When Tyler's children are asked, "What's one thing you wish your father would do more often that he doesn't do nearly enough?" without hesitation, each child separately expressed some version of "be more himself," "be more accessible," "be less judgmental," and "love me for who I am, not for what I do."

In therapy, Tyler was asked about his relationship with the future. At first, he seemed genuinely puzzled by this inquiry. With further context about how his experiences with his father shaped his parenting and ability to be the parent he always wished to become, Tyler began to make contact with his anxiety. He shared a constant sense of worry and dread that the way he was parenting his children was not enough. When given greater therapeutic space for exploration about this felt experience, Tyler sensed he put too much emphasis on providing for his family and not enough effort into nurturing the people he cherishes the most. Had he become his father?

Interestingly, and quite fortunately, when asked to travel back in time and imagine what he might say to his father if he was still alive, Tyler echoed an eerily similar statement about his father. He connected the dots. Somehow, yes, he had become his father, or at least a version of the parent he always respected but from whom he never felt deeply loved. This insight sparked inside Tyler a desire to step out of his habituated way of parenting from a distance. It helped him begin to reshape his parenting style into something that more accurately reflected and naturally synchronized with his personality, his values, and his long-treasured wish to be the father his father never was to him. By doing so, Tyler courageously put much of his past behind him and gracefully stepped into being the person and the parent he always was meant to be.

Do you see how Tyler's willingness to examine his trauma and listen to his anxiety opened his capacity to become more himself?

Mind Rule Life Lesson
The Mind Is Time Blind

The past, present, and future seem to be so obviously different. Yet your mind often gets confused. For example, to your mind, trauma causes your past to collide into the present, reminding you of the worst moments of your life. When your trauma is triggered, it's as if you get stuck in the past. Because of the way trauma is stored and behaves inside your nervous system, your worst memories can surge back when you are least prepared, leaving you with a desperate wish to forget.

Then there's worry, which causes your attention to shift from the present to the future. And while all of us worry from time to time about this or that, excessive worry causes you to dwell on difficulty or troubles repetitively and with increased negativity. Normal worry allows you to think ahead and plan accordingly. This type of time shifting makes a great deal of sense, especially when there is something of importance that requires your time and attention.

Excessive worry, meanwhile, hijacks your attention from what is happening and causes you to overfocus on events or ideas that are unlikely and extremely remote. When worry fails to yield to your better judgment, this type of worry can torment you and cause you to remain attached to the type of thinking that has no real purpose.

In these ways, trauma causes your mind to stay stuck in the past, while worry makes your mind get ahead of itself. Knowing the mind rule that your mind is time blind invites you to take the time and slow down. A great course of action involves thinking about what's next and then finding that sweet spot in your mind where you find that time is on your side. This is a felt experience of when you're not being bullied by your past or being abducted by the future.

CHAPTER 12

The Mind Expands by Learning

*When We Open Our Minds to New Experiences,
Our Perspective Shifts*

How and what you learn determines everything. Beyond instincts, which are available to you without asking, learning reflects your interaction with our external world and your ability to internalize information and replicate behavior with increasing mastery.

Infants progressively master their use of cries and sighs to get their needs met. In the toddler years, something is learned every day that brings delight to parents. Next, walking is accomplished, speaking begins, and the child's temperament and personality become increasingly evident. Adventure and discovery appear to be the young child's modus operandi.

In middle and late childhood, a child's aptitudes and interests begin to reveal themselves. The young person experiences consistent growth, and motor skills become increasingly adept. They start the process of developing unique ways to handle life events and manage daily hassles.

Then, of course, adolescence is a period when everything changes. During the teenage years, learning happens at a faster rate than anyone can truly appreciate. This is the developmental period in which children begin to match, if not outpace, the strengths and natural talents of their parents. This life span development is reflective of the fact that learning occurs across time, which reveals how you become your unique sense of self.

Learning by Example

Much of what a child first learns is accomplished by engaging in a playful version of follow-the-leader. Along these lines, the child's journey into maturity is guided by their exposure to different models and their capacity for imitation.

The practice of early learning is a prolonged game of copycat. The young child carefully watches you wave your hand and say, "Bye-bye." Then, before your eyes, the child mimics some version of bye-bye and waves their hand in a manner roughly consistent with what you just modeled.

The neuroscience behind this extraordinary mimicry method of learning new behaviors involves a group of neurons or brain cells in your premotor cortex. This part of your brain is responsible for planning out actions before another group of neurons being activated in your motor cortex, which initiates muscle movement. These neurons are called *mirror neurons* because their action mirrors the activity of the same neurons in the person that is being observed.

As the child grows, their capacity for copying other people's behavior is substantially generalized. Because of this, a child can come home from school and exhibit a brand-new behavior, such as saying, "Gross," when served dinner.

This new behavior was likely absorbed from observing another child at school or daycare. When the child begins expressing dislike for a specific type of food, this is an example of their mind expanding as a direct result of learning.

Easy to Remember, Hard to Forget

Let's go back to Tyler's story of emotional deprivation at the hands of his alcohol-abusing father. This is a classic example of how a child is markedly and unknowingly shaped to become the parent he never wanted to be. In Tyler's case, not being emotionally validated as a child clearly influenced his own parenting style, which, in turn, his children interpreted as him being chilly and unaffectionate.

Interestingly, while Tyler is nothing like his father in terms of developing a substance abuse disorder, he did end up mirroring his father's absence of nurturing behaviors. Fortunately, aided by therapeutic nudges, Tyler came to notice the pattern and determined it wasn't too late for the old dog to learn new tricks.

Let's also return to Rachel's predicament. The last time we discussed her situation, she had decided to postpone or avoid sharing with Todd her newly minted desire for motherhood. Like Tyler, a brief examination of Rachel's upbringing may shed valuable light on her delayed recognition of maternal leanings and current hesitancy to openly discuss this with her life partner.

Rachel was the middle of three children. She had an older brother, who was the star of the family, and a young sister, who was always pampered and essentially allowed to get away with anything. When asked to describe her role in her family, without hesitation, she characterized herself as being the peacemaking middle child who didn't dare add any commotion to her noisy family.

Rachel says her older brother was a natural at everything. He excelled in sports, got perfect grades, and always seemed to be the most popular kid on campus. Since everything came easy to her brother, Rachel's parents frequently heaped praise upon him for his endless accomplishments and achievements.

Her younger sister, who was the rebellious one in the family, was raised with different rules. Rachel recalled always having a curfew, being prodded to try much harder, and having her parents seem to be incredibly judgmental regarding her friends. By contrast, it seemed her sister could stay out all hours without punishment, and her underperforming grades were excused because of her *creative nature*.

As Rachel remembers, although her sister's friends were, by any definition or standard, reckless and reputationally suspicious, to

Rachel it seemed her parents never sat down and talked with her sister the way she remembered being routinely *guided* over and over.

In Rachel's mind, as the middle child, she grew up in a no-win situation. She wasn't as naturally gifted as her brother and was placed on the losing side of the double standard that her sister was raised by. So Rachel found herself feeling regularly misunderstood and mistreated by her parents.

Additionally, following the lines associated with the quintessential middle child syndrome that involves the development of a set of feelings and relationship style, Rachel started feeling left out, invisible, forgotten, and underappreciated by her parents. Rachel's feelings match up with her frequent experience of disappearing between her siblings.

Fast-forward to Rachel's adult dilemma involving her discovery of desiring to have a child despite a long-held and much publicly asserted preference for remaining childless. In an earlier chapter, remember, Rachel had decided to put her desire on the backburner and act as if nothing had changed. Her decision was in line with the mind rule that *avoidance is the mind's natural reflex.*

There seems to be an obvious parallel between Rachel's childhood as the middle child and the way she presently handles her current life situation. That dynamic of feeling neglected and overlooked may prove instrumental in helping Rachel move toward resolving her inner tension between desiring a child but not wanting to rock the boat with her life partner.

It's also possible that Rachel's middle child syndrome, which made her feel a need to stand out on her terms, could combine with her deeply embedded sense of not being noticed to offset feelings of having to prove herself.

Given her upbringing, it's not surprising to see that Rachel is the type of people pleaser who rolls out the red carpet for those who have yanked the carpet out from under her. Armed with strong convictions and a hidden desire to protect her yet-to-be-discussed child from feeling her feelings, Rachel's earlier decision to not have children is broadly consistent with her experiences growing up. Now, Rachel's experiencing an unsettling dissonance brought on by her life lessons that are up against this brand-new and deeply primal desire to bear a child.

Will Rachel stand by her developmental propensity to keep the peace and hold fast to her prior commitment with Todd and remain satisfied with their partnership without a child? Or will Rachel allow herself to connect with her newly discovered conviction, let go of some of her middle child baggage, and choose to talk with Todd about her family secret? We'll find out in the coming chapters.

Mind Rule Life Lesson
The Mind Expands by Learning

When learning happens, your mind expands. We know this because as you are exposed to new experiences, your perspective grows, which stretches your mind. Think of a young man who has recently expressed a growing interest in national politics. While his life experiences likely do not provide him with enough context to develop a well-informed opinion, following his attendance at a political rally for a particular candidate, he comes home filled with enthusiasm and heartfelt conviction. From a neuroscientific perspective, this young person's mind has been modified, secondary to his choice to have a new experience. From a brain development standpoint, this is fantastic, regardless of the candidate he supports.

Something to put into our pocket is knowing that the neurobiological benefits of new learning are amazing, even life promoting. In fact, the 411 on keeping your brain working optimally, beyond following a healthy diet focused on choosing the right fuel for your brain, along with regular exercise, the process of engaging in lifelong learning serves to reshape your neural pathways. As you take on a new skill or challenge your mental abilities by performing tasks that require cerebral horsepower, you are building up cognitive reserves. Such reserves are how your brain can cope with biological adversity, such as dementia, and slow the aging process. Another side benefit is that learning is also closely associated with increased happiness.

See, I told you, amazing.

CHAPTER 13

The Mind Is a Pattern Detector

The Mind Jumps to Conclusions Based on Limited but Trending Information

Tic-tac-toe is a game based on pattern detection. The rules are simple. The first player to mark three consecutive rows with an X or O either up, down, or diagonally is the winner. Since the mind is predisposed to analyzing information rapidly and detecting patterns, the game appeals to the mind's embedded interest in pattern detection.

This proclivity is referred to as trend analysis. This type of pattern detection is used to predict such things as future stock prices, how a professional athlete is likely to perform, or even whether a person likes us enough to accept being asked out on a date.

Here is an example of how being presented with simple and limited information can dramatically influence your interest or disinterest. Think of the diagram below as representing three data points across time of a particular company's performance. Given this sparse data, which graph appears most favorable?

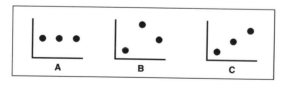

ABC DOTS

Although the above information is ambiguous, it's quite likely figure A was visually accepted as representing steadiness, while figure B showed variability, and figure C showed an upward trend. If the challenge was heightened to involve you investing serious money in one of the three companies listed above, after reviewing the above annual performance metrics, chances are great that you would be convinced to invest in company C. This example illustrates your mind's susceptibility to being easily influenced by trending information.

Our Past Reflects Our Habits

Because of your mind's fondness for connecting dots, you are extremely vulnerable to repeating your past. If, for example, you've always enjoyed a nice cup of coffee, and you come across an eye-catching coffee shop after driving a long time on a stretch of highway, you'll likely make a stop. This simple, everyday behavior exemplifies the power of habits, which, in essence, is nothing more than a biographical game of connecting the dots.

The following nine-dot puzzle provides a classic example of your mind's fondness to see patterns that, in turn, influence your behavior. The goal of the puzzle is to link all nine dots using four straight lines or fewer, without lifting the pen and without tracing the same line more than once. Each line must start where the last line finished. Give it a try. Be patient and good luck.

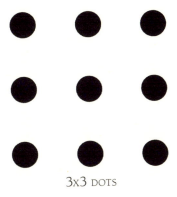

3x3 DOTS

If you've never seen this puzzle before, then it's likely your efforts were met with a degree of frustration. Don't worry, this is not a test of intelligence. Rather, this puzzle reveals the power of habits.

In your first efforts to solve the puzzle, you looked at the nine dots and saw a square or a box. When information shows up in a particular configuration, you've been conditioned by experience to automatically organize the data in a certain way. In this case, it's by seeing a square or box. If you see a square or box, the answer to the puzzle will evade you.

By bending your mind to the rule that makes you inclined to see patterns, you find that the answer is rather simple. By thinking outside the box here, so to speak, your chances of solving the problem improve measurably.

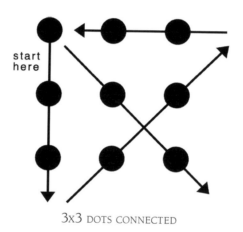

3x3 DOTS CONNECTED

When Will the Pattern Stop?

Susan has a story that illustrates the mind's proclivity for pattern detection. A middle-aged woman, Susan, is amazing. In addition to being successful in her line of work, she maintains a large, active network of close friendships. She has the type of personality that people are naturally drawn toward. Despite all of this, however, Susan has struggled in the romance department.

When you learn how Susan was raised and see what her

relationship history has been, it might provide you with insight into her difficulty creating romantic relationships. Susan was put up for adoption when she was six months old by her biological mother, a drug addict, when it became obvious that she was incapable of providing for her daughter's basic needs.

Promisingly, Susan was adopted into a wonderfully loving and supportive family. Throughout the next phase of her life, Susan's adopted parents doted on her and treated her just like one of their biological children. In truth, Susan never doubted her adopted parents' motivation, devotion, and love. It seemed Susan had truly lucked into an incredible lifetime opportunity.

Then, in the middle of middle school, something began to change. Her adopted mother's chronic, low-grade depression began to surface. Suddenly, her mother was sleeping longer or becoming moodier. Before long, these distracting traits became more obvious and harder to ignore.

For about a year, her mom became more and more unavailable, staying in her bedroom for extended periods, sometimes days at a time. Susan and the other children adapted by taking over the lion's share of the domestic and parenting activities, from cooking and cleaning to packing lunches and providing transportation.

Although Susan was concerned about her mother, for the most part, Susan's life stayed on track at first. Then, out of nowhere, her mother packed her bags, moved to Arizona, and proceeded to divorce herself from her husband and children. Just like that. Susan's mother was gone. In her absence, Susan became loosely detached from her other family members. Fundamentally, she felt different from them and began to be confused about where she belonged.

The immediate connection she enjoyed with her siblings began to feel forced and unnatural. In therapy during her adult years, Susan's reflections about this moment in her life made her realize she felt guilty about being brought into the family and believed she was largely responsible for her adopted mother's depression, which led to her decision to walk away from the family.

To calm her anxiety and sense of social awkwardness, Susan threw herself into her friendships. She accepted every opportunity for overnights. She joined various after-school activities and became extremely active in multiple sports. This resulted in Susan not being home much at all.

After graduating high school, Susan went to a nearby college, where she fell deeply in love almost immediately with Peter. Her feelings were stronger than anything she had ever felt. Her love-at-first-sight experience convinced her that Peter was her soul mate. The passion between the two was obvious to everyone. When not in class, they spent every waking moment together, whether they were hiking, studying, or discussing their dreams. After completing her first year in college, Susan and Peter decided to live together. Their relationship quickly intensified. Now, they found themselves doing everything together, from cooking and cleaning to shopping and sleeping together.

To wit, Susan was happier than she had ever been. She felt complete. She felt safe. She believed she was living happily ever after, and she was able to stow away much of the earlier sense of her being inadequate, detached, and responsible for someone else's misery. Susan and Peter got married before they finished college and moved into married student housing. Their rent was affordable. They made new friends together. Life was good.

Then Susan noticed that Peter was acting funny. He felt more distant. He was less conversant and seemed to find more things to do away from them than together. Knowing in her gut something wasn't right, Susan began to explore. Painfully, she didn't have to look far. Peter was having an affair with a younger college student.

When this indiscretion was brought out into the open, what Peter said next changed Susan's life abruptly and forever, even though he seemed to be genuinely disappointed in himself. In a let's-get-to-the-bottom-of-this moment, Peter shared that while Susan was his best friend, he had found his "true love," and it wasn't Susan.

Susan and Peter broke up immediately. Their divorce was

quick—very quick. The remainder of Susan's college years were a blur. Although she graduated the next year near the top of her class, she no longer felt in control of her life. Contemplating what to do next, she knew she couldn't go home, whatever that was. So she moved to another part of the country and started over again.

When Susan started her professional career with a brand-new company, everyone fell in love with her. Her vibrant personality, fun-loving spirit, and incredible capacity to bring out the best in others shined through. Nobody would have ever guessed that Susan had experienced such pain, grief, and heartbreak in her life. Around her friends and colleagues, Susan was adept at pushing her setbacks to the side and acting as if everything was no problem. But Susan did have a problem. She was insecure and emotionally unstable when it came to relationships she depended upon and did not have control over.

This is where the dots connect with Susan's attachment history. Her biological mother was mentally incapable of nurturing her. She was adopted into a loving and established home. Her new family provided her a revived sense of belonging. Her adopted mother fell into depression, left the family, and moved far away during Susan's formative years.

As a coping mechanism, Susan threw herself into friends and activities, from which she gained deserved attention and validation. After going to college, Susan fell deeply in love, only to have her heart broken stunningly and dramatically when Peter was unfaithful. Bouncing back from sorrow and confusion, Susan relocated and threw herself once again into her friends, colleagues, and activities.

Clearly, Susan is resilient. When life knocks her down, she gets right back up. She knows she is likable, but her lifetime of connected dots reminds her that deep down she may not be lovable. She also carried around a fear that the people she loved would disappear.

Mind Rule Life Lesson
The Mind Is a Pattern Detector

Whenever you're asked to solve a problem, make a decision, or ponder a riddle, you should allow your mind to do what it does best—look for a pattern. If the pattern is not easily detected or the chosen pattern doesn't solve the problem, then think outside the box. You need to ask, is your mind jumping to a conclusion based on trending or historical information? If so, perhaps the trend is not helpful, and it might be hindering, even detrimental.

An anecdote to breaking patterns that your mind is keen on following is to practice being curious. Curiosity is code for an open mind. When you actively choose to be curious, you are giving yourself a chance to connect the dots a different way. Let's explore one more example of the influential nature of your mind's fondness for pattern detection.

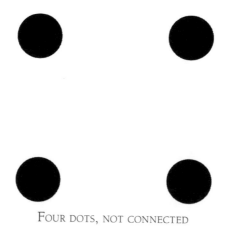

FOUR DOTS, NOT CONNECTED

Above, you see four dots. That's all, nothing more. Or maybe there is something more. Does your mind detect a pattern? If so, what is it?

If you're like nearly everyone else (that is, normal), then, in your mind, you connect the dots to form a square. Once your mind sees the square, it's hard to not see it, even though the square exists only in your mind.

The diagram below is what the pattern your mind detected looks like.

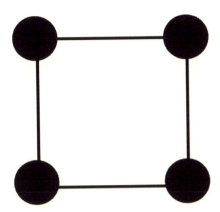

FOUR DOTS CONNECTED

Using the power of curiosity, by opening your mind and allowing it to see more than just a square, you might detect the following patterns and others.

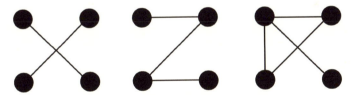

THREE IMAGES OF FOUR DOTS, SIDE BY SIDE

Now that you understand how your mind is designed to make sense of information as quickly as possible by using its instinctive partiality for pattern making, by turning on your curiosity, you are practicing how to open your mind, which may greatly expand the prospects in your life.

Think of curiosity as the key to open your imagination. Once activated, your imagination can create worlds that never existed, worlds that once forged then become secured in your mind.

CHAPTER 14

The Mind Is Hypersensitive and Struggles with Empathy

The Mind Is More Aware of What Is Being Done to It Than What It Is Doing

Here's a closely guarded secret: Humans have a desire to care deeply about one another, but their mind gets in the way. As humans, we are hardwired to be selfish and insecure. This selfishness shows up in our mind's underlying preoccupation with self-preservation. The mind's natural reflex is to shield you from obvious and real signs of danger, as well as threats perceived to be real and only imagined.

Your insecurities are tucked deep within your identity, embedded by competing degrees of rejection, exclusion, and devaluation. When you experience any dose of such social put-downs and brush-offs, your sense of self destabilizes. Soon self-doubt takes over, and you privately wonder whether the off-putting feedback received reflects insight into your faulty makeup. If the reaction from others is negatively saturated and occurs repeatedly, such moments of invalidation become unforgettable, even though you may not be able to easily recall them.

From such unwanted social experiences, the central theme of insecurity can ignite and express itself in a variety of ways. While insecurity is a universal phenomenon for all humans, how you experience your insecurity is unique. A careful unpacking of the familiarity of insecurity reveals vulnerable feelings of inadequacy, inferiority, incompetency, impotency, and insignificance. By examining your moments of insecurity, you can discover a great deal about what's going on deep inside. When you reflect on your felt experience of insecurity in context with the backdrop of your upbringing and relationship history, you become better acquainted with your psychological weak links and blind spots.

Is Selfishness Virtuous?

Because your mind is hypersensitive to what is happening in your surroundings, especially those situations that create inner confusion or threaten to harm your reputation, your mind naturally defends itself by assuming a protective stance. This defensiveness on the part of your mind is personal and spontaneous. Knowing that your mind reacts to attacks is reassuring.

Your mind also effortlessly glides toward moments that promise validation. Occasions for attention, affection, acknowledgment, approval, and applause are compelling, even seductive. When your sensitivities are admired, the resulting affirmation and confidence inspire you to move boldly in the direction of becoming the person you were always meant to be. Such urges are welcoming and revitalizing.

Conversely, when your surroundings make you feel trapped, out of control, vague, or lacking inward power, your mind becomes vulnerable to such unfavorable moments by questioning itself. When unwanted moments recycle, your mind becomes prone to turn on itself. Believing what it's being told, instead of protecting your interests, your mind's instincts short-circuit, take on features of its surroundings, and believe what others are doing, thinking, or saying. You become your worst critic. If left unchecked, your inner critic can spiral out of control, reinforcing itself, warping your perspective, and causing you to feel trapped in a web of invalidations of your own making.

Invalidation comes in different forms. The most common attributes include being ignored, hurt, dismissed, rejected, and made to feel insignificant. Gaslighting is the term that describes what happens when invalidation is taken to the extreme.

Specifically, this happens when another person undermines your reality by persistently denying what you say, believe, or feel. When gaslighted, you question everything about you—your understanding of right and wrong, your right to have an opinion, and your sense of fairness, honesty, and integrity. With your reality fully twisted, you may even doubt the reflection of yourself in the mirror.

When your mind detects an unfavorable social pulse and suspects an invalidation may be inevitable, it routinely copes by either devising an escape route (avoidance), lashing back (attack), or choosing to do nothing and, thereby, tolerate intolerable behavior (surrender).

When you choose to escape and move away from an undesirable situation, you are acting on primal instinct for self-empathy. When your identity falls into a state of confusion and no one is around to protect you or remind you of your worth, your mind turns inward. In this fashion, your mind focuses on getting your needs met, the most basic first. This is especially true during times when your safety and security are threatened. During such moments, your mind instructs you to hunker down to prevent further harm.

Lashing out is when you defend yourself from a barrage of negativity; this is another way your mind protects itself. While fighting back may not be the smartest thing to do, as it predictably escalates tension, the process of putting up a good fight, in the moment, feels right and good, good enough to keep doing it even in the face of better judgment.

On the surface, surrendering doesn't sound like a wise choice. After all, isn't it cowardly to give up? The thing about surrendering is it works, the fighting stops. If your mind is focused on not making things worse, then surrendering makes sense.

Going even deeper, when you intentionally decide not to fight or put-up resistance, you are reclaiming your life space and demonstrating emotional regulation. What is not well known or often forgotten is that times of conflict are not the best time for problem-solving or teaching a lesson. By reframing surrender as a form of conflict resolution, what is gained are ways to stay safe during a crisis, regain self-control, and recover to move forward constructively.

Whether your mind chooses to move against, away from, or alongside unpleasant moments, your mind's default mode for self-empathy is what makes selfishness a virtue. Self-directed empathy functions as a type of antenna. It detects opportunities to recognize and understand the pain inside you stemming from episodes of disappointment, discouragement, and disapproval. When you feel your pain, deep and familiar pain, you can adapt in different ways by shielding yourself from times of social nullification.

Is selfishness virtuous? Like so many other human behaviors, when selfishness is taken to the extreme, its virtuosity descends rapidly. But when selfishness is measured against Aristotle's principle of the golden mean, which introduced the benefits of moderation, then your mind's instinct to self-empathize by protecting itself is completely virtuous. What's more, it's based on merit and conferred by better judgment.

Looking Closely at Others

Self-empathy is one thing; empathizing with others is quite another story and a rather elusive one at that. Empathy is feeling and grasping what another person is feeling. When you respond to another person with an emotional response that is like what they're feeling, you're channeling empathy. You know you've hit the empathy bull's-eye when the other person expresses a sense that *you get me*.

In developmental psychology, it is generally recognized that children around age two begin showing flickers of empathy. Yet, developing and honing the capacity to experience and express true empathy in real time is a long and twisted road, with some of us ending up being much better than others. What does this mean? Empathy is an innate faculty that needs to be developed and practiced over time.

In the field of neuroscience, certain parts of your brain have been pinpointed to be actively involved in your capacity to have a vicarious experience—to feel what someone else is feeling. By using advanced brain imaging studies (functional MRI), research has shown that the insula and cingulate cortex are intimately involved when you are feeling another person's pain and intimately recognize their suffering.

For a quick reference, the insula is an often overlooked area of the brain that is responsible for giving you that felt sense of someone else's distress or sorrow. The cingulate cortex, sometimes referred to as your fifth lobe, deals with your capacity for self-regulation—emotion regulation, thought management, productive decision-making, and sound judgment. Together, these two anatomical structures inside your skull make up vital neural underpinnings of your capacity for empathy.

Let's look at empathy at work. Consider what happens in the workforce between different genders. Some men can be extremely insensitive toward women. This lack of empathy is demonstrated by gentle touching, banter about sexual topics, telling dirty jokes, expressing off-putting innuendos, using offensive language, and just generally engaging in bad behavior. In these cases, when discovered and verified, a common practice by a human resources department is to mandate the offender attend sensitivity training.

What is taught at sexual misconduct and awareness training? Without getting into the weeds on this complex and multifaceted topic, an overarching emphasis of this specialized training focuses on teaching empathy and its precursor—what you are doing without realizing what is being done.

When you examine empathy carefully, you discover that empathy involves an emotional state, a cognitive process, and a smidgen of imagination. The emotional component of empathy is the practice of synchronizing with another person's private experience by feeling their pain, understanding their emotion, and acknowledging the unique way they must feel. By feeling another person's private experience, your empathy allows you to take on the perspective of the other person.

The cognitive or thinking part of empathy relates to your self-talk or inner dialogue. It is one thing to feel someone's pain. Taking empathy to a higher level occurs when you contemplate what they must be going through. Do they feel trapped? Are they overwhelmed and feeling exposed? Are they alone and hoping someone throws them a lifeline?

Feeling a person's pain and thinking from their perspective gets you closer to appreciating the person's private experience. But to land squarely in the zone of accurate empathy, to understand what the other person is indeed experiencing, you need one more ingredient—imagining yourself being the other person in their situation.

Social research has shown that the greater your imagination, the more empathy you can experience. On top of that, the more accurate your empathy, the better you become at mitigating the human suffering of another person. You can see how empathy is so powerful and stunningly effective. When your felt emotions for another person intersect with thoughtfulness and creative insight, congratulations—you've hit an empathic bull's-eye. The diagram below illustrates the intersecting aspects of empathic accuracy.

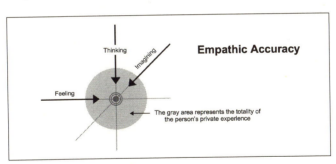

EMPATHIC ACCURACY

Perhaps you've read about another person's horrific life story and thought, *I can't imagine*. Or closer to home, maybe someone in your extended family experienced a tragedy beyond words. Whatever the case, to make sense of what you can't fathom, your imagination gets to work. To the best of your ability, you feel their pain, sense their sorrow, and identify with their anguish. By using your imagination, you have grown closer to that person. Welcome to the true power of empathy, in which you draw closer to that person without moving.

Empathy is extremely useful for deescalating conflict, repairing broken connections, and making sure things don't go from bad to worse and worse to ugly. While empathy is innate, it needs to be developed by switching on an intentional mindset. Empathy is not automatic. It requires deliberate practice. Empathy, therefore, is a learned behavior that emboldens your character, enhances your reputation, and keeps your life from getting messier.

Put simply, empathy cannot be experienced as an abstraction or from a state of detachment. On the contrary, empathy requires a willingness and capacity to connect compassionately with others while relying upon an envisioned sense of what is happening in the other person's mind. The degree of effortfulness demanded by empathic accuracy reflects why your mind struggles with empathy.

Mind Rule Life Lesson
The Mind Is Hypersensitive and Struggles with Empathy

Empathy is learned across time and experience. Being empathetic requires intentionality and a willingness to deliberately focus on your internal emotional state as it focuses on another person's internal emotional state. Then the task is to dial in your experience so that it closely matches what you believe the other person is experiencing. This process can be called psychologically synchronicity. To get in sync with another person's private experience requires you to either tap into your treasure trove of life experiences that approximate what you think the other person is going through or turn the controls over to your imagination and let your sensibilities guide you accordingly. Don't be too hard on yourself if your efforts fall short; your ability to accurately understand and respond to the thoughts and feelings of another person requires practice. Be patient and kind toward both you and the other person.

So when you see and feel another person's pain or discomfort, this is an excellent time to get out of your mind. By allowing yourself to envision what the other person is feeling, you then permit yourself to act on that feeling. When you do, amazingly, your capacity for empathy is strengthened, your sense of self is bolstered, and your connection with other people deepens.

Another groundbreaking benefit to practicing empathy is how it produces relational equity. As you attempt to feel what another person is feeling, you cannot be standing against, encroaching upon, be in competition with, or otherwise exert dominance over the other person. Instead, empathy invites mutual empowerment. Sharing power is foundational to valuing the connection with another person and placing in high esteem the relationship. Empathy builds trust, promotes truth, sets into motion commitment, and is a prized form of intimacy.

Unfortunately, as we age and mature, many of us become settled into our opinions, beliefs, and convictions. It's as if we have had enough experiences to last a lifetime, which gives us agency to allow our minds to shut down. What we all need to keep in mind is that without new experiences, learning stops. A surefire way to open your mind is to look for empathic opportunities. You can never go wrong caring about another person.

CHAPTER 15

The Mind's Favorite Color Is Black

The Mind Is Highly Sensitive to Negativity, Keenly Detecting Hints of Danger and Threat

Few things are as frightening as believing your life is in danger. When confronted by a near-death experience, your autonomic nervous system shifts into overdrive. Jolted by fear, your fight-or-flight instincts take over—the stress hormone norepinephrine surges, your heart rate rises, your breathing becomes shallow, your emotions swell, your vision narrows, and your reflexes sharpen.

Without knowing how or how much, extreme experiences tend to reshape your inner map and model of the world. Fortunately, though, such moments of raw intensity are not something you experience frequently in everyday life. You do, however, experience relative stressors and strains that impact you, resulting in subjective distress that leaves behind indelible traces of lived experiences that color your world.

For some people, the world is seen in black and white. Against a backdrop of poverty, parental abuse or neglect, household dysfunction, abandonment, and other adverse childhood experiences, a child becomes more at risk for poor mental and physical health.

When a child merely survives their way through their upbringing, as opposed to thriving, they develop a binary worldview. The world is seen as being fair and unfair, for example. People are viewed as either good or bad. Actions taken are either right or wrong. With little room for free choice, a lack of nurturance and allegiance throughout development leads the child to flourish on their own. In a black-and-white world, the overlooked child's worldview lacks color, and, by proxy, their perception lacks depth and significance.

Fittingly, when discussing near-death and other forms of extreme stress, the color of such harrowing psychological experiences is represented by the color black. And just as black absorbs all light in the color spectrum, during your greatest psychological struggles, your world likewise turns darker and darker. Take, for example, the experience of depression. What words or phrases come to your mind when you think of being depressed? Perhaps you associate this common human condition with being down in the dumps, or dismal, or sad and unhappy, maybe gloomy, bummed out, in the doldrums, or feeling a little melancholy?

Interestingly, the root word of melancholy from Greek (*melankholia* or "sadness") literally means (an excess) of black bile, which itself represents one of the four bodily humors or fluids recognized back in the days of medieval science and medicine. For the betterment of humanity, the discovery of germ theory long ago replaced the archaic notion of humors, with an imbalance of the four humors being once accepted as the root cause of all diseases.

Not All Emotions Are Created Equal

Black-and-white photography is powerful and solitary. This type of photography evokes emotions and resonates details that are difficult to put into words. As shown below, such images speak a universal language, one that draws your attention, captivates your interest, and taps into your deepest psychology. What you see, you see alone. Stripped of color, photographs become compositions of consolation and possibility, intensely private and enduringly engaging.

PHOTO, BLACK AND WHITE OF WOMAN
PHOTO BY JACOB MAJICANOS ON UNSPLASH

The purity of the woman's image invites you into her psyche. While color enhances, it can be distracting. The monochromatic snapshot depicted above is timeless. Everything about her seems relevant and interesting. There is beauty in both light and darkness. Perhaps most intriguing, identifying with her is effortless and uncomplicated. The quietness of the picture reveals the starkness of life's extremes. Colorless art confirms, indeed, less is more.

Another example of the deeply influential nature of the color black involves how humans experience feedback. A classic example happens frequently at work when a person undergoes an annual performance evaluation. This process, when done correctly, is a fair and balanced summary of one person's experience of the other person's job-related strengths and weaknesses.

Putting yourself in the employee's shoes. During the yearly evaluation, the supervisor typically begins sharing a host of highly positive and ego-inflating descriptors, such as dedicated, driven, personable, well-liked, sensible, thoughtful, honest, and hardworking. This positive and encouraging feedback sounds great at first, right? If we visualized what the employee heard, it might look something like the diagram below.

SEVEN RED DOTS IN A ROW

All the red dots represent forms of validation. Attention, acknowledgment, affirmation, and applause—pieces of information they were hoping to hear. Next, however, the supervisor's focus turns to the employee's work traits, which are less than spectacular. Perhaps they're told they need to work harder on becoming more organized and really step it up in time management.

Overall, the performance evaluation appears favorable. However, psychologically, the employee walks away from the evaluation feeling a bit dejected and unsteady. Why? Because the negative feedback really stuck. If we visualized their overall performance evaluation, it might look like the following diagram.

SEVEN RED DOTS IN A ROW WITH ONE BLACK DOT

While most of the feedback was upbeat and confirmed their experience of the employee's performance over the past year (shown by the red dots), the part of the evaluation that really caught their attention was the negative feedback (reflected by the black dot). This demonstrates the power of negativity. It's hard to take your focus off the black dot.

Negativity Is Contagious

From a psychological perspective, the color black is equivalent to the experience of negativity. As you likely noticed growing up, or even now, negative experiences feel stronger, hit harder, and are more long-lasting than positive ones. It appears the mind magnetically attracts negative experiences. But why?

First, consider that attitudes and moods are contagious. You know this to be true from the way you looked up to your father, adored your mother, or were brought down by emotional entanglements with your first lover. A previous discussion introduced the concept that there are mirrors in the brain. When you watch another person do something, mirror neurons located in the motor cortex of your brain fire as if you are doing what they are doing. This neural mechanism allows you to learn something without being aware that you are learning.

The method of mirroring can save you a lot of grief. For example, if someone takes a sip of milk and immediately spits it out, because of the power of observational learning, with your mirror cells firing madly like rockets into the sky, you are likely to ask for water instead. Clearly, there is an upside to learning from other people's mishaps. However, there is also a downside.

Psychologists have developed a concept called negativity bias, by which people are influenced more profoundly by negativity than positivity. The neuroscience behind negativity bias is robust and complex. There is a specialized region in the epicenter of the emotional brain called the amygdala. As the brain is divided into two halves, there is one amygdalae on each side, both of them being almond shaped and responsible for determining, at lightning speed, whether something in your surrounding environment presents a threat or danger.

In essence, the amygdala is like a smoke alarm that detects the emotional intensity of a situation. When it comes to discerning intensity, the amygdala is hardwired to sound an alarm more easily when confronted by negative and threatening situations rather than positive and comforting stimuli.

It has also been shown that negative stimuli hold greater information value than positive stimuli and, therefore, attract more attention at a higher cognitive level. Stated another way, you spend more time contemplating negative information because it's more confusing and requires greater distillment. From an evolutionary perspective, it has been proposed that negativity bias assists you in exploring your environment to avoid harmful situations, now and in the future. While positive information may keep you on course, negative information urges you to adapt and steer a new course.

Finally, much like a virus that spreads like wildfire, neuroscience has discovered that negative behaviors are similarly contagious. Research reveals a contagion effect in which negative behavior begets negativity, and rather easily. That is, you have a built-in tendency to unconsciously mimic the emotional expressions and behaviors of other people. Fear signals the potential of something dire, while happiness does not. So it makes sense that your mind is designed to readily detect and stay focused on unwanted, undesired, and undeserved stimuli.

The compelling qualities of the color black, from the standpoints of the arts and sciences, is rather easily explained and shown. But what about your mind? Why is black your mind's favorite color?

Mood over Mind

When your mood is saturated, everything seems to change. The way you feel, think, and behave is often impacted suddenly and seemingly outside of your immediate control. You experience a range of deeply private experiences, from sadness to aloneness, from confusion and contemplating self-harm to being disengaged and sleeping too much, to collectively being weighed down by rival degrees of guilt, gloom, and worthlessness. In a word, depression creates detachment. You disconnect from your sense of self, your perspective of the world shifts, and your willingness to interact voluntarily, thoughtfully, and cheerfully in the world slips through your fingers.

As humans, one thing we all have in common is the experience of suffering—pain individualized and scaled beyond endeavor. While suffering shows up in competing degrees, shades, and duration, if asked what color best represents the universal experience of suffering, without much debate, the consensus vote would be black. To help illustrate why this is, allow the picture below to reveal an elegiac answer.

Photo, black and white of crying boy
Photo by Kat J on Unsplash

To offer further clarity as to how negativity and, by proxy, the color black hijacks your mind, let's revisit Charlotte. Her story, as you may recall, involves a descent into the depths of chronic disability, set against a backdrop of persistence despite unobvious hope.

Feeling trapped and impatiently overlooked by her family, time and again, she struggles with grasping the purpose of her life. Her unrelenting pain leaves her immobilized, suffocatingly dependent, and constantly fighting thoughts that others would be better off without her presence, as they would be released from their burden.

Charlotte's psychological tug-of-war involves her routinely reclaiming victory over her unsolvable struggle, while at the same time occasionally falling victim to believing her directionless life lacks purpose. What's captivating about Charlotte's reality that pivots along with an existential fight-or-flight axis is that her mind believes itself to be correct either way it swivels.

At times, Charlotte's mind is convincingly forceful when she fights through her pain, as she navigates another day, hoping for a better tomorrow and perhaps even a medical miracle. But when her mind shifts, she believes her situation is beyond hope, her despair never will reverse, and most disheartening of all, she will never become the person she was meant to be.

When Charlotte's mind turns black, she is swayed to believe that today should be her last day. She contemplates consciously how to end her life. She cries out and pleads with her family to assist her with putting an end to her misery, to help her stop being such a burden and make it so she no longer feels the desolation of not belonging.

With no extrinsic reward in sight and no sense of intrinsic value within, the blackness of Charlotte's mind speaks a disquieting truth that sinks her into hollowing gravity that does not remit, does not let go, and moves her closer and closer to the unimaginable—that the possibility for relief does not exist and likely never did, not for her.

Tears fall but not because she's crying and not to see if anyone cares. For Charlotte, tears fall because, in her mind, there is nothing else to do. In the darkness, when Charlotte's mind turns black, her emotional core compels her to find a solution. Sadly, in a state of unpredictable confusion, if Charlotte listens to what she believes her mind's instincts are telling her to do, she may accidentally end her pain by giving up her life.

Mind Rule Life Lesson
The Mind's Favorite Color Is Black

It has been said that to be human, pain is mandatory, while suffering is optional. This statement implies there is a marked difference between the experience of pain and suffering. The former cannot be avoided, while the latter must be negotiated. Sooner or later, directly or indirectly, like all of us, you will be hurt by someone. Your experience of livable pain comes in many forms, including grief, discouragement, disappointment, rejection, exclusion, invalidation, and, of course, trauma.

The experience of pain is different from suffering. When you suffer, the original pain lingers longer than expected and deeper than desired. Suffering impacts your emotions and disrupts your thinking, altering your perceptions of yourself, your world, and the interaction between them. The chain reaction of the internalized negativity that suffering causes is harmful and potentially self-destructive.

Suffering shows up in the faces of many clinical disorders, such as anxiety, depression, anger, malaise, sadness, and hopelessness. While suffering appears initially to be a state of mind, when left unattended, the unrelenting psychological torment begins to eventually cause wear and tear on your body. In this sense, without attending to your emotional wounds, suffering can create physical discomfort. When this happens, you get caught in a type of toxic cycle where psychological pain leads to emotional suffering, which, in turn, creates physical pain and behavioral difficulties.

Understanding that pain is inevitable while suffering is optional, how you cope when life gets you down substantially offsets your experience of suffering. Learning to be intentionally aware of your pain is the key to resolving the entrenched experience of suffering. This comes from acknowledging and sharing how your life is being impacted, analyzing the altered dynamics that have shifted your perception, and becoming more adaptive and flexible to your difficult life circumstances.

To be resilient in the face of adversity requires you to maintain consistent contact with trusted family members and friends, to focus on solving problems that are under your immediate control, while maintaining a sense of lightness and remaining committed to a routine that focuses on improving self-care and your general state of well-being.

CHAPTER 16

The Mind Self-Regulates

*The Mind Is Designed to Restore Stability,
Rapidly Returning to Homeostasis*

During times of tension and upset, you're more likely to feel imbalanced, confused, and shaken. Such inner turbulence is part of the natural fabric of being human, caused mostly by your interacting with other humans. While restless moments are common in life, remaining out of balance goes against the grain of your basic neurophysiology.

Outside of your immediate awareness, there is an internal mechanism in your critical neurology that governs your body's vital functions. This is called your autonomic nervous system (ANS for short). If you're familiar with the expression *what goes up must come down*, this sentiment explains, in a nutshell, how the ANS works.

The ANS is part of your nervous system that controls involuntary actions, such as the beating of your heart, your breathing rate, the constriction of your blood vessels, and even your states of arousal. The marvel of the ANS is not so much what it does, which is crucial and abiding, but how it operates. Behind the scenes, your central nervous system functions as your internal command center, self-regulating and operating independently, serving as a humble and obedient servant to its master.

Working outside of consciousness, the ANS is made up of two separate divisions. One part of this system, the sympathetic nervous system (SNS), gets to work in unexpected and emergency situations. This is often referred to as your fight-or-flight network.

When provoked, the sympathetic division (the animated side of your ANS) sets your system into motion by way of a sudden jolt of chemicals and hormones that flood your body. Because of this action, you get fired *up* for the situation and hopefully react in a way that helps you stave off injury or worse.

Here's where the *what goes up must come down* comparison comes into play. The autonomic nervous system's response for bringing your body *down* involves the parasympathetic nervous system (PNS). The parasympathetic division (the calming partner to the SNS) applies the neural brakes and assists your body to return to a state of relative peace and quietness. Just as the SNS is famous for its fight-or-flight instincts, the PNS is known to be active when you rest and digest.

When the machinery of your ANS is synchronized, your body masterfully responds to its surroundings. When the conditions around you are pleasant, your PNS is humming. Then, when conditions change and become stormy—when you are startled, for example, or something unpleasant occurs—your SNS becomes dominant. Working together, these two divisions of your ANS are driven to help you maintain a biologically balanced condition called homeostasis.

Mind Control versus Controlling Mind

Your mind consumes an incredible amount of brain food (glucose) when it's active. So, when not needed critically, your mind goes into a conservation mode. The best way for the mind to conserve energy is to restore balance or self-regulate as quickly as possible. This process of returning to and maintaining a relatively stable internal state is what homeostasis is all about. This unique word derives from the Greek words for "same" and "steady," which, to your mind, represents a great place to kick off your shoes and chill out.

The image of a bulb shining dimly can be handy when trying to understand why your brain is so motivated to return your body to a state of rest. Remembering that as a lightbulb brightens, the amount of energy consumed increases directly reflects how your mind works under times of duress. In fact, this explains why you feel so drained after an extended mental effort, such as cramming for a final examination or driving across the country.

PHOTO, LIGHTBULB
PHOTO BY ALEXANDER JAWFOX ON UNSPLASH

To illustrate how your mind self regulates, take for instance the following scenario. You are hiking in the woods, enjoying the morning sunshine and gentle descent toward a favorite resting spot when, out of nowhere, you spot a snake on the path. The lightbulb inside you instantly lights up and goes to full brightness. Quite likely, your ANS is operating at the equivalent of a 1,000-watt bulb.

The disproportionately unequal response of your SNS puts you into a "Let's do whatever it takes to stay alive, and let's do it *now!*" mode. When you are threatened or perceive something as a threat, your ANS upsurges and rapidly activates the SNS division. Fight or flight are the most obvious options, but there's also freeze as an alternative. By choosing the appropriate and necessary option, congratulations, you've increased your chances of surviving your snake encounter.

Remember, the brighter your bulb, the more wattage or energy is consumed. The longer your bulb stays blindingly lit, the more quickly your brain resources are depleted. Think about a stressful situation you experienced that required your lightbulb to shine blazingly for hours. How did you feel afterward? It's likely you were wiped out, exhausted, and ready to drop. Welcome to the messy world of acute stress, where emotions run on full tilt, thoughts scream and scramble, and the body pays the price.

Your mind prefers you to be at rest. It grapples with your ups and downs by coordinating with your ANS how to respond to any given circumstance, whether it's dealing with intense, imminent, and unexpected threats, like running into snakes, or chilling out and enjoying a sip of tea. If you are in panic, your SNS is being activated. If you are in a state of peace, thank your PNS for its calming down and chill out qualities.

These two divisions of your ANS are partners. Working closely together, they seem to understand each other in unique ways. In fact, they have a codependent relationship with each other—one can't live without the other. Just the same, they speak a different language, and when stuff happens, they react in different ways.

Knowing about your ANS and its two divisions provides insight into an incredible opportunity to better control the wattage of your inner lightbulb. While your ANS works behind the scenes and outside of your immediate awareness, now that you know about this hidden neurophysiological jewel, you are in a greater position to better influence how much it influences you.

Minding Your Own Business

Contemplate the following visual puzzle and focus on what happens to our mind's wattage. Pay attention to the energy being consumed as you noodle about how to solve this challenge. The puzzle is relatively simple. Based on the pattern of the five grids below, where should the blue square be placed in the final grid? While this problem is not complicated, it certainly requires you to turn up the wattage a bit to solve the problem.

FIVE SQUARES WITH A QUESTION MARK

Let's try another challenge. Trace out a ten-letter word in any direction, using each letter only once. If you're like most, it's likely this second puzzle will require you to use more brain power (or wattage).

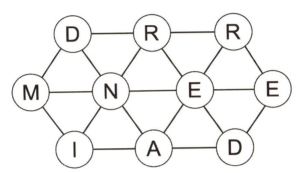

ARRAY OF LETTERS CONNECTED WITH LINE

Both visual puzzles are examples of how your mind is designed to restore stability by finding a solution as quickly as possible. As soon as the puzzle is completed, your wattage goes down noticeably, and you experience a type of calming, which is your experience of being returned to homeostasis. Of course, if either problem proved to be unsolvable, then you would have noticed how your mind remained active and unsettled. (To help your mind be subdued, for each puzzle, the answers are provided below.)

When you are stressed and life goes a bit off the rails, the lightbulb increases in intensity and gets noticeably hotter, requiring substantially more energy to stay bright. Once the stressful period has passed, you should experience some amount of mental fatigue and emotional exhaustion. This is the by-product of your lightbulb burning too hot for too long.

Mind Rule Life Lesson
The Mind Self-Regulates

There is such a thing as good stress. It is the type and amount of stress under which you perform at your greatest potential and optimal efficiency. Good stress helps you perform at the top of your game. But when stress stretches beyond your in-the-zone tipping point, your performance begins to decline. Knowing when you've peaked and when you are beginning to head downhill is critical and an insightful life skill. You'll know that you've extended beyond your tipping point and have begun the descent to become protective and defensive when you experience a generalized imbalance internally and your mind begins to work overtime—using excessive wattage.

Essentially, this mind rule that highlights how your mind self-regulates underscores the importance of knowing your limits. Checking the temperature and brightness of your inner lightbulb will inform you when you're beginning to reach your limits or when you've gone too far and have surpassed your limits.

When your life situation increases in intensity and you remain oblivious to how your surroundings are heating up your ANS, you're much more likely to blow a fuse and act like someone you'd rather never have met. It's critical to bear in mind that your inner world of thoughts, emotions, memories, and perceptions become distorted when strong emotions come into play, such as anger, hate, guilt, shame, and the other names assigned to the shadow world of our inner workings. Contemplating the brightness of your inner lightbulb during times when you're fired up functions to help you offset the chances of having a perfect storm moment.

Answers to Visual Puzzles

The answer to the first puzzle is shown below. The pattern in this puzzle involves the blue space moving counterclockwise in a stepwise fashion. That is, from the first to the second grid, the blue box moves one space. Then, from the second to the third grid, the blue box moves two spaces, and so on, until, from the fourth to the fifth grid, the blue box has moved four spaces.

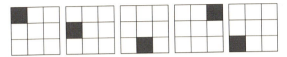

FIVE SQUARES WITH QUESTION MARK REMOVED

The answer to puzzle number two involves playing around with the letters until you find the word *mind reader.*

CHAPTER 17

The Mind Is Directly Connected to the Past

The Mind Vividly Remembers Its Worst and Best Days, in That Order

The mind is filled with knowledge and brimming with memories. Some of what you know, you learned intentionally and hope to remember forever. The rest comprises pieces and parts of your life experiences that didn't especially catch your attention, things you either don't remember or have no need to recall, or things you prefer to stay far away from.

Your mind only knows what it has been told. Everything you recollect, know to be true, or anticipate is essentially a version of what happened in your past. In this way, your mind is directly and crucially connected to your past. This sentiment is assuredly what Charles Darwin had in mind when he said, "A moral being is one who is capable of reflecting on his past actions and their motives—of approving of some and disapproving of others."

Good, Bad, and Ugly

Your past is filled with a broad spectrum of life experiences that range from good to bad to ugly. The good stuff you hang on to and revisit as frequently as you can. When you look through a photo album, for instance, you go back to your favorite moments and reminisce about the good old days, reflecting on how lucky you are to have the loved ones that you have and for the opportunities afforded to you.

The part of your past that is bad likely involves situations that you wish you could do over. While you try to make the best decisions along the way, if you're like most of us, you have regrets, frustrations, and irritations about some of your choices. Hopefully, though, in the long run, you've learned more from your disappointments and discouragements than it cost you.

Then there are those ugly moments in your life, the times filled with unspeakable and unshareable life experiences. Some of us, for example, survived our upbringing. We were raised by parents who suffered from substance abuse, were physically or sexually abusive, were strict to the point of us feeling imprisoned, or were cruel and filled with disdain for us.

Others of us, meanwhile, may have had parents who didn't lash out but were largely absent, either physically or emotionally. Feeling abandoned, we unknowingly carried our unresolved insecurities into adulthood, and, feeling inadequate or insignificant, we seem unsteady and never consistently stable in close relationships. Being mistreated and/or abused, we were never able to relax. We avoided being vulnerable and remained constantly on high-alert status for the possibility—no probability—of the next developmental betrayal.

In all the above cases, we grew up in families characterized by emotional dishonesty, a lack of trust, or an absence of nurturing, and, as such, we were released into adulthood with difficulties experiencing, identifying, and expressing emotions. Quite likely, as a result, we have struggled with depending on and trusting anyone other than ourselves.

Because of a lack of safety, loving reflections, and internal validation, it's also likely we learned that a way to get attention was how we behaved and performed for others and what connection was all about. In this case, we were misguided by our past.

What Is Hidden Is Not Gone

Your mind works to predict the future by referencing the past. Since your mind is focused on self-preservation, your mind follows a worst-first policy, a dynamic in which your mind keeps memories of your worst days up close and personal. Why? Because you cannot afford for your history of disappointments, bad decisions, failures, mistakes, and trauma to be repeated.

Let's briefly revisit the story of Rachel, who, as you might remember, is navigating a challenging relationship dynamic like the one mentioned above. When we last checked in with Rachael, she was struggling with whether or not to express her desire to have a child. Not wanting to mess up the best thing that had ever happened to her—her forever relationship with her husband, Todd—she grappled with telling him.

Typifying the mind rule that *avoidance is the mind's natural reflex*, Rachel decided to put her private thoughts on hold, at least for a while. Is this an example of her being in control of her mind or her mind controlling her? Likewise, the mind rule about how *the mind expands by learning* provides insight into how that rule applies to her upbringing.

As you might remember, Rachel was the middle child of three. Her older brother could do no wrong and was the star of her family, and her younger sister, the baby, was pampered like a princess. As the middle child, Rachel became the peacekeeper and was guided loyally by the phrase *don't rock the boat*. Rachel's recent decision to keep her boat steady is strikingly consistent with the role she played growing up. Raised in a noisy family, Rachel became highly skilled at keeping quiet, doing things under the radar, and getting quite good at not having the spotlight shine on her inner world.

Rachel's past life experiences and practice conditioned her to develop a habit of aloofness, to remain tactically detached, partially estranged, and interpersonally static. Mostly unrecognized and unnoticed, Rachel experienced a childhood that provided her an admixture of solitude and anonymity. An upside to Rachel's remoteness was that she was able to skate through her early years without being punished for having done or not done something.

Steering clear of family drama, Rachel was not forced to feel psychologically vulnerable. Since she shielded herself from being exposed, what she felt, observed, thought, and experienced were not met with judgment. When asked to describe her childhood in one word, Rachel would say, "Untroubled." Her years of playing with paper dolls, fitting together one-thousand-piece puzzles, devouring books, penning diary entries, and daydreaming away countless summer days taught her how to occupy and enjoy time by herself. For Rachel, privacy became her best friend.

The downside to Rachel's neutrality and independence was that she never discovered her deeper truths. Her instinct to remain withdrawn led her to believe that what she needs, wants, desires, and deserves is not praiseworthy. Rachel describes this aspect of her childhood, without blinking, as "misunderstood." Since intimacy requires confidentiality, while Rachel's heart desired to be known, her mind kept her safe instead.

Although trauma did not invade her childhood and drama was something she mostly observed rather than participated in, the worst part of Rachel's upbringing did not happen on any day; instead, it's what happened across too many days. Unidentified, unnamed, and unnoticed, Rachel never developed a sense of self that progressed away from feeling tentative and unsteady. Even though she truly loved herself and could list many things that she considers likable about herself, Rachel remained distant from knowing what makes her unique and worthy of having her needs met by others.

Rachel's rudimentary road map about how to handle life's ups and downs was plotted using mostly a straight line—stay the course, keep quiet with her head down, don't make noise, and be happy that you're not unhappy.

True to her nature and obedient to her nurture, Rachel's reluctance to share her maternal inclinations with Todd keeps her stuck. What she is slowly realizing is she cannot manipulate her truth, cannot get out of her stuckness, by keeping her thoughts, emotions, desires, and cravings to herself. By hiding her truth from Todd, in fact, Rachel is coming to realize her thinking does not stop, her emotions do not settle, and her longings do not disappear.

Perhaps, just perhaps, Rachel will find the nerve to question her significance, challenge her identity, and defy her past by breaking away from her behavioral scripts, action tendencies, and ingrained habits of keeping the good stuff to herself.

Mind Rule Life Lesson
The Mind Is Directly Connected to the Past

Your past must be viewed with raw honesty, awareness, and acceptance before you can truly understand the difference between who you are and what you've endured. If your learned practices and unwanted life experiences continue to repeat, you essentially remain trapped in your past by your past. The critical point to know is that your past is something you went through, something that happened to you. It is not who you are or who you are meant to be.

While your past can never be undone, actively exploring your yesterdays and deciphering the life lessons that you learned during the times you weren't aware you were being taught helps you foresee and, therefore, forestall your worst days from repeating.

Allow your exploration to be guided by your instincts. If you let go of the present—really let go, as you've never let go before—you will go where you need to be. Much of your life has happened without you really knowing. Much like the billboards and signs along the roads you've traveled, you've seen a lot and remember only bits and pieces.

Putting these pieces together is like assembling a complex jigsaw puzzle. At first, it seems overwhelming and nearly undoable. Befuddled, you might sit frozen for a while. Then, after you've found the corners and made progress on the borders, you gain momentum and become adventurous and daring. The more progress you make, the more confident you become.

So sit still. Very still. Let your thoughts meander, weaving in and out, up and down, even sideways. Don't try to catch up with your thinking. Your thoughts are a guide to your emotions. Now bring your awareness to what you're feeling. Don't judge or label your feelings. Recognize that your emotions are amazing.

While your feelings do not tell you what to do, they don't lie. Your emotions will be comforting and nurturing, and fascinating and completely surprising at times. Feeling what you are feeling opens your mind to revisit what you've pushed down, locked up, or pulled away from.

Your emotions are adding color to your thoughts. Begin to trust your adventure. You are moving in a direction on purpose and with purpose. What is coming to your mind may seem random. But honestly, what is happening is that your world is getting bigger and bigger. Your mind is expanding. Pieces of your past are coming back to you. What was once a silent memory is now, again, an experience with a voice.

Listen. Learn. The hidden conflict inside of you is coming to the surface. Listen. Learn. You are tapping into your unmet needs. Listen. Learn. What you've unburied is trying to tell you something. Your discovery is your truth, your deep truth.

Now, like a bird in flight, examine your deep truth from a different perspective. If you're not scared of heights, by looking down on your truth, you will more clearly see, understand, and appreciate what you've been hiding. The little girl or little boy inside you will whisper to you amazing things.

Listen. Learn.

Finally, if you dare, share what you've learned with another person. Doing so has a healing power.

CHAPTER 18

The Mind Is Designed to Reduce Pain

*When Threatened, the Mind Quickly
Devises a Plan to Minimize Suffering*

Without even realizing it, you probably have a plan in mind as you live your day-to-day life, deliberately doing things this way or that, all to ensure that your needs are met.

When you wake up, for instance, and prepare for the day, if you know the day is going to be tightly packed and stress filled, chances are you wake up early and start tackling tasks right away. On less stressful days, meanwhile, you might be more likely to sleep in and take your time getting ready, perhaps tapping the snooze button a few times before falling back asleep.

Think about the route you take to work or school. It's probably planned to maximize efficiency and decrease your chances of running into roadblocks or frustrations. On the way in, you might stop to fuel up with a fresh brew at your local coffee shop. On some days, maybe traffic is at a standstill, so you take a shortcut through a neighborhood to bypass the bottleneck.

Even if you take a long way in, say a route that winds its way through a dense forest, you get a glimpse of nature's beauty before you put in your full day. If all goes well, if your plan goes off without a hitch, when asked, you will likely say you had a good day. If so, why? Would you say it's because your day went according to plan?

Whatever your plan, focusing on meeting your needs is a primal passion of your mind. While this statement may seem obvious, how your mind goes about its business may surprise you.

People Are Easy to Predict, Hard to Know

In your daily life, one area that is particularly tricky to plan for is how other people will respond when you say or do something. Invariably, since your life involves people—and we all know how great and/or ghastly folks can be—it's a matter of when, not if, people will cause you to experience some level of discomfort, disappointment, discouragement, or distress. In the ordinary world, it is common for other people to upset your applecart without much effort. While the applecart represents your carefully laid plans, the apples reflect the inner workings of what makes you, you.

How do you like them apples?

Over the course of your life, it's assured that you will interact with two types of people, the *up* people, those who bring you up, build you up, lift you up, and pull you up, especially during moments when you're down and you need a little boost. And then there are your *down* people. These people let you down, bring you down, put you down, or pull you down.

In the latter case, when people are propelling your pain, without knowing it, you are given a choice. You can suffer through the slings and arrows of those types of personal interactions, letting them get the best of you. Or you can learn the lesson that conflict is trying to teach you. Contextually, it's worth noting that the catalyst for nearly every conflict is an unmet need.

The diagram below provides a visual reference to the model presented above. To reiterate, life involves interacting with people. Some bring you up, while others let you down. When your downs eclipse your ups, you experience pain. Pain comes from your needs being unmet. In pain, you can either suffer or learn. Choose wisely.

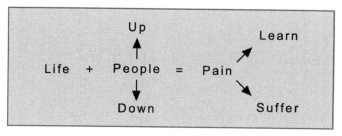

LIFE + PEOPLE = PAIN

Learning how to listen to your pain brings you closer to recognizing what is missing in your life and what you truly need from other people. Such listening moments require you to be wide-eyed and curious, have the patience of a saint, and be willing to make contact with experiences that have happened to you that you may not want to revisit.

A Natural Painkiller

Now that you know that life's discomforts, disappointments, discouragements, and distress all stem from your life not going according to plan, let's ask what your mind is doing during such moments of pain.

Your mind is highly sensitive to pain and discomfort. It's trying vigorously to prevent your unwanted past from happening again by forecasting when familiar and unpleasant moments may reappear. And when they do, your mind rolls up its sleeves and gets to work.

Your mind is designed to reduce pain rapidly by devising a plan that minimizes the sting. What does your mind have in mind? Being economical by nature, your mind digs into its arsenal and offers you three popular choices: attack, avoid, or surrender.

Attack is what you do when you feel like fighting back is necessary. In moments like this, the fighting spirit inside you broadcasts to others that you should not be taken lightly or for granted. If threatened, you will rise to the occasion and put up resistance. However, as you may know from experience, sometimes fighting is not the wisest choice. In fact, if your attack style is not well polished, things can go from bad to worse and from worse to ugly in the blink of an eye.

Avoidance is another obvious option. To some extent, we all avoid something. Maybe it's sidestepping a strained situation with our significant other by grabbing a few drinks after work instead of going straight home. We might also put off potential provocation otherwise by staying silent and refusing to share our opinion with a person with whom we have conflict. Or perhaps it's task related and not relational, and we procrastinate by preoccupying ourselves with some pleasing distractions, such as playing around on our smartphone, shopping till we drop, working in the garage, gaming, and exercising to exhaustion.

Whatever the case, the problem with avoidance is that it works. In fact, because of its effectiveness, avoidance is the root of addiction. Why? Because when we avoid our inner conflict, we experience relief. But the more we suppress what we need, the more our needs go unmet. When this happens, we repeat the cycle.

Conflict is both exhausting and painful. Any method you can find and implement to find relative peace and reduce pain is highly attractive, if not seductive. In this way, paradoxically, you can become conflict addicted.

Think about it. Anything that you do that provides you a sense of relief is enormously attractive. What is a major source of relief? Doing something you prefer over doing something you should be doing. This sentence explains the powerful reinforcing properties associated with all types of addiction, be it alcohol, drugs, gambling, sex, shopping, overworking, food, golf, gaming, and so on.

Another form of avoidance involves surrender. This type of pain reliever is quite effective yet not always healthy. If you learn to master the technique of giving people the impression that conflict does not bother you, or you extinguish conflict by always agreeing with the other person, then conflict doesn't immediately get worse, but it never goes away.

Of course, conflict doesn't go away when you don't do anything about it other than tolerate intolerable behavior. Hence, surrendering is a form of pretending that being misunderstood or mistreated doesn't bother you. Surrendering sets the stage for things in your life to progressively get worse, eventually becoming unacceptable and intolerable.

Barricaded Pain

The story of Susan, mentioned in a previous chapter, is illustrative here. By every metric, her life thus far has been sad, painful, and remarkable. The hand she was dealt made things difficult from the start. As you might remember, Susan's mother was drug addicted and unable to keep Susan in her focus. After being adopted into a new family filled with amazing promise, the luck Susan had along the way also let her down.

Her stand-in mother fell into the darkness of depression. Seeking to find an escape, she abruptly packed her bags and relocated far away. In her bedroom, Susan felt the grip of guilt. Going to college, she fell in love with Peter, who eventually betrayed her. Leaving Peter and college behind, Susan threw herself and her heart into her career and friends.

In balance, informed by misfortune, Susan's life has been painful. Yet, relying upon her resilient nature and steadfast focus on controlling things in her control, Susan has remained hopeful but not happy. Her upbringing and relationship history cast a shadow over her that seems to keep her a step or two away from flourishing. While Susan's resourcefulness has kept her balanced and she has learned to strategically harness its reins to adapt to life's unexpectedness, her experiences of deep sorrow and tragic loss, like unwanted developmental milestones, caution her against taking chances on letting people into her private world.

Susan's mind has become hypersensitive to the pain caused by people she allows to get close to her. What's next? To Susan's mind, the answer is to keep it superficial and nonthreatening by investing in friendships and career-related achievements. If Susan could hear what her mind cannot tell her, it might be "Don't you dare even get close to that door of intimacy." If you do, she is reminded, you will only be let down, deeply hurt, and left alone.

In response to her controlling and safeguarding mind, despite tremendous efforts of friends and colleagues to match her up with a great guy, Susan has gone years without dating or even contemplating the idea of stepping into a close relationship. Her mind is obliging by distancing her from the greatest source of pain—the loss of love.

Mind Rule Life Lesson
The Mind Is Designed to Reduce Pain

A universal truth about the human experience is that pain is mandatory, while suffering is optional. Knowing the difference between these two deeply human and humbling life experiences is key to learning how to move beyond forces and factors that weigh us down, pull us down, and bring us down.

As you loosen your grip on hardship and life's all too familiar discontents, you become more in control of life rather than life controlling you. When you gain mastery by short-circuiting the suffering that persists in the wake of unresolved past disappointments, discouragements, resentments, and private wounds, life begins moving again. In motion, you improve the odds of finding a better direction, which heightens the chances of your needs being addressed and gratified.

Think about your choices. Without moving forward, nothing changes. Life remains a series of frustrations and disappointments. The limits placed upon you become internalized, and you begin to limit yourself. Postponing opportunities for improved well-being become a way of being, and satisfaction is recognized as a distant memory. No longer being in the world, a life compromised by pain and suffering leaves you focused on the chances you're not willing to take. In such circumstances, reflecting the authority of mind rules, your mind has taken control as it dutifully employs its tactics to reduce pain. However, by doing so, your life as you once knew it fades into the background, and you become progressively unaware of how you are missing out on opportunities to get out of the mindset of suffering.

Everyday life is comprised of encounters with obstacles and resistance. Paradoxically, it is learning how to navigate such challenges that provides the lived experience of being satisfied. In this way, frustration becomes necessary to fully appreciate and eventually seek out prospects for taking in life on its own terms. Much like threading a needle, navigating the distance between pain and suffering requires focused attention and a willingness to be frustrated, yet you keep trying.

Knowing that learning is the opposite of suffering increases your awareness of when your mind is avoiding pain rather than pursuing new and mind-expanding experiences. Bolstering your personal power to break the cycle of avoiding life that reduces pain starts inside of you and is especially needed when people let you down or your world crashes around you. Remember, when you experience frustration that comes from feeling gridlocked, you may not be immediately aware of what your mind is doing, but now you know it's always following a plan.

In such moments, having a plan B is helpful. A deceptively simple rule of thumb involves splitting apart pain and suffering. The former does not necessitate the latter. Instead, when you experience the unique type of pain associated with being human, know that you have the power to choose to live, albeit within limits, and you do not need to stay imprisoned by the suffering that so convincingly attaches itself to your thoughts.

CHAPTER 19

Under Times of Duress, the Mind Imagines the Worst

Needing to Be One Step Ahead of Discord and Chaos, in Times of Despair, the Mind Predicts Adversity and Projects Negativity

What does your mind do when things don't go according to plan? Do you go full tilt bonkers? Do you hunker down, go back to the drawing board, and push through harder the next time? Do you find yourself nailed down by frustration, frozen in place, and unable to move?

Your mind needs to be one step ahead of anything bad that may happen. This is a basic principle of survival—stay alive! Since your mind comprises events that have occurred in the past and your personalized memories about such experiences, under times of pressure and threat, your mind has a critical decision to make, and that's *what's most important?*

To your mind, the decision is a no-brainer. The most important materials to retrieve from the deep vault of your memory bank are facts and fears necessary to prolong your life. Accordingly, your mind has achieved an incredible capacity for imagining the worst.

Forecasting Doom

A common quirk among many humans is a fear of spiders. Even without being traumatized by spiders in childhood, many of us share the same reaction when a spider crosses our path; we recoil immediately and sometimes dramatically.

Is this intense reaction an evolutionary relic hardwired into humans? Does culture dictate what is scary and what is not? Does your witnessing of other people's overreaction to spiders teach you that you, too, should be afraid? Or is it because of their leggedness? Is the prevalent fear of spiders just because they look creepy?

When you look at the picture below, do you have an immediate and powerful response? Interestingly, for some, coming upon a spider's web is enough to elicit a rapid, intensely eerie feeling. For others, not so much.

Photo, spider
Photo by Peter dos Santos on Unsplash

The experience of your spider reaction is a simple example of how the mind tends to make things worse than they really are. When you see a spider, your mind is forecasting doom.

In your daily life, this phenomenon is especially true when you are experiencing a level of distress. On edge or exhausted from your day, this level of heightened mental stress can be enough for you to react unreasonably and foolishly, fueled by your mind's tendency to expect the worst.

Everyday Doom

Now, imagine your typical day. Nothing much is happening. In fact, it's rather routine. You're sitting out in the backyard enjoying a pleasant spring day. Then, out of nowhere, you hear something. It's the sound of a small branch breaking, coming from a small grove of trees about twenty feet away.

What does your mind first imagine? Probably something far more sinister and threatening than what is creating the noise. Your reaction is intense. You're startled. Your heart rate shoots up, and your breathing becomes shallow. While it might seem that you're overreacting, really, you're doing exactly what your ancestors did when they were sitting outside their cave and heard a similar sound.

It's completely normal to jump when you hear an unexpected sound. Since the sound is sudden, your mind has no immediate context from which to make a rational decision. So reaching into its survival handbag, your mind jumps to the conclusion that your life is being threatened. While this reaction may seem far-fetched, it keeps you alive.

To view how everyday doom impacts a person's life, let's check back in with Tyler, who was raised by an alcoholic father whose high expectations and lack of parental engagement created confusion within his son. Tyler grew up compliant, hardworking, loyal, and steadfastly committed to meeting the needs of other people.

Fast-forward to Tyler's adult predicament. He is married with four teenage girls. They know their father loves them immensely, but Tyler's focus on expectations and a lack of engagement in their private world has left them starving for moments of tenderness, opportunities to swap their vulnerability for paternal understanding, a few giggles here and there, and fewer barbs of judgment and criticism.

Inside the walls of therapy, Tyler responded amazingly. He acknowledged that his father was the person who influenced his life the most. He shyly confessed to not wanting to be like his father but becoming more like him the older he gets. When asked to describe his sense of humor in one word, Tyler stated he never had much of a sense of humor.

After being told he sidetracked the question, he paused for quite some time when asked again. Starting to speak, he hesitated and then said, "Infrequent." Tyler's therapist made a mental note that given Tyler's oblique answer and difficulty in accessing his lighter side, they needed to work on giving Tyler permission to remember what it is like to be playful.

Weeks into therapy, when asked to express the simplest truth that he could in words, Tyler shared that he doesn't think he's very lovable. He quickly added that he strongly loves God. Tyler's relationship with God was explored. He said he feels at home when he's at church, helping others, giving back to his faith community, and making stronger connections with fellow parishioners through shared church activities and fellowship.

Tyler was then asked to consider his sense of being "at home" as reflected through the mind of his girls. Although he stumbled through the exercise, displaying a lack of familiarity with the idea of seeing the world through the eyes of another person, Tyler seemed to genuinely enjoy the challenge of growing psychologically.

Tyler's therapeutic journey is allowing him to grow in ways his upbringing never allowed. Now, instead of being ambushed by his past scripts, the ones borrowed from his father, the ones that would cause him to be fault-finding toward his girls, Tyler is starting to find more room for him to move alongside his daughters.

By joining them in their moments of laughter, in their discussions about their future, in their passions and play, Tyler has begun to stay out of his everyday doom, which left him feeling distant, disconnected, and unworthy of companionship. Tyler's progress revealed itself one day when he blurted out, for the first time ever, "I don't feel like my day starts with me lost in a maze."

Mind Rule Life Lesson
Under Times of Duress, the Mind Imagines the Worst

When you find yourself struggling more than usual, believing there is little hope for things to improve, and forever thinking others have it much easier, you need a global assessment. You need to separate the past from the present while keeping the future at arm's length. Without doing so, during times of distress, your mind imagines the worst, and your thoughts along with your emotions go to the same place, which is back to your past.

When conflict erupts quickly and endures convincingly, these are the moments that your past is taking over. Remember, you get into this position because, in times of despair, your mind predicts adversity and projects negativity. To get out of times of discord and chaos, you must be willing to step out of your past and remain one step ahead of your mind's reflex of defending itself.

During these moments, chances are things are not as bad as they seem. Chances are that under the pressure of distress, your mind is simply imagining the worst. Chances are, by removing yourself from your past, you will begin to realize that the sound of a breaking branch is not equivalent to your life about to end.

To keep yourself from slipping back to your unwanted past, the trick is to practice radical awareness. The first step is to bring your awareness to the moment you sense that your mind is taking over control of the situation. You may know your mind is trying to take over, but noticing this phenomenon helps to pause your mind from taking any further action.

When you know something, it commonly exists in your peripheral vision. When you notice something, however, you are placing it right in front of you. Your focus is intentional and unwavering. Everything else goes away, and what's left is your targeted attention on what your mind is trying to do.

Once you've steadied your attention, step two is to acknowledge your private experience by making a public announcement to yourself.

By talking to your mind rather than your mind telling you what to do, you've reversed the internal dynamic.

Try saying something like "I know what you're doing. You're keeping me safe. But I need you to step back and let me take over." This type of active self-talk is synonymous with what a coach says to her players at half-time. Beyond providing motivation, the talk provides perspective and articulates a revised road map to victory.

Next, you need to give yourself some time and space to analyze what part of your past is being activated. You'll be surprised what you can accomplish by giving yourself thirty seconds of contemplation. This analysis involves you seeking old patterns, rules, and assumptions that your mind relies upon.

Just like science creates unifying ideas from experimental observations to help us understand the complexity of the world, this step involves the process of radical awareness, asking you to keep your eyes wide open as you look for a pet theory as to why your mind is doing what it's doing. If the creation of earth via the big bang theory can be explained in thirty seconds, then, of course, much can be accomplished when you take this slice of time to examine your internal solar system.

Finally, you need to learn how to adapt rather than react during moments when the pressure around you is mounting and the stress inside you is following suit. The process of adapting involves revising your internal working models by examining the principal mindsets that dictate how your mind operates.

This examination process is explained in detail in the final chapter. In fact, while the identification of mind rules is necessary, they are not sufficient to elicit deep and lasting change. For that, you will need to study and practice the process of how to change your mind by shifting your mindset.

CHAPTER 20

The Mind Has a Blind Spot

Much of Your Past Happened without You Knowing It; In This Way, You May Never Know What Really Happened, but You'll Never Forget

Your life is literally happening right before your very eyes. Yet you'd be challenged to consciously detail what has transpired in a meaningful way. Naturally, you remember the ups and downs, the great times, and the not so great times, but everything else, the stuff that fills the gap between your best and worst memories and moments, is blurry. You know it happened, but it didn't stick.

All the same, even though you don't readily recall much of your life's journey, that doesn't mean it never happened. While much of your past remains hidden from speedy and accurate recall, events that keep moving further beyond your reach with each passing day are recalled at times when you're least prepared. Your mind is remarkably capable of summoning back experiences you thought were long gone and even those you wish would stay gone.

For instance, what would come to mind if you were asked to recall your favorite Christmas present of all time? Your first vinyl record? Do you have any scars? Other questions might require a bit more thought. Are you a sore loser or a good sport? Have you ever been at the wrong place at the wrong time? What is the best thing about you?

Then there are those recollections you may have never contemplated, such as what was your parents' greatest sacrifice? What happened to you to put you at your lowest low? What secret are you keeping from others? Even deeper, what secret are you keeping from yourself? By answering these questions, you retrieved memories stored long ago that were nearly forgotten. Your past is inside you but needs to be triggered for you to recall. Unfortunately, not everything that comes back to you is pleasant.

Hidden Trauma

Even though you may not be aware of some of the troublesome things that have happened to you in your past, they did indeed happen, and sometimes your mind and body replay the episode when you least expect it. This is how hidden trauma works. These are your unwanted life experiences that were displeasing, perhaps even appalling, that have been silenced by tolerance, deactivated by avoidance, disconnected by dissociation, and dampened by long-standing intentional forgetting.

Troubling as it might seem, what is hidden is not gone. An unexpected thing happens when you are routinely exposed to intolerable situations over time; your mind reshuffles the deck when it comes to what's normal and redefines it. Although your subjective experiences of the distressing events, by every account, were disturbing and unacceptable, over time, you gradually came to believe they weren't so bad. Your ability to tolerate intolerable behavior is a survival mechanism that comes with unwanted and unexpected consequences.

This explains why you do what you do after being invited to share an uneasy story from your past. While others sigh or cringe as you flashback, you buffer your narrative and temper their quiet discomfort by adding, "It doesn't bother me anymore," or "It wasn't as bad as it sounds," or "It could've been worse."

The way your mind adapts by minimizing recurring hardship is like how the brain tunes out constant background noise. Whether you're exposed to the steady whir of a fan or live close to an airport and regularly hear, over time, you stop noticing the noisiness.

The neuroscience behind this amazing phenomenon involves the brain having a natural noise-canceling circuit. Essentially, when a new noise becomes an old sound, the brain's auditory cortex tells its inhibitory neurons to selectively cancel out the sounds it has learned to be predictable. The result is your brain can make sound disappear.

Your mind also has a type of noise-canceling feature. Just as your brain can tune out the everyday ruckus, so too does your mind neutralize the background noise of continuous unpleasantness. This is how trauma becomes hidden in plain sight. Your memory of what happened is too painful to forget and too painful to remember, so your mind stores it in a place not easily found—your blind spot. It's there, and it will always be there, but either you don't see it, or you don't go looking for it. Instead, it comes looking for you.

In one way or another, everyone has had hard times. Getting through the most difficult periods of life is what allows your character to grow and for resilience to be harvested. Consider a time in your life you wished never happened. How did you bounce back? Did you recover slowly? Did you pull through just barely? Were others around to help you? Did you get over it but find yourself being pulled back in now and again? Was your rebound partial or complete? Assuming you're now out of the woods, what strength have you gained from this experience?

Hopefully, whatever darkness you've been through never happens again. These are the times you try to put out of your mind and restore balance to your identity but that can ricochet back at lightning speed during times of vulnerability. By keeping your unwanted and strange days in the past, your mind has developed a blind spot, an attentional blink.

The mind has created a way of protecting you from your unwanted past, your emotional injuries, your wounded self. It accomplishes this amazing feat by putting your distressing experiences and dark memories in hard-to-find places. Because of this tactic, you may never really know what happened, but you'll be reminded now and again, and forever.

Your Blind Spot

Welcome to the blind spot test. Below is a rectangle with a plus sign and a filled circle inside. Follow the directions below to see what happens.

RECTANGLE WITH + AND DOT

1. With your nose centered between the plus sign and the filled circle, look straight at the image above.
2. Cover your left eye and focus on the plus sign with your right eye. Try your best not to look at the circle. Concentrate your focus on the plus sign.
3. Now, slowly move your head closer to the image. Keep your focus on the plus sign.
4. At some point, between ten to fourteen inches, the circle will disappear from your peripheral vision. Your mind will read the surrounding white color and fill up the empty space.
5. When the circle disappears, you've found your visual blind spot.

This experiment gives you a hands-on understanding that your visual system has a natural blind spot. From a technical perspective, the spot where your optic nerve connects to your retina has no light-sensitive cells, called photoreceptors, so you are blind in this area. What's true for how your eyes perceive the world also happens to be true for your mind.

Because you prefer certain truths (the plus sign) at the expense of other less favored realities (the filled circle), the mind's blind spot makes you fall prey to nearsighted ways of perceiving the world. Your tendency to turn away from or dismiss competing truths, ones that clash with your belief system and preferred worldview, is how mind blindness explains much of the conflict between you and others.

Also, since you can't see when you're blind, your mind's dead spot can ruin your reputation, get you fired, make other people steer clear of you, cause you to bet against a sure winner, and destroy your sense of adventure. Your mind's blind spot is explained by the gap between your perception of what you believe to be true and what is the truth.

When it comes to navigating through your daily life, you rely upon your mind to handle matters ranging from simple to complex. To help you, regardless of the level of challenge in front of you, your mind uses mental shortcuts, or heuristics. This mind trick lets you decide quickly between right and wrong, good and bad, and to differentiate the important from the unimportant. However, mental shortcuts have a built-in snare that falls outside your awareness due to a concept called attentional blindness.

Perhaps the most common heuristic that occurs during times of critical reasoning and opinion making is called confirmation bias. This shortcut happens when you gather facts that support a favorite conclusion by being selective of what evidence you value (wheat) versus disregard (chaff). Another example of your mind's blind spot in action happens when you engage in wishful thinking or optimism bias. This is when you want to see things in a positive light, which can distort your perception and thinking.

Out of Sight, Out of Mind

Charlotte's story of being trapped by her medical condition illustrates the power of the blind spot in the mind. Her imprisonment by circumstances beyond her immediate control has caused her to fall into a hole so deep and dark that no light, no hope, no relief can enter.

When Charlotte's mind loses moral energy, she gives up trying to find a way to crawl out of the darkness. The gravity of despair takes over, and everything she once thought was possible slips away, leaving

Charlotte feeling empty, detached, and beyond consolation. In her mind, even her suffering seems wasted and unworthy.

When her father is beckoned, his hope is that his love, his affection, his devotion, and his admiration for his daughter reach her in time. In his mind, he searches for words that might help. Nothing. In his heart, he feels her pain, her emptiness, her misery. Everything. The divide leaves him motionless. Worse, in her darkness, Charlotte refuses his love.

She screams to be released. Her endless cycle of suffering devours. She is brave but has lost her courage. She is strong but has lost her power. She is determined but has lost her direction. In Charlotte's mind, her blind spot has taken over. Her presence has been conquered. She is left feeling nothing but absence.

Charlotte's life is extreme. Fortunately, a lesson can be drawn from her rare life experience. That is, the mind's blind spot is a deeply significant force that, when left unexamined, leaves you vulnerable and exposed. Once examined, however, what emerges are new possibilities for how to move, how to build, and how to live. As Charlotte's mind is silenced, her best hope is to move forward and risk the danger of believing her life is worth living.

Mind Rule Life Lesson
The Mind as a Blind Spot

An incredibly important step for advancing self-awareness is understanding what happened to you long ago without your permission or approval. This process requires you to focus on what didn't happen. While your grown-up self may believe your parents did the best they could considering their circumstances, this does not undo what was done, intentionally or otherwise.

The intent here is not to blame parents for their deeds and misdeeds, their effort or lack thereof. No. The focus of this mind rule asks you to revisit your past, which is tucked away in the deep recesses of your mind, and to do so intentionally and curiously. The process of self-examination, combined with a brave willingness to ask and receive feedback from others you trust, opens your mind and reduces your blind spot.

Whether you experienced the advantages of healthy and balanced parenting or were casualties of mistreatment or neglect, by opening your eyes to your past, you will receive insight to better understand the implications associated with being given everything you wanted except for what really mattered.

In other words, since everyone has a blind spot, including you, it's helpful to open your mind by asking at critical times, "What's happening before my eyes that I'm not seeing?"

CHAPTER 21

The Mind Struggles with an Attention Deficit Disorder

The Mind Knows What to Do but Doesn't Always Do What It Knows

It's a chaotic world we live in. Every day, it seems, we're bombarded with a dizzying number of distractions. Not to mention the cacophony of our internal world, the thoughts, emotions, images, desires, and cravings that drive us. It's as if everything is vying for our attention all at once. Amidst this barrage of noise and activity, something invariably gets lost. To the mind, what typically gets lost is precision and control—not knowing what's most important at any given time.

In psychology, this phenomenon is called sensory overload. The notion is based on the theory that humans have a limited capacity to handle increasing environmental stimuli and, as such, eventually become overwhelmed. If you find yourself feeling agitated, anxious, irritable, lacking focus, or feeling extremely stressed, chances are high you're in sensory overload.

When the environmental load surpasses your capability for processing, your mind responds by filtering the incoming information. Attention is a finite resource. Subsequently, it's impossible for you to consciously attend to all your sensory input at once. You'd go crazy. So, rather brilliantly, your mind employs a filtration system by which it chooses to focus intently on some things and ignore or suppress others.

The upside of this sifting the wheat from the chaff, as it were, is that the things that you bring to your attention are vividly embraced and focused on with vigilance. The downside is that you may be ignoring important details that are relevant to your situation in the process.

To illustrate the mind's curious ability to serve this function, how when too much information is coming, your mind acts as a filter and screens out some while allowing in other stimuli, think of the mind as a bottleneck. As information comes into the bottle (the stimulus all around you), your mind selects certain sensory input and waves off the rest.

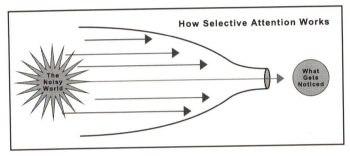

BOTTLE TIPPED OVER

The above illustration demonstrates this interesting phenomenon—just because you didn't tune into and remember something doesn't mean it didn't happen.

Distraction Is the Rule

While you seek to understand your environment and stay balanced, you will become distracted by whatever grabs your attention. Against this backdrop, paradoxically, your desire to be in control of your surroundings gets upended when your world takes psychological control of your attention.

In everyday life, you are challenged to remain focused on what's important. You may think that you're in full control of what captures your attention, but to one extent or another, forces outside your immediate awareness try to steal your attention. In this tug-of-war over your attention, how successful are you? Let's see how you're doing in a few critical areas that can steal your attention or make staying focused on what's important tricky.

Do you struggle with time management? Throughout your day, do you keep time in mind or do you lose track of time? Do people bring to your attention or complain about your lateness or tendency to procrastinate? Without reminders, do you forget appointments and other scheduled activities? If so, then you may suffer from time blindness, which is a type of attention deficit.

If this sounds like you, here's some insight: the thing that makes paying attention to detail harder from day to day is that you live in a world without time. Instead of viewing your daily activities as a string of events and traveling along a linear path, perhaps you are instead enraptured by the process of *becoming* rather than being present in the moment. It's almost as if time is pushed to the side as you concentrate your attention on your entanglement with what's in front of you.

How's your working memory? Do you struggle with holding new information in your mind as you connect it with other information? Mental math is a great example of working memory. For example, Bob has four children. If each child gets five apples every day for seven days and each child shares four apples with a less fortunate friend each week, how many apples each week do Bob's children have altogether?

If your answer is "They have a lot of apples," then your working memory could use a boost. If you needed to read the problem several times to yourself but eventually came up with the right answer, then your working memory is likely average. If you answered the question rapidly and correctly, congratulations, your working memory is excellent. This type of problem tests your capacity for attention, short-term memory, and complex reasoning—or working memory, for short. Think of this form of memory as sticky notes in your brain.

Do you consider yourself to be a highly emotional person? Do your moods change quickly? Once upset, is it difficult for you to calm down? When corrected or criticized, do you take things personally and have strong emotional reactions? If so, then your emotional self-control needs to be exercised.

When emotions take over, your thinking brain goes offline. This explains how emotional disorders interfere with your ability to stay focused, concentrate, and make wise decisions. Emotions, especially strong ones, sidetrack your ability to stay in control of your surroundings.

Time management, working memory, emotional self-control are all examples of executive functions that assist or hinder your attentional capacity. In the end, what is important to keep in mind is that being distracted is the rule, not the exception.

Addiction Is a Distraction

Let's talk neuroscience. When your attention is drawn toward something interesting, something exciting, a burst of dopamine is released in your brain. Dopamine is a chemical messenger that plays a major role in your brain's reward pathway. It's what signals your brain to send you out seeking a second helping of whatever seductive stimuli you've just experienced.

The magnetism of this potent chemical is mesmerizing. Once you've found something that really gets you going, beware; you could be entering into an addiction cycle. And once addiction takes hold, the mind's blind spot explodes. While the rational mind may know the dance of addiction—that any behavior can become a habit, habits can transform into compulsions, and compulsions are a quick step away from full-blown addiction—the impulse to act overrides the wisdom of knowing better.

The science of addiction teaches us that when the brain's reward system is repeatedly activated, the mind loses the plot. Addictions come in many shapes and forms, whether it's working out, playing golf, shopping, gaming, having sex, drinking alcohol, doing drugs, or even being on your phone. Does any of this sound familiar? Has anyone mentioned to you that you overindulge in one of these activities?

When attempting to balance reward and punishment, the addicted brain tilts predictably toward reward. Every time. Although there are plenty of negative consequences associated with addiction, when tempted, the mind fails to appreciate the downside of indulgence. So, when you feel the relentless pull of pleasure, it's handy to hardwire a blinking neon reminder inside your mind's blind spot to take it slow before you give in to your indulgence.

In a nutshell, anything that feels good and is rewarded—from behavioral fixations to chemical compulsions—has acute addiction potential. Do the math: inside this seductive reality is that whatever is rewarded grabs and holds your attention, which increases the odds that learning occurs. What's learned then becomes fixed in your mind, regardless of whether what you've learned is what you had hoped to have learned.

Mind Rule Life Lesson
The Mind Struggles with an Attention Deficit Disorder

It's known that your mind often decides what's important without asking for your input. The combination of instincts and unconscious behavioral patterns, commonly known as habits, explains much of your day-to-day actions. Science points out that 40 percent or more of how you think, what you say, and what you do happens when your mind drives your decisions, as opposed to those times when you're making conscious decisions.

This explains how so much happens in your blind spot. Think about what you do when you're concentrating. Perhaps you click your pen, chew the top, twirl your hair, or bite your nails. Although you may be aware that you do this or some other involuntary tic, because you're focused on something else, your mind turns its attention away from your repetitive behavior.

However, when someone shares their annoyance with your behavior, your mind shifts back to your pen. Then you stop—at least for the moment. Because of the power of overlearned behaviors, it's likely your clicking, chewing, or twirling resumes in short order.

It feels like your nervous habits when you concentrate have been bundled, such that without your pen in hand, your attention is scattered.

For the most part, your habits are a good thing. Life happens fast, sometimes too fast, and there's not enough time or mental energy to discern the trivial from the vital. Consequently, your mind provides an invaluable service. The route you drive to get to work, you do so without thinking. You crack an egg and flip it once, easy over without a thought. On your evening walk, you're home before you know it because when your mind wanders, it doesn't track time.

On the other hand, some habits can be damaging to your interactions. When you receive criticism, for instance, you shut down. When you fight with a friend, you say things you don't mean, but they're very mean. It's what you've always done. You didn't deliberately choose to switch off, shut down, or chew out your friend; you do what you do because it's your habit, it's been drilled into your mind to do what you've always have done.

The power of habits allows your mind to focus on what catches its attention. However, and this is important, just because something catches your attention doesn't mean that it deserves or needs immediate action. Wisdom guides you to remain discerning and actively curious of your surroundings and be intentional with what you perceive and how you choose to respond to your perception.

CHAPTER 22

The Mind Prefers Repetition

Because of Our Preference for Doing the Same Thing Over and Over, the Mind Guides Us down the Same Path, Even When the Path Isn't the Best Choice

As humans, we love what we know. In fact, we love what we know so much that we tend to think, feel, and do the same thing over and over. The power of repetition is quite alluring, even hypnotizing. We're creatures of habit, as they say. Maybe you have the same thing for breakfast every day. Or maybe you skip breakfast altogether and settle for a cup of coffee, a morning ritual where you fill your first cup at the same time almost by the minute.

Your other habits can be more subtle and nuanced, such as where you place your toothbrush, what order you put on your shoes, whether you back up or pull straight into a parking spot, and what side of the bed you sleep on. Like all of us, you have various quirks, customs, mannerisms, practices, rituals, routines, and ways of life that you are not fully conscious of when you're doing them. You just do them.

If asked to examine and count your private habits, starting with the moment you wake up until you put your head back on your pillow at night, it's likely you would pinpoint dozens of routines that you seriously rely upon during your everyday life. On this basis alone, much of your living is dictated by this cluster of overlearned behaviors. And the extent to which they influence the rhythm of your life is stunning.

When habits make life easier, it can be said you're in a groove. On the flip side, when habits make your life harder, you're in a rut. Whether your habits are healthy or not, when you do the same thing many times over, these sculpted habits of mind, there must be a reason.

Lather, Rinse, Repeat

How is it that without even trying habits develop? Even more perplexing, why do bad habits seem to flourish so readily while good one's demand effort and self-control?

When a person is shaped by healthy habits, whether it's adhering to a vegan diet or training to become a marathoner, an outpouring of positive descriptors prevails. Words like *tenacity*, *determination*, *perseverance*, *fortitude*, *grit*, *resilience*, and *indefatigable* frequently get tossed around. Different words, meanwhile, come to mind when contemplating the character and actions of people who are controlled by unhealthy habits: *addicted*, *dependent*, *hooked*, *weak*, *powerless*, *out of control*, or *damaged*.

Curiously, while bad habits seem effortless, as if having a mind of their own ("I don't want to drink, but I can't stop," admits the problem drinker, trapped by an appetite for not feeling), no amount of effort seems sufficient to disentangle them from their addictiveness. The stories of individuals afflicted by addiction appear to be controlled by them rather than authoring their own life story.

The power of repetition cannot be underestimated. From learning our ABCs to checking into a rehabilitation center, much of what we learn comes to us by virtue of what we are exposed to over and over. To bring home this point, in Benjamin Cheever's novel *The Plagiarist*, a fictional advertising executive adds the word *repeat* to his client's shampoo. What happens? Sales skyrocket. Behold the power of repetition.

What's important to keep in mind is that your mind is fast and frugal. Once exposed to a stimulus, especially something inviting and captivating, the mind anchors this experience with relevance and importance. Against this backdrop, like a mantra, what's learned gets repeated.

Time and Again

Reflecting on the interplay between time and identity, two elusive but imperative human concepts, it can be said that people who are driven by health habits intuitively know and appreciate the value of now. Such people are making good use of their time. They're keeping time in mind. They're not allowing time to slip by. Instead of killing time, they're focused on making time. They believe that time is on their side.

In the end, they cherish and understand meaningfully the preciousness of time. They seem to know at a deep level that yesterday is gone and tomorrow will take care of itself. Equipped with this wisdom, they repeat what serves them well and eliminate whatever distracts them from their destiny. Put simply, for these people, time flies because they're chasing the sun. The mysteries, complexities, and intricacies of life are coupled with beliefs that miracles do happen, dreams do come true, and people can live happily ever after, if, and only if, you keep time in mind.

Others, meanwhile, lose their sense of time when driven by distraction or overwhelmed by debilitating stress. Like clockwork, they make choices and take chances that increase the odds that yesterday's relief becomes today's distress. Instead of living in the moment, they fall behind the times and end up wasting time. To these folks, the mysteries, complexities, and intricacies of life are overwhelming, and they end up wishing and hoping they could turn back the hands of time.

The lesson to be learned is that over time, much of what you've learned happened step by step. First, you were exposed to something novel. Next, you rehearsed something over and over. And then you received positive reinforcement for doing so. Over time, your learned behavior became deeply ingrained and could be activated automatically. Because of this learning process, you no longer must think about what we're doing; you just do it.

Interestingly, the process of learning involves a critical shift. When you're first exposed to something new, this experience is registered in your brain as a short-term memory. Like remembering a person's phone number, short-term memory decays rapidly, lasting from seconds to a few minutes. Why? If the information you received has no lasting value, you dispose of it. Once you've placed the phone call, you no longer need the number, and, like magic, it vanishes from recall. However, if what you've been told is important, it needs to be transferred into long-term storage. When the transfer is completed successfully, it's learned.

There are three ways of consigning bits of knowledge from short-term to long-term memory. The first involves urgency. When something you've experienced has a high emotional value, such as being involved in a bike accident, for instance, the intensity of the experience becomes seared into your long-term memory, likely for the rest of your life, even though it only happened once.

This explains why you feel anxiety when you ride through the intersection where the accident occurred. As you approach the intersection, your mind is recalling your past experience combined with feedback from your body, such as a shortness of breath, resulting in a few alarm bells ringing inside you.

The second way to move information from short to long-term memory involves association. What you've previously learned is stored, waiting to be retrieved. Associative learning reveals your brain's fondness for taking shortcuts. This learning principle states that ideas and experiences that reinforce each other become mentally linked to one another. Basically, your mind loves to group things together. By doing so, the process of learning is made easy but not always correctly.

For example, assume that you've learned the phrase *blonds have more fun*. Then you go to a party and are introduced to a woman with blond hair. Your mind rapidly places your new experience into an already existing file folder, and you believe this person you've just met is probably fun. Even though you've only known the woman for fifteen seconds, because of the power behind associative learning, with your mood boosted, you engage in the conversation with the thought of having a good time.

Third, there is repetition. Being exposed to something over and again is the backbone of the formal educational process. You remember the process of how you learned your ABCs. The whole class looked up to the alphabet wall strip at the front of the classroom and, in unison, chanted "A, B, C ..." Day after day, this routine was repeated. Until, as if by magic, one day you no longer needed to look at the strip because through repetition, the alphabet strip made its way to the inside of your mind.

While repetition is your friend and a powerful tool to learn complex material, such as memorizing human anatomy, it can also trick you into learning something that is not factual. When this happens, it's called repetition bias. When you've been told something enough times and by various sources, your willingness to believe what you've heard increases. This explains how the most ludicrous conspiracy theories, quack medicine, bogus science, and fake history gain head-shaking traction.

Repetition also explains the popularity of homework, at least from the perspective of school boards, principals, and well-meaning parents. Recognized as the first principle of learning, repetition is simple. However, its simplicity also creates a problem that every student knows too well—boredom.

To make learning really pop, the power of repetition requires a splash of creativity. As something is presented redundantly, the stickiness of the material improves when material is introduced in different ways, such as factually first and then replayed in a story format. Then the material becomes embedded at a deep level, and mastery is gained when the student becomes the teacher and retells what's been learned.

Let's explore the neuroscience behind repetition. It's known that repetition influences how your brain processes information. For example, if you live near a busy airport, at first, the sounds of planes taking off are unbearable. But, over time, you learn to ignore the sound of air traffic, as though, by magic, the once unbearable sound vanishes.

Another example involves fear. When you are exposed to something frightful enough times, your fear response becomes less intense, less disturbing, and less scary. This type of learning is known as habituation, which implies the process of how you learn not to respond or react to stimulation. Pretty amazing!

Quite by accident and most unfortunately, your ability to do something repeatedly can also get you into a great deal of hot water. We are referring to the world of addiction. Addiction is basically defined as the continuation of a behavior in the face of unpleasant consequences to your life or health, often despite well-intentioned efforts to cease and desist.

Some of us have rather innocent and quite insignificant addictions, such as collecting porcelain pigs, musical instruments, or the fastest streetcar. Some others of us have an addiction we keep under lock and key. These types of addiction are driven by an unbridled desire for patches of happiness.

When impulse overrides intention, when acting on a whim takes the place of shrewd forethought, addiction wins. Once this type of addiction gains control, authority over the future is abdicated, and recovery becomes harder than anything else you've ever attempted, by a long shot.

Habits are clearly universal. Some habits are kind and gracious, providing a rhythm of life that would otherwise be a struggle. On the other side, the dark side, some habits are extremely damaging and completely devastating to our identity, our reputation, our potential, our relationships, our future, and our sense of time. Oftentimes, these uncontrolled habits are so overpowering and controlling that only three options are left—hope, prayer, and time.

Mind Rule Life Lesson
The Mind Prefers Repetition

Since the mind prefers repetition, now and again and forever, make a point of examining the everyday things you do without thinking. Take an inventory of your habits. Once you've identified your steady habits, go back and separate them into three piles, the good, the bad, and the ugly.

Pile one consists of habits that are healthy, easily discussed with others, and fill you with pride. Pile two, meanwhile, involves actions that are unhealthy and move you away from your pursuit of becoming the person you've always wanted to be. Pile three is made up of those things that you do that hurt those who you love the most.

The things that belong in the first two piles are easy to spot and differentiate. They're like night and day, black and white, two sides of the same coin. Then, there is the last pile, the destructive habits that wound others. Ugly habits are harder to detect because of two factors: thinking and feeling.

The first involves a convincingly oblivious awareness of innumerable alternative possibilities. The impulsivity of the moment impairs common judgment and logical objectivity. The second entails an overwhelming experience of giving in to temptation and external pressure and, in turn, abandoning good judgment thoroughly and pervasively, doing things that others might now and again contemplate but rarely employ.

As a human being, you are meant to ascend, to rise up and strive toward your greatest potential. Your habits can facilitate this trajectory. They can also cause you to descend, get caught in a rut, and find yourself further and further away from remembering, let alone actualizing, your potential.

Your unhealthy and harmful habits make it easier for you to stall and fail. Don't let your habits win. Take back control. Complete your inventory, set your priorities, ask for accountability, track your behavior, and be willing to learn from mistakes. The gift of self-critical attention and examination is life affirming. In the end, you are left with either choosing your future or your future will choose for you.

CHAPTER 23

The Mind Believes It's Constantly Being Judged

The Mind Thinks It's Being Judged at a Much Higher Rate Than What Is Actually Happening in the Real World

Humans have a particularly unique vulnerability. We believe we're constantly being judged. Whether others are looking us up one side and down the other or we're the ones measuring our own worth, it seems the experience of being evaluated is a full-time endeavor.

Think of all the ways you've judged yourself throughout your upbringing and extending into adulthood. You may have thought you had too much of something; maybe you're too slow, too shy, too thin-skinned, too gullible, too sensitive, too dependent, too heavy, too anxious, too compulsive—you get the picture. Or maybe you have dwelled on not having enough of something and judged yourself inadequate in such areas as confidence, charm, good looks, athleticism, humor, height, intelligence, wealth, or social grace.

Then there's the way you experienced the evaluation of others. They may have felt judged as being attention starved, arrogant, conceited, bitchy, self-indulgent, controlling, entitled, high-minded, impulsive, paranoid, overly competitive, headshaking difficult, incredibly intense, or way too insecure.

Whether you are busy judging yourself or worrying about how others are assessing you, your mind believes it's being judged nearly all the time. But is your mind right? Further, if judgment cannot easily be sidelined, do you remain forever susceptible to the pushes and pulls of life's irregularities? Even more, at best, can you expect nothing more than imperfect control over your mind's inbuilt methods and tactics?

Mind Your Own Business

It is abundantly clear that as you go through your typical day, sooner or later, whether you're aware of it or not, someone will judge you for what you say or do, or conversely, for the things you don't say or do.

Judgments of magnitude cannot be easily ignored or readily deflected and can have deep and lasting impact. When a child is bullied for any number of reasons, the experience is remembered forever. When someone jeers at an overweight person from across the street, the searing intensity of humiliation transforms into permanent invisible pain.

The core issue in being judged cruelly by others is a clash of realities, involving a distorted sense of what reality once was hitting hard against the headwind of what is rapidly becoming. Although the authority of such destructive acts and words is motivated by a deficiency of conscience, which is patently obvious to most but convincingly oblivious to the bully, the subjective emotional significance is tangible, setting into motion a downward self-revision.

What makes such disdainful acts of abuse and cowardness so immediate, so imposing, so impactful, and so devastating is the deliberateness of its delivery. The quality and intensity of put-downs, digs, and other types of belittling comments and disparaging acts are dispensed with targeted accuracy. On the receiving end, the internalization of demeaning and nullifying attacks is hastened by a felt sense of personal relevance.

Why is judgment so sticky? What is it about another person's negative comments that muddles our sense of self? Are we truly unknowable to ourselves, so much so, in fact, that the opinions of others act as a type of mallet that shapes and misshapes our own self-image? Is our selfhood so fragile that it cracks under the weight of the slightest put-down or off-color comment?

How rapidly judgment is processed and considered appears to be the Achilles' heel of our identity. What explains our inherent insecurity and susceptibility to the viewpoints of others is what we carry around inside of us, a deep little secret: the belief that if people knew who we are, really knew all about us—our thoughts, feelings, cravings, hopes, and fantasies, along with the things we've said and done—they would walk away and have nothing else to do with us.

You know well, sometimes far too well, what's wrong with you. You're not, for example, as smart as others believe and, consequently, see yourself as an imposter. Or you feel less significant compared to others, so you've mastered the art of telling tall tales about your travels, achievements, and conquests.

While being consciously aware of your false projections of a make-believe self to the world, it's far better, says your insecurity, than being no one and having no relevance. In any case, what's vital to your self-concept is that whatever your deep little secret might be, even if it's hidden in plain sight, it absolutely needs to stay secret.

Great efforts go toward keeping your secret concealed. When someone's audacity reveals your secret, you feel exposed. This unwanted and unsolicited disclosure lends itself to the awakening of old habits that are defensive and self-destructive, sometimes even fatal.

External insults permeate your sense of self, corrupt your internal balance, and manifest as a primal source of human suffering. The words and actions of others may alter your self-definition by destabilizing and devastating your sense of reality. Judgment also comes in subtle and nuanced ways, barely noticed but clearly visible, be it a smirk, an offhand comment, a dismissive look, a condescending attitude.

In the early seventies, related to such experiences, Howard M. Pierce, a Harvard University psychiatrist, coined the term *microaggressions*. This tag astutely reflects and explains the brief, blatant, and commonplace indignities thrust upon racial and ethnic minorities by way of denigrating messages given to them without warning or permission.

According to this research, these barely visible but never missed put-downs show up in three forms: microassaults, microinsults, and microinvalidations. Take note, microaggressions apply to all human interactions, regardless of color, ethnicity, and preferences.

Microassaults encompass verbal or nonverbal attacks. Examples of partially disguised ethnic strikes range from name-calling ("colored") to discriminatory practices (serving a white guest fist and a person of color last) to purposeful and "old-fashioned" hate signaling (waving a flag with a swastika). Microinsults, on the other hand, are muted communications that explicitly convey rudeness and indifference. A hidden but readily decoded insulting message, such as when an employee of color is asked, "How did you get promoted?" stings with the venom of racial hostility and abhorrence.

Finally, there are microinvalidations. Like all invalidations, whether big or small, statements that nullify another person's private experience are simultaneously confusing and demeaning. While microinvalidations may be broadcasted in the form of a mixed message ("Don't be so sensitive" says the white friend after her Latina companion shared her experience of receiving blatantly inferior service at a restaurant), all share one thing in common; intentionally or unintentionally, at a bone-deep level, they cancel the person's experience, perception, and sense of self.

What's most upsetting about microaggressions is that whether they're willful or inadvertent, occasional or frequent, they are difficult to prove and even trickier to respond to with confidence. They happen under the radar, so to speak, and outside of the obvious perception of others.

Consequently, you can be mistreated by being overlooked, underrespected, and devalued without anyone but you, and only you, knowing that the aggressions are traumatically unfair and objectionable. Even the quietest forms, detachment and disinterest, create psychological messiness and personal unsteadiness. In your mind, you're wishing that everyone would mind their own business and keep their judgments to themselves.

The Pursuit of Attention

What's curious about the impact of judgment is that while it comes with an obvious downside, the gut punch of being invalidated, it also has an irresistible upside. Being judged by others in a favorable manner illuminates your inner vibrancy and seductively boosts your ego. For good and bad, judgment runs through the texture of everybody's life, something both immensely detested and deeply desired.

When you hear "Way to go—great job!" as you cross the finish line, it makes all your hard work seem worthwhile. When you're judged positively with accolades like "You're the best," "The work you put into this project was amazing," or "Your commitment to your family is extraordinary," such acknowledgments inflate your ego with pride and confidence.

When you choose to wear stylish or eye-catching clothes, others will take notice. When you speak up for yourself or ask a question during a public assembly, others will turn their attention to you.

In short, how you look, sound, and act may capture the attention of others, as well as your own. This is good and bad news. If you mean to get someone's attention and you succeed, that's good news. When you receive unwanted or undeserved attention, that's bad news, and it feels like a failure.

To help mollify the force of being judged, it's critical to understand, for the most part, other people are observing you with only passing interest and casual judgment. That is, while people may notice how you look or what you're doing, after registering this observation, rather quickly, their focus and attention shift to something else.

Ultimately, when people do judge you, for good or bad, it's likely momentary. Just the same, in your mind, like standing trial, such moments are likely to linger longer than desired and persist without restraint or consideration of your best interests.

For instance, think of a moment in your life when you did something embarrassing. The reaction from others may have included them chuckling, smirking, or glancing sideways. For the chucklers, such moments are like snapshots: they're taken, looked at, and put away. But to you, the situation seems more like a viral YouTube clip, something that gets played and passed around continuously.

Still skeptical? Remember the saying, "Are they laughing with you or at you?" The first is easy to live with by simply going with the flow. The second is another beast altogether. Thing is, even if people are laughing at you and, worst-case scenario, they carry their spitefulness with them throughout their day and amusingly share their hurtful anecdote about you with others, it is vital to remember that what they're remembering is what you did, not who you are. This difference makes all the difference in the world.

The person who hurts you by spreading gossip about you likely doesn't know you and never has and never will. Their motivation for defaming you is likely self-serving. While such people may gain some aspect of pleasure by harming others, more likely, their behavior to devalue you, in their mind, heightens their perceived value in the eyes of those with whom they gossip. The strategy of a person improving their social status by putting you down reflects severe pathological insecurity.

While this explanation may not remedy the sting of being the victim of cruel gossip or unremitting bullying, it does extend an invitation to you to distance yourself from the abuser, both physically and psychologically. Instead of being someone's hapless scapegoat, you come to understand the best way to manage an unsolvable problem is by recognizing underneath every conflict is an unmet need. Then you can begin to explore and identify inside you what it is you need. Under most times of duress, what is needed is safety, support, or validation, which is just feeling like you're being understood and treated with respect.

Mind Rule Life Lesson
The Mind Believes It's Constantly Being Judged

Your mind is firmly and directly connected to your insecurities. It's as if you can never really let go of what holds you back, what brings you down, what hinders you from becoming the person you were meant to be. Everyone struggles to one degree or another with insecurity, which is broken down into various feelings of inadequacy, inferiority, ineptness, ignorance, and insignificance. The truth is, since we all are insecure, it's not realistic to believe we can stop being insecure. Therefore, to be human is to be insecure and to seek increased security by securing and sustaining connections with other people.

Your insecurities, oddly, function to keep you humble and striving to be a better version of yourself. While you can be preoccupied with the notion of not measuring up to other people's standards and suffering unnecessary anxiety, you also can listen—really listen—to your insecurities for what it is you need. From this perspective, your insecurities serve as a type of barometer, highly sensitive to detect fluctuations, that measures the extent to which your needs are being satisfied or rebuffed.

The key life lesson from this mind rule is remembering how important it is to loosen your grip on the insecurity that is felt intensely following the experience of being judged. This type of awareness and action permits you to be more in control of your insecurities as opposed to your insecurities controlling you. By becoming aware of your insecurity, your mind remains open and permits you to choose among the options of what to do next.

Whether you are feeling judged or you're judging yourself, the experience of judgment causes your mind to close. This can be remedied by refraining from being convinced and delaying the tendency to be confused, keeping your mind open and filling it with what is not yet known. This means putting energy into shifting your mindset from being certain to being actively curious.

Your willingness to be inquisitive will not only open your mind but widen your perspective about your current circumstance. When you've stepped back and seen the big picture, not only might you perceive your situation differently, but your emotional reaction to it will be better managed, from which alternatives for action become more readily possible.

Take heed. The process of being curious about your insecurities rather than judging them takes enormous amounts of deliberate practice. Also, while you may believe that others are busy judging you, in truth, how you are judging yourself is your true nemesis.

CHAPTER 24

The Mind Resolves Conflict by Repeating the Past

During Times of Conflict, the Mind Rapidly Recalls Useful Memories and Avoids Being Injured by Doing What It Has Learned to Do

In a deeply real sense, your self-image reflects your learning history. What you've experienced and what your mind has stored becomes the backdrop of how you see yourself, who you've become, what you believe and disbelieve, and how you approach life. For this reason, as you stand here and now, what you experience as being your true sense of self is really a composite of what has happened then and there. As you reflect on your past, therefore, yourself appears.

When life is good, naturally, your mind stays focused on the here and now. It's easy to go with the flow when nothing is getting in your way. When your life is on track and everything is going according to plan, you might say, after knocking on wood, that you have no complaints, you are content and pleased with what's going on in and around you. If pushed further, you might even confess that you are pleasantly surprised and happy, even.

But when things get tough, it's easy to get distracted and become confused. During such moments, your mind shifts direction and heads back to the past. Why? According to your mind, the past holds all the answers. Think about it. This completely makes sense. Remember, your mind only holds onto information it has determined to be correct.

For example, one plus one equals two. It always has and always will. Regardless of information to the contrary, such as a captivating conspiracy theory involving "new math" that tells you in a plausible-sounding manner everything you've been taught about basic arithmetic is total malarkey and 100 percent nonsense, without further contemplation, your mind remains unconvinced and goes back to one plus one equals two. Why? Because what your past tells you is true is more convincing than what others say is true.

By extension, it's sensible that your mind disregards what it determines to be faulty or wrong. Much like fitting a square peg into a round hole, what your mind has anointed as being *right* determines the roundness of the hole, while competing and square-like information is, therefore, lightly considered, respectfully declined, or wholly rejected.

But just because you believe something to be true does not make it so. There is often a sizable gulf between the world as it appears and the world as it truly is. The concept of *belief perseverance* explains your human tendency to cling to what you believe to be true even in the face of overwhelming facts that refute such beliefs.

If you've consistently been a good student, earning A's and B's along the way, for example, but you get back a test one day that reflects a much lower grade, this unexpected performance would not cause you to reexamine your faith in your academic capabilities. This lower than expected grade would be accepted as being an exception to the rule, and you would persevere in believing in your capabilities.

Motivated reasoning is another useful term that cognitive scientists have coined. This concept exposes how emotional reasoning colors a person's thinking process and motivates them to justify their position or conclusion by strategically relying on arguments that support their thought process and deliberately disregarding information to the contrary. When motivated reasoning and belief perseverance are combined, it's easy to see how wild ideas spread like wildfire, especially nowadays in the digital world that has become so turbulently divided.

Think of the impassioned stance taken by individuals who are

Holocaust deniers or global warming naysayers or those who believe that 9/11 was planned by a "deep state" within the US government. In such extreme cases, this type of thinking reveals the mind's preference for being right rather than being motivated to get the right answer.

While such true believers may be hard to understand to many, their way of thinking—albeit more overtly extreme and polarizing—is not uncommon. Just like you and me, they cherry-pick their facts, reject whole cloth contrary evidence, seek out others who hold the same attitude, and—here's the kicker—they identify opposing opinions as muddled thinking and misinformation. By doing so, they create an even more stark divide between fact and fiction, which fuels their commitment to their proud possession of "real" truth and final knowledge.

To understand the pervasive impact that your belief system has upon your perception, your choices, and your actions, it can be handy to view your beliefs as being a silent partner—constantly involved but not intrusively. In a nutshell, much of what you know and believe to be true is because of an admixture of past circumstances, selective attention, involuntary cynicism, and a preference to hang out with others of like minds. Do you see how your mind can hijack your thinking process outside of your immediate awareness?

So, using this logic, your greatest prized possession, which is your sense of self, is crafted by an interplay of past events, remembered diffusely and assembled haphazardly. The experiences you've been exposed to are sifted by your truth from the fantasy filter that results in your version of truth, which guides and explains your behavior, especially in the presence of perceived or actual threat or stressful circumstances. In this way, the past truly does predict the future as it shapes your identity.

How you've been judged in the past and how you've come to judge yourself determines the type of feedback you are vulnerable to moving forward. Further, when a pattern of unfavorable judgments has been leveled against you and you've connected the dots, the outcome produces your felt sense of insecurity. Knowing your insecurities at a deep and committed level helps to reduce the frequency and intensity of how future judgment may influence you under challenging conditions.

Here's the bottom line: you'll never completely know how completely in control of your thinking you may or may not be. Once you've had the same thought repeatedly, something truly amazing happens; your thinking turns into a belief. Once formed, your belief system functions as a filter through which you discern right from wrong, good from bad.

Having achieved an efficient way to reduce complexity into manageable and bite-sized chunks of knowledge, the next step involves transforming your beliefs into an overarching faith that permits you to rapidly discard and reject information, to distance you from the possibility of being discarded and rejected.

Remembering the Future

The phrase *the best predictor of future behavior is … wait for it … past behavior*—let's unfold this popular maxim a bit more. While your mind is on to something by believing the answer to today's trials and tribulations is stored in the past, this mind rule reveals an amazing observation about the human condition. While your mind may hold the answer, it also carries around countless other pieces of knowledge, trivia, bits of wisdom, and its share of nonsense and noise.

Amidst this bounty of information, your challenge is to learn how to separate the sheep from the goats, so to speak, by choosing the best solution to the problem at hand from all that you know. When you're confronted by a wealth of options, however, in good faith, you might become overwhelmed and end up picking the most convenient and familiar truth, not necessarily the most helpful truth and skillful action.

Because of your mind's partiality to draw from the past, you repeat yourself all the time. Then, with every repetition, your mind becomes more convinced of its capacity for choosing wisely. Your mind's fondness for repeating itself can be extremely helpful and efficient when you're doing something simple and routine, like looking for your keys. When you put your keys in the same spot every time, then every time you need your keys, like magic, they appear in the same spot. If life was this simple, you would be in great shape.

But life is often messier and more demanding than merely finding keys, requiring you to be more discerning about what to do, when to do it, how to do it, and with whom to do it. This means you have choices, and sometimes you have too many choices, but really not as many as you might think.

When a situation arises involving conflict, your mind's inclination is to go back to basics and select something that has worked in the past. What your mind does not know is that it is heavily influenced by repetition bias, a partiality to believe what it has told itself most often across a repeated number of incidences. When this happens, your mind may strand itself on an island that it personally helped to create.

Why would the mind fall prey to simple repetition? Because the mind is designed to keep you from being hurt or injured, it gets to work rapidly and devises a strategy to keep you out of harm's way. There may be no better strategy to rely upon, especially in a pinch, than to remind you of what has worked in the past.

The downside to repeating yourself is revealed through the wisdom of Henry Ford, who stated, "If you always do what you've always done, you'll always get what you've always got." So, for example, if you find yourself in a hole and don't know what to do but scream, over time, you become very good at screaming. And if no one hears your scream and you still can't get out of the hole, what do you do next? According to this mind rule, you reach for all you have and scream louder and longer.

Now, knowing that your mind resolves conflict by repeating the past, especially during times of intense distress or high conflict, you are in a better position to decide whether your mind has made a good choice or if you should keep noodling and searching for a better solution. That is, the process of getting out of your mind is equivalent to stepping out of your past and into another experience that your mind cannot yet imagine.

Another way of making the same point is by asserting that when the past (what is known) and the future (what is not yet known) compete, the present (what needs to be known) is often overlooked. What exactly is meant by this statement?

It's clear that what you've learned from your upbringing, relationship history, and formal education never goes away. Certainly, some pieces are far more memorable than others, some indelible. What is known and most knowable as your truth is revealed through the pursuit of truth, that, by itself, confirms the results of what has previously been pursued. In short, you know what you know because what you know is established and preferred over what you don't know or don't care to know.

You're aware that your mind detects patterns rather easily and distinguishes good from bad with impressive speed. In this way, the past is extremely persuasive in making sense of what is happening related to your current state. Your past creates mental models across time and past experiences that are an extremely powerful factor in influencing your actions. A mental model is the explanation you tell yourself how something works in your surrounding world. Like a blueprint, your mental models function as a psychological drawing you reference now and again to deal with this or that. Think about how easily you navigate around parts of your house without the lights on. So, too, your life experiences become the blueprint from which you navigate your life, especially during times when things get complicated or sketchy.

Remember the reference to round holes and square pegs? Your mental models represent *holes* in your mind. The shape of the pegs represents the particulars that your mind is being asked to process. When you hear something that sounds *right* to you, it is the roundness of the information that attracts your attention. To your mind, anything that lacks roundness is often readily dismissed. As if being guided and misguided by your mental models weren't challenging enough, there is another force that distracts you from staying present—that's your tendency to worry.

Amazingly and fortunately, the human brain has evolved to the point where you can forecast the future. In fact, our ability to conjure up scenarios that have not yet happened appears to be one thing that separates us from all other species. By anticipating what might happen, you can be persuaded to feel feelings, think thoughts, and imagine images that may never happen, but you act as if they most certainly can. Because of this phenomenon to forecast something that may never happen, but we act as if it already has, worry and anxiety represent mental models of a future world that may be nothing more than a figment of our imaginations. Real or imagined, your mind struggles to differentiate, so it defaults to recalling what has happened in the past to predict the future.

In combination with your past mental models, your future viewpoint causes you to often remain distracted from your present circumstances and, consequently, be overly fixated on what has happened in the past or what might happen next. Because of the push of the past and the pull of the future, your biggest challenge is learning how to stay focused on the present so that you can optimize your functioning.

Mind Rule Life Lesson
The Mind Resolves Conflict by Repeating the Past

Your ability to revisit the past is an incredible, amazing, and truly human phenomenon. The fact that you can look back in time and reflect upon your past life experiences allows you to prepare for the future. But not always.

The life lesson drawn from this mind rule is that since your mind is hardwired to quickly resolve conflict by repeating the past, you need to remain astutely aware of whether your mind's first inclination or instinctual urge is the best choice. Simply put, you have the option of stepping out of your past and into a better future by deliberately making better choices in the present. This is accomplished by understanding the power behind one of our greatest gifts of being human: mental flexibility.

Mental flexibility is a mindset, a mental state or attitude that impacts your emotions, guides your thoughts, and directs your actions. From a relational perspective, flexibility is defined as having options and bending so connections don't break.

When flexibility is viewed along a spectrum, at its extremes exist rigidity and permissiveness. Rigidity occurs when flexibility is extremely low. It is demonstrated by a person who is set in their ways, does not give in easily, and hangs onto views even when it causes problems. Taken to the extreme, such people not only concentrate intensely, it seems as though they're always concentrating. Everything they do is deliberate, driven, and completed with impassioned directness.

At the other end is a person who shows too much flexibility. This person pleases others at their own expense and gives in easily. In trying to reduce conflict, their own needs get lost. Lacking confidence, this person comes across as being ambivalent about nearly everything. To others, their passive style may be perceived as a weak character, evinced by not being able to stand up for what they believe, need, want, and desire.

Succinctly, too much flexibility can be just as clumsy and improficient in a transactional world as having too little flexibility.

To be mentally flexible in a healthy manner incorporates three interwoven skills. First, there is the skill of adjusting to circumstances by tolerating the gap in knowledge of what is not fully understood. Intolerance of uncertainty is a psychological muscle that needs to be exercised. If you insist on things remaining the same, rigidly adhere to routines, and have a reputation for not tolerating change, then it's time to throw on your sweats, hit the gym, and begin pumping some mental iron to strengthen your tolerance of what you essentially have little control over—uncertainty. Perhaps you may find some comfort in being reminded of the old saying *the only thing certain in life is uncertainty.*

Second, there is the skill of creativity, which is reflected by your capacity to develop unique options to sticky problems. Too often, your mind will be frozen in time and not know what to do or go back in time and return to old ways of doing things. In either case, your mind is not compelled to innovate. That's your assignment. Stretching the envelope, thinking out of the box, generating and celebrating wild ideas, musing unconventionally, and brainstorming are all ways to get your mental muscles moving in new ways. The beauty of innovation is that it breaks down barriers and pushes to the side old ways of doing and being. In simple terms, being creative opens your mind.

Third, the skill of anticipation involves the ability to expect the unexpected and stepping in rather than running or digging in. To reference an enormously overused quote by Wayne Gretzky, who is famously accepted as being the greatest hockey player who ever laced up, "I skate to where the puck is going to be, not where it has been." While this quote is densely overworked to the point of becoming a cliché in sports and business media, it makes the point with incredible clarity. Working on becoming more anticipatory will keep you from falling back into your old ways of living.

In a nutshell, when tolerating, creating, and anticipating are combined and deliberately practiced, your mind will expand and become increasingly flexible. With your new limber mindset, you will yield new ideas that will motivate fresh outcomes.

CHAPTER 25

The Mind Is Often Approximately Correct and Absolutely Wrong

Being Great at Detecting the Gist of Something, the Mind Can Misinform, Causing Us to Believe in Something Absolutely, When Likely We Should Keep an Open Mind for Being Approximately Correct

If we're honest with ourselves, we can admit that we all jump to conclusions. What's more, we enjoy connecting the dots, finding the right answer, and receiving over the top praise for what we've accomplished. When this happens, at least in the moment, it's as if we're standing on top of the world.

When these two cognitive trends collide, when we make a snap judgment and feel smug in doing so, we discover that humans are quick-thinking smart alecks. Case in point: As you probably know from your early schooldays, it feels good when you master the math problem of the day. It feels even better to be the first person to raise your hand, get called on, and proudly show off your masterwork in front of the whole class.

This drive to hastily gauge the situation and respond accurately is fueled by your desire to experience a state of uplifted energy. Whether it's a question that is answered correctly, a baseball hit squarely, or a first-date request that is executed successfully, these experiences grab your attention and make life worth living. Although these occasions don't last long enough, such moments give you a taste of what it feels like to be alive.

Pendulum

There's often a difference between facts and opinions. Sometimes, reality and viewpoints coincide; other times, they don't even come close. When a discrepancy occurs, you can be fooled into believing that what you see is what everyone sees. Or you may see what no one else sees and, therefore, believe supremely in your perception.

On a clear day, you look up to the sky and see blue. Unless their vision is altered by a psychedelic, people around you would readily agree, "It's a beautifully blue, sunny day." In response to such routine questions, the distinction between being approximately correct and absolutely right does not come to mind. It's as if your mind says, "It is what it is—let's move on." But when the world becomes increasingly complex, as it often does in the world of politics and religion, not to mention relationships, people have widely different perceptions of and opinions about the color of the sky.

Compared to the trivial nature of the sky's color, ponderous questions like "Is there a God?" and, if so, "Is God benevolent?" can spark highly contentious debate, even fisticuffs, or, as detailed in countless history books, multigenerational conflicts that are seemingly endless. Infused with a flurry of stated facts that are merely well disguised and frenetic opinions, these types of inquiries are rarely settled with a polite yes or no answer or agree-to-disagree verdicts.

Instead, as if a person's true existence depends on the answer, the stance taken is typically undergirded by *proof positive* justification along with chapter and verse citations. To such people, being right about their vision of God is existentially essential and linked inextricably to their identity, cultural significance, and wholehearted pursuit of everlasting life. In the end, at least when God is involved, the stakes couldn't be higher. Consequently, the mind swings like a pendulum convincingly toward being absolutely correct. It's as if your mind says, "I'm right. You're wrong. Shut up!"

The quarrelsome topic of God, which can be the breeding ground of cultural convulsions and generational upheavals, reveals how your mind is motivated to *get it right*. While being right feels good, sometimes amazingly good, when this is accomplished by putting someone else down or not showing interest or concern about the other person's perspective, an impasse is created, and disconnection arises. This dynamic reveals how the mind's tendency to be at least approximately correct can be absolutely wrong, in the end.

When your opinion or position is delivered in such a manner that the other person feels misunderstood, invalidated, humiliated, or injured, then such truth telling doesn't likely accomplish what you were intending. Being understood and treated respectfully is built into the conversational fabric of productive and satisfying dialogue.

Moving forward with authenticity requires your mind to find a way to stand up for yourself without putting the other person down. Here's another relational trinket: anticipating how your delivery will likely impact the other person is another essential ingredient in the recipe for navigating a successful narrative exchange.

Understanding the Gist

Being great at detecting the gist of something, the mind can misinform you without you knowing it. Take, for instance, a common experience such as a restaurant review. Good or bad, a strong review can have a sizable impact upon the bottom line of an establishment. An impassioned review can cause the doors of the restaurant to swing wide open with an influx of new business. The same doors can be slammed shut if the review is devastatingly draconian.

The purpose of a restaurant review is to serve up a thin slice of how the cuisine, atmosphere, and service were experienced. While prospectively helpful, it's hard to know whether the reviewer is biased and if the opinion truly reflects what is typically experienced. As would be expected, most food reviews are approximately correct and absolutely wrong. That is, the reviewer's experience truly may have been favorable or unfavorable, but this limited sampling of the restaurant's overall quality may be completely off base and, therefore, not necessarily representative of a typical dining experience.

The mind handles your daily life challenges in much the same way. Take, for example, something you look at everyday: your mirror. Your reflection is a deeply personal experience. During this private moment, your mind's tendency is to detect the gist (the overall reflected image of you), while also providing detailed information (the smoothness of your complexion) that can be prospectively misleading (you end up hating what you wish you didn't see).

When you look in the mirror, what do you see? Beyond your reflection, you perceive details—your favorite features, your beauty, your aging skin, your imperfections, your flaws. If your focus zooms onto a blemish in your complexion, then, quite often, the appraisal of your looks is harsh, and the consequences are rather severe. You feel ugly, you think you look unattractive, and you avoid situations where others may catch a glimpse of your hyper-focused deformity.

The mind's tendency to be approximately correct and absolutely wrong is illustrated by the expression *beauty is in the eye of the beholder*. While this example demonstrates what seems trivial, what your mind does with this limited information it has at its disposal can have disappointing and devastating effects on your self-image. More to the point, any defect detected in your appearance can cascade, causing you to judge yourself harshly and change your general attitude for the worse.

In such cases, while your observation of your blemish may be accurate, your assessment as to how such a blemish disrupts your overall looks is absolutely wrong. But the mind doesn't know this, so you need to remain astutely aware of when you're making a mountain out of a molehill. In psychology, this phenomenon is known as *catastrophizing*—when you believe something is far worse than it is.

Below is a simple experiment to bring home the idea that your mind can be approximately correct and absolutely wrong. Turn your gaze to the image below and answer the question, "How many black dots are inside the grid?

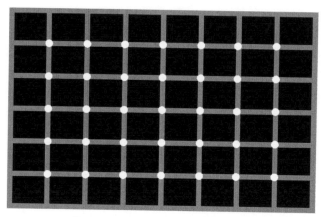

OPTICAL ILLUSION, FLOATING DOTS

This image is hypnotizing. As you examine the dots within the grid, they appear to change color, shifting from white to black. In fact, as you attempt to focus on the black dots, they seem to scatter, giving you the impression that the dots are trying to avoid detection. This optical illusion provides evidence that despite what your eyes are telling you, what you see is not always what's real.

By the way, the answer to the challenge above is zero. While you're sure you see black dots, in truth, there are no black dots. What you see, much like a mirage, is an illusion—but don't bother telling your mind; it won't believe you.

Mind Rule Life Lesson
The Mind Is Often Approximately Correct and Absolutely Wrong

Since your mind can be both approximately correct and absolutely wrong, you need to be on guard during times when you are being influenced by a wave of strong judgment. During such situations, it is helpful to ask yourself, "Am I looking at a situation through a microscope or telescope?"

Some situations require a telescope, which provides you with the ability to see faraway objects and the vantage point of an expanded perspective, enlarging your knowledge and providing you a deep understanding of how things around you work together. A telescopic view of a life situation can be invaluable, especially when you can benefit from gaining perspective and broadening your frame of mind.

By contrast, a microscope is excellent at detecting details not apparent to the naked eye. The microscope functions by taking a small sample of something, sectioning it into small slices, placing it under magnification, and gazing into a fascinating new microworld. Using a microscopic viewpoint promotes your ability to detect aspects of your lived experience that deserve time, thoughtful reflection, and considerate action.

The life lesson of this mind rule is knowing when a particular situation needs you to take a step back to gain a wider view, or when you should step in a bit closer and examine something more carefully. Having flexibility to back up or step in provides you a capacity to be more in control of your mind as opposed to your mind controlling you, especially when it may be trying to protect you by misinforming you.

CHAPTER 26

The Mind Has a Low Pain Threshold

*The Mind Struggles with Knowing the Difference
between Being Hurt and Being Injured*

Pain is humbling, but it's also useful and serves a purpose. Besides signaling to us that perhaps something is wrong, it also reminds us of our limitations and keeps us honest. More than that, pain is the indisputable equalizer. It's the tide that raises and lowers all boats. Regardless of wealth or status, fortune or misfortune, pain is the one thing that stops everyone in their tracks. Without exception, pain shows no mercy and demands great patience and even greater respect.

The presence and urgency of pain makes the mind restless and prone to wandering. Ping ponging from the past to the future to the present, the mind at once revels in the romanticism of fond memories before it begins sifting through best- and worst-case scenarios and finally settling into stagnation spurred by debilitating discomfort.

Before you know it, pain sends you spiraling into an almost suspended state, where instead of moving forward toward the person you aspire to be, you're pushed into being a person you never intended to be. In times like this, pain has an uncanny way of narrowing your perception to the point where only slight glimmers of hope can be seen.

It's hard to find consolation in pain; it ensnares you, taking control over what you can do, prefer to do, and dream of doing. Trapped by circumstances beyond your immediate control, your mind struggles to comprehend its predicament. Typically motivated by instincts to protect you from being harmed, once injured, your mind finds itself in unfamiliar and disempowered territory, especially when that pain is sudden and sharp.

What's more, when pain becomes chronic, the clarity of what you once envisioned for yourself becomes cloudy. In the wake of relentless suffering, the prospects of personal advancement become obscured by shades of somberness and self-doubt, and your confidence takes a hit. Pain also affects relational interactions. When pain becomes prodigious, the mind shuns being social. Thoughts of fitting in or any anxiety about standing out dissipate and slowly lose their relevance. In its place, the dominance of pain causes the mind to shift its focus from social affairs and connection to self-protection and survival.

All told, the only thing that really matters when you experience pain is relief. And when pain abates, your focus returns to satisfying your essential needs for self-definition and relatedness. Striving for autonomy and mastery while merging and fitting in with others through social bonding, it becomes possible once again to move in the direction of becoming the person who you were always meant to be.

Neurons of Pain

There is an amazing paradox when it comes to pain and the brain. Although the brain is responsible for creating the experience of pain, the brain itself does not feel pain, and that's because it does not possess pain receptors. This partially explains why patients undergoing brain surgery remain conscious and are not given general anesthesia.

A fascinating coincidence occurs deep within the brain. The experience of physical pain (a broken bone) and social pain (a broken-off marriage proposal) share the same underlying neural circuitry. So, whether you trip and fall or get blindsided by your expected life partner, similar brain pathways light up. As noted above, pain can be useful. It warns your body about potential or actual harm or damage.

When pain is felt, the body takes appropriate action so things don't go from bad to worse.

Imagine a life without pain. People born with congenital analgesia—a genetic disorder in which pain-sensitive nerve endings are not present—don't have to imagine such a life. They're living it, burdened with being unable to feel any type of touch or pressure. Without the ability to feel physical pain, life can be perilous. Given that physical pain is vital for survival, a pain-free life would place you in physical danger of being lethally injured without ever even knowing it. So, while living life without pain might sound wonderful, pain keeps you alert to what can eventually kill you.

The experience of pain involves nearly every part of the brain. Yet there is a suite of brain regions that work together to produce the felt sense of discomfort. When detailed, the pain perception process in the human body is incredibly complex. To begin with, the part of your brain that detects touch—the somatosensory cortex, along with the insular cortex—the information integration center, registers what part of the body has been impacted.

When a child touches a hot stove, for instance, electrical impulses from damaged skin tissue travel to the brain's relay station, the thalamus, via the body's main control center, the central nervous system. Upon arrival, the thalamus routes the pain signal to specific parts of the brain that pinpoint the source of the pain and registers the intensity of the injury.

Next, since the brain is designed to protect you, when the pain reaches a threshold level, the pain signal is routed to another area of the brain, the supplementary motor cortex and motor cortex. As reflected by the term *motor*, this area of the brain takes appropriate action by escaping from the pain stimulus.

In the example above, without thinking, the child yanks his hand away from the stove. This entire pain process happens automatically, and since pain travels as rapidly as touch, fortunate for your survival, you feel pain instantaneously and take prompt action so things don't get worse.

While immediate physical pain is handled by specific neural circuits, the brain doesn't stop there. Located behind the thinking center of the brain (prefrontal cortex) and resting above the part that connects the two cerebral hemispheres (corpus callosum; a thick band of millions of two-way nerve fibers connecting the two cerebral hemispheres) lies the anterior (front) cingulate cortex, or ACC. The ACC is the brain's main connection in the limbic system, the emotional brain. The ACC is known as being the self-regulation center and is a hub of activity when pain is felt and during situations that spike upsetting emotions and troubled thoughts.

During the experience of pain, the ACC's mission is to determine the emotional significance of pain and to decipher its salience (what's most important) related to the upsetting moment. Think of the ACC as the part of your brain that helps to emotionally decode the signal (what's important) from the noise (what's not important).

When the neuroanatomy of pain is dissected, two aspects of pain are revealed. These distinct yet intertwined facets involve the sensory (physical) and the psychologically distressing (mental) aspects of pain. Sensory pain is what you feel when you get a flu shot. The stabbing sensation of the hypodermic needle pin-pricking your skin sends a message to your brain that something unusual just happened. Upon the arrival of the sensory signal, the brain reacts by sending an alert message causing you to wince as the vaccine enters your system.

And, as you know from seasonal experience, all this neuronal activity occurs in microseconds. Yet, while the feeling of being injected may be extremely brief, the intensity of the shot may cause you to never forget. This explains why the emotional memory of the flu shot makes you hesitate as the next flu season rolls around and you find yourself, for no particular reason, putting off getting the vaccine.

The experience of psychological distress is commonly referred to as social pain. In your everyday walk of life, as you meet people, there lingers the possibility of being hurt by their words or actions or inactions. While there are countless ways in which others can hurt you, topping the list of social injuries includes being rejected, excluded, and devalued (or RED, for short). Like physical pain, the pain of social loss can be distressing and debilitating.

What makes the experience of *seeing red* so difficult and painful is that it often occurs when least expected. Being blindsided is when someone does something hurtful to you that you never saw coming. Further, when it does happen, when you are ignored or rebuffed or flatly discarded, it feels so deeply personal. When you *see red*, as the expression goes, anger piles up rapidly, and it can be overwhelming, making you prone to an emotional outburst as it takes control.

The fast and furious adventure of road rage is a great example of how seeing red can happen intensely and abruptly. While the psychology of road rage involves a complex mixture of competing internal and external factors, the short-fused nature of a person's hostile and aggressive action is often sparked by an everyday happenstance—traffic congestion, an unexpected slowdown on the road, or a minor traffic accident.

In the heat of the moment, the road rage incident is fueled by the person being overly stressed and feeling offended that whatever is happening is happening to them. The rager's displaced anger reflects their lowered threshold for social aggravation and reflexive action to discharge negativity. The upside to road rage is that it works. To the person releasing their explosive anger, which is an integral part of the fight-or-flight mechanism, they are solving a problem. In their mind, their action is justified, and their behavior is constructive.

The downside to road rage is its vicarious destructiveness. To the person on the receiving end of road rage, their experience is the equivalence of social anarchy. At once, they are being villainized and victimized. When, out of nowhere, things get out of control and there's nowhere to go, the intensity of such trapped circumstances is enough to trigger uncharacteristically hostile reactions. When attacked, after all, it's only human to attack back.

While road rage illustrates a distressing and dark side of humanity, there are other sides that are similarly unattractive and harmful yet more discrete and devious. Plots to undermine a person's reputation, bullying, workplace harassment, gaslighting, and other forms of social intimidation and psychological terrorism exemplify the types of despicable acts humans are willing to do to other humans.

When subjected to such cruelty, the level of social pain can be immense and eventually intolerable. In fact, the intolerability of relentless social pain can cause a person to choose the ultimate form of human destruction—suicide. The decision to end one's life is motivated by the desire to escape from unbearable psychological pain and the private torture that stems from believing the world is a better place without them and their presence is burdensome to others.

The news is filled with too many stories of individuals, young and old, who suffer silently under the oppressive weight of rejection, exclusion, or being devalued. This type of REDness is more than disheartening; it's disorienting and disturbing. When the social pain becomes unshakable, it alters the person's view of themselves, their world, and their confidence to navigate the interaction between the two. Nothing seems worthwhile, and everything appears hopeless.

The private struggle is often made worse because it isn't shared, at least not openly and intentionally. Instead, dark thoughts and darker emotions are locked away. Even when loved ones know something isn't right, because they don't know what to do, too many times, they choose to act as if everything is fine. Curiously, the act of doing nothing can make things even worse, as the silence validates the person's internalized shame and lack of worth.

Knowing the close relationship between physical and social pain provides greater insight into the process of feeling another person's discomfort. While the cost of social pain can be immense, feeling another person's pain and identifying with their emotions, a transactional experience called empathy, is the crucial ingredient to enhance social connection and dispel the person from their feelings of unworthiness and helplessness. When empathy is practiced actively, accurately, and authentically, it just may be enough to save a person's life.

Asking questions and listening longer are ways to show interest in another person's life. In sequence, when that person *feels felt*, they become more willing to be vulnerable and share crucial details about their internal living experience. The willingness to open the psychic door to another person's perspective is key to understanding their story, their inner narrative, and the way they connect the dots of their life experiences to create their version of reality. This is how to be brave and real when talking to another person about when they say they don't want to talk about. This is how to save a life.

Pain Is Pain

The felt experience of pain involves the two interconnected cerebral spectacles of perception and reaction. When a stimulus fails to reach a threshold of discomfort, no reaction is needed. The soft touch of a feather against your forearm, delicate and barely discernible, is felt as something pleasant, something that relaxes you, and certainly something that doesn't require any reflexive action. As a result, you attach favorable qualities to feathers so that the next time you come across something feathery, you may find yourself feeling wonderfully relaxed.

A paper cut is another story entirely. Albeit unusually small and shallow, when you pick up a sheet of paper that cuts your finger, an immediate stinging sensation of pain is felt. How can something so small hurt so much, you ask? The science of pain answers this curiosity. The nerve endings in your fingers and hands are densely packed together. This also explains how a blind person can read.

Braille is read by moving the hands from left to right, allowing the fingertips to lightly brush across a line of raised dots that represent the letters of the alphabet. The history of braille is astonishing. During the early 1800s, a man named Charles Barbier was serving in Napoleon's French army. Because the light shining from lamps would identify where soldiers were located, making them easy targets for the enemy, Barbier developed *night writing*, which allowed soldiers to communicate at night without being killed. Night writing involved a series of raised dots representing letters or phonetic sounds.

About a decade later, Louis Braille modified Barbier's night writing system, allowing fellow blind individuals to communicate with one another more efficiently. Braille was a young man who lost his sight after he accidentally stabbed himself in the eye with an awl belonging to his father, a leather worker who used the tool to poke holes in his leather goods. Braille spent nearly ten years perfecting his system, which is used worldwide by people who are blind and severely visually impaired.

Knowing how fingertips allow people to read helps us to appreciate the mystery of why paper cuts hurt so much. The ability to discriminate between two physical stimuli close in space is called spatial acuity. The density of spatial acuity in the fingertip makes recognition of touch extremely effective, which allows a blind person to read about 125 words per minute using braille. The downside of this acuity is that a paper cut, if you've never had one, can hurt more than you can imagine.

What makes some people suffer more from paper cuts or undergoing a medical procedure is explained by unpacking the concepts of *pain threshold* and *pain tolerance*. While pain is pain, the minimal level of intensity at which a person begins to perceive pain is called their pain threshold. The maximum amount of pain a person can endure is their pain tolerance.

Interestingly, gender appears to influence pain thresholds. When injured, the body releases a flood of pain-relieving substances, especially beta endorphins, a natural opioid. For many women, their bodies produce fewer natural painkillers, which causes them to feel pain more readily. As reflected by the miracle of Mother Nature, when a woman is giving birth, their pain threshold increases. Other factors that impact pain perception include genetics, age, stress, mental illness (depression, panic disorder), social isolation, and past experiences.

The effect of past experiences is astonishing. For instance, individuals who live in frigid climates become accustomed to extreme temperatures. When the thermometer dips well below zero, instead of complaining, they bundle up and mutter to themselves something like "It's just another normal day." Their lifelong experience with cold weather conditions increases their tolerance to plummeting temperatures that would cause a person who grew up in Miami to say, "You're crazy—this isn't normal. It's like the dead of winter out here."

The other side of pain tolerance happens when a past experience causes you to have an unusually strong pain response to a relatively minor situation. For example, if you've had an extremely bad experience at the dentist, then your tolerance for even minor procedures can be lowered. Why? Because your past experience (dental trauma) has set an expectation in your mind for what can occur when you visit the dentist.

At the extreme end of the lowered pain tolerance spectrum, allodynia is a neuropathic (nerve pain) condition that causes people to be extremely sensitive to the slightest touch. For such people, such everyday events as brushing hair, wearing a light shirt, having their hand lay on an armrest, or the blowing of cold air from an air-conditioner can be quite painful, even unbearable.

For some of us, the lucky ones, pain is kept at a distance—far enough removed so our lives are not imposed upon or restricted but close enough to remember we, too, have limits. For others, pain is chronic, unrelenting, and disruptive. When such pain takes over, it's easy to feel ambushed, pinned down, cornered, trapped by circumstances, and left without much choice but to hunker down and weather the storm.

Whether you are fortunate enough to be distant from pain, or if pain is constant and inescapable, for many reasons, we experience different types of pain differently.

Medical Purgatory

Going back to basics, we are reminded that the mind is designed to protect us from being harmed. In our past, at one time or another, we've all been disappointed, discouraged, and distressed during the journey through our upbringing and relationship history. We have all felt some type of pain. Due to this universal developmental experience, we know that pain is not optional—it is compulsory.

Because the mind is so keenly attuned to times when we may be hurt, the mind quickly responds to any detection of possible harm. Accordingly, the mind needs to have a low threshold for pain, especially the familiar kind, to deal with what is happening and keep at arm's length what may be harmful.

However, the mind has a difficult time distinguishing between when you've been hurt as opposed to being injured. Being hurt, needless to say, is an occupational hazard when interacting with others. As part of being a social creature, your feelings will get hurt. This is the drama of life. Others will let you down, put you down, or even drag you down. Some moments are harder to take than others.

Being injured is another story altogether. When you are injured by others, you fall prey to becoming convinced deep down that something vital is wrong with you. This is how trauma impacts the soul. You may doubt your worth and can even question your existence. Your vulnerability to being injured is influenced by your childhood, your personal development, your social history, and, basically, the hand you were dealt. When the sum of your personal losses is greater than your wins, your susceptibility to being injured by others markedly rises.

The story of Charlotte touchingly reflects the mind's low threshold for pain. While Charlotte persevered over decades dealing with an unsolvable medical problem that left her with debilitating pain and extremely limited quality of life, the absence of having a life caused her to frequently contemplate whether her life was worth living.

Her father would argue vociferously that his daughter had a low pain threshold. In fact, he would almost certainly counter by saying her threshold for tolerating intolerable pain was extremely high, evidenced by how she survived and pushed through her day-after-day unwelcoming life.

While he is absolutely correct that his daughter displayed magnificent courage and resilience, what Charlotte learned about herself by way of cold and unsympathetic feedback from various family members and countless medical doctors was that she was the biggest problem. Time and again, Charlotte was told by medical personnel that there wasn't anything wrong with her and that the problem was in her head.

At the same time, different family members at different times in different ways slowly began to believe Charlotte's problem was a figment of her imagination, something she chose to bring attention her way. Being surrounded by a host of voices that disbelieved her reality drove Charlotte to become confused and demoralized. During moments when her physical pain reached epic levels and her rawest emotional state of mind was ignored or shunned, Charlotte found herself being provoked into spasms of *yell begging*.

What was she yelling about? What was she begging for? Charlotte routinely struggled with finding a reason to keep living. Her futile interactions with medical personnel left her feeling brushed off and helpless. Her family's bias against her caused her to feel abandoned and hopeless. Yet there was her father—there was always her father.

Charlotte's father served as her beacon of light. His unceasing optimism and never-ending support became the one and only reason for her staying alive. He provided her the only source of validation, which partially quenched her otherwise feelings of deprivation. His singular voice proved sufficient to keep Charlotte from ending her life.

Knowing that her identity was shaped by the judgments of those who surrounded her, Charlotte's greatest challenge was to repeatedly beat back the chorus of naysayers and remain convinced that her father's affections were genuine and that she remained worthy of his allegiance and sacrifice.

Across time, Charlotte suffered the consequences of neglect. She regularly felt unimportant. She viewed her life as being a failure. Her self-image was relegated to feeling unworthy, a disgrace, a nobody. Her yell-begging was an existential scream for confirmation and endorsement. She craved for others to understand her dilemma and treat her with respect so she could learn how to love herself again.

After countless breakdowns throughout her adolescence and adulthood, Charlotte had lost hope for a breakthrough. Then, out of nowhere, it happened. One day, while listening to a podcast, she was reminded of something she had forgotten. What she heard was trite, nearly inconsequential, yet the timing of her listening was perfect. She was ready.

What she heard allowed her to look at her life from a different psychological angle. Charlotte learned that only she could give herself permission to change—change her perspective, change her self-worth, change her point of view, and change how she felt about everything, including her future.

Equipped with this new mindset, Charlotte began to experience welcomed relief and a sense of hope. When asked about her newfound freedom, Charlotte stated, "It's so refreshing to see myself without the burden of all those insults and injuries." Accessing the power of the mind, Charlotte had decided to increase her pain threshold actively and intentionally.

Mind Rule Life Lesson
The Mind Has a Low Pain Threshold

Pain is invisible and readily forgotten but always remembered. No matter how hard you try, you can't recreate the pain you felt while giving birth or having an acute attack of appendicitis. In this way, the physical part of your pain experience is left behind and forgotten, but the factual and emotional memory of having had intense pain lingers.

While you may differ from others in terms of your pain tolerance, your mind remains highly attuned to detecting any and all signs of possible harm. What you need to remain aware of is that the mind has difficulty distinguishing moments of drama when you are left feeling hurt from times of trauma, when you are injured and your sense of self along with your worldview are permanently revised.

By understanding the difference between being hurt and being injured, you are more inclined to be assertive when activity is needed and yielding when it's appropriate to distance yourself from those who are willing and able to inflict lasting pain. Pain comes in different forms. Most obviously, there is the physical side of pain, ranging from discomfort and general achiness to prolonged soreness and suffering to a sudden and life-threatening attack.

Then there is emotional pain. At some level, we all know about heartbreaking pain. When you experience a loss of a loved one or much-loved family pet, something is felt deep down. When a relationship ends, suddenly or somewhat expectedly, a shift inside of you happens. When you get bad news, whatever the variety, something inside of you sinks. Anytime life catches you off guard and unprepared, and you are forced to redefine normal, even when doing so is the last thing you want to do, your emotions remind you of how much life is outside of your immediate control.

The purpose of your emotions is to remind you that you are vulnerable. During such times, without even meaning to do so, your emotions communicate to others what might be going on inside. Perhaps others pick up on your facial expression, tone of voice, body language, or, more directly, what you say or don't say. In any case, your emotions often give you away and allow others to read your mind.

You know your emotions are being received by others when they ask, "What's wrong?" or "What's wrong with you?" The first question conveys a degree of empathy, while the latter is overflowing with judgment, as if being delivered a verdict against your character.

Moving on, you also experience psychological pain. When your needs go unmet for extended periods, you feel deprived and, quite often, become confused about your sense of self. When your life is filtered through a lens consisting of moments when you've been rejected, excluded, or devalued, you may feel abandoned, abused, emotionally deprived, defective, entitled, or a failure. In all such cases, what has been altered as a direct result of your psychological needs being unfulfilled is your true sense of self.

Psychological pain is different from emotional pain. When you feel wounded, empty, and imbalanced because of being disconnected from others, you may question your sense of significance and adequacy. Psychological pain, when felt deeply and pervasively, causes you to contemplate the meaning of life, the purpose of your life, and whether life is worth living.

It is. Just ask Charlotte.

CHAPTER 27

The Mind Never Lies, but It Doesn't Always Tell the Truth

The Mind Warns Us When Something Might Be Wrong, but It Doesn't Tell Us What to Do; It Does, However, Make Suggestions

Your mind prefers to be at rest, lying low, staying relaxed, and consuming as little energy as possible. But when something attracts your mind's attention, it springs into action and gets busy—very busy, very quickly.

When the mind wakes up, it does so with purpose in mind. As a rule of thumb, your mind comes alive when something unexpected happens that demands a quick response or when something indeterminate develops that requires thoughtful analysis and deliberation. These two ways of processing information, speedy and steady, are discussed in instructive and scholarly detail in Daniel Kahneman's groundbreaking book titled *Thinking Fast and Slow*.

Dr. Kahneman refers to these ways of thinking as *systems*. System 1 involves the mind operating automatically and quickly (fast). Sometimes the thought can enter and exit the mind so fast that later it won't be easily remembered. The second system (slow) kicks in during conditions involving effortful and more complex mental activity.

When you consciously engage in active thinking, the kind that requires you to weigh your options and consider future outcomes, you are using System 2 thinking. This type of slow thinking comes in handy when you're looking for your car in the airport parking lot after having been away for a few days, or when you finally sit down to do your taxes.

System 1 is all you need when you are asked what's the answer to one plus one, or when your life partner rolls their eyes. Referencing these two examples, thinking fast is handy but can also land you in some hot water. You know you're using System 1 thinking when you react to something rather minor, and the other person asks you, "What were you thinking?" and your answer is "I wasn't."

Drive-By Annoyance

Let's explore these systems a little further by considering the everyday experience of driving through your neighborhood on your way to some local destination, say Starbucks or something. Because you have driven this route a zillion times, it's likely your mind is focused on what's in your future once you arrive safely (a grande, peppermint, white chocolate mocha with oat milk) and not thinking that much about the actual process of driving.

Now, let's change things up. During your journey out of the neighborhood, as you approach a stop sign, you notice another vehicle converging at the same intersection from a different direction at about the same time. Again, no big deal, you think; this happens all the time. But on this occasion, the advancing car doesn't make any effort to slow down. Instead, the driver breezes right through the stop sign without any concern in the world. This situation quickly gets your attention.

System 1 turns on. You become enraged with the driver's lack of concern for the safety of others. Or, perhaps, your blood boils because of this person's apparent selfishness and recklessness. Either way, your mind answers the call to action and rapidly devises an explanation for the rogue behavior. Thinking fast, your mind tells you that this is a bad person who, sooner or later, is going to harm or kill someone.

Then, once you're satisfied with System 1's initial version of what you just witnessed, you are compelled to slow things down. You pick up your cell phone and call your best friend to vent. "Why do people act this way?" You can't wait to share the you-won't-believe-what-just-happened story. Together, swapping System 2 ideas, you kick around various explanations for why some people choose to be indifferent toward others and glaringly disinterested in the public contract. Digging even deeper, System 2 brainstorming compels you to ponder whether this type of behavior represents a deeper and disturbing societal trend moving in the direction of flamboyant self-absorption and trademark arrogance.

As these systemic bursts of neural activity are examined, you'll notice something quite remarkable about the actions of your mind. Since the mind's lightning-quick rendition of events appears to be plausible and convincing, you don't question whether you have told yourself the truth, the whole truth, and nothing but the truth—or merely a version of the truth that fits your preferred view of the circumstances.

Accordingly, when it comes to what your mind tells you about what just happened, your firsthand translation of reality is accepted at face value and without debate, which, in turn, feeds the gossip mill of how flawed human nature has become as it slides toward increasing intolerance, smugness, driven by a diminishing interest in the common good and lack of appreciation for the utility of a shared morality.

Think about the implications of fast and slow thinking. Exemplified in the story above, the elaborate contemplations involving the dismantling of the common good and decay of morality were derived from a single experience of one person having witnessed another person electing to do something in a split-second situation that did not reflect favorably on all of humankind. Makes you wonder how many philosophical manifestos, political treatises, and psychological dissertations that have floridly exposed the various injustices in and curiosities about the world were conceived from such trivial moments.

Truth Is a Frame of Mind

The mind is a way station of extremes, a medley for likes and dislikes, pros and cons, pluses and minuses, and other ways you discern good from bad and right from wrong. To the mind, there is little negotiating room between extremes. The mind is inclined to pick a side and then look for reasons why its choice was selected. Even more, the mind typically relies upon information that cannot be easily measured or counted.

In the scholastic world that studies human judgment and decision-making, the mind's penchant for gathering facts that support certain conclusions while disregarding other facts that support different conclusions is popularly referred to as confirmation bias. This mental shortcut rapidly sifts through confusing and competing information, focuses on finding what it's looking for, and, like magic, presto, that's exactly what's found.

The mental activity that rapidly takes a position or selects a side is extremely useful when making a hasty decision or when being imperfect is perfectly acceptable, such as picking a winner at a horse track. This cognitive shorthand functions to confirm what is preferred to be true as opposed to what may or may not be true. But when the stakes are higher, such as when jurors deliberate before reaching a verdict, it is hoped the process of reaching a decision is methodical and reliant upon salient features of the facts, which serve as guideposts to their final judgment.

Think about how your mind makes up its mind. Do you vote as a Democrat, Republican, or independent? Are you the type of person who sits in the front of the class or occupies a space more in the back? Do you like peas over carrots? Are you the kind of person who would rather read a book or work on a car? Do you make lists or do things at the last minute?

The answer to these questions is based on the complex and distinctive mixture of nature and nurture. How your biological design and biographical experiences come together shapes the way you gather information, study human behavior, determine relevance, and interact with the world.

The interplay of these two factors serves as the building blocks of your worldly perception and understanding of how the world works and doesn't. Another name for your worldview is a *frame*, and framing is what you do to make sense from nonsense. When you've determined what you like and don't like, you've created a frame of mind.

Let's explore the difference between a subjective and objective frame of mind. What you're exposed to influences how you think about something. If the exposure is repeated and a pattern of information is detected, your mind commences to inconspicuously yet unabashedly formulate your beliefs that guide your behaviors and determine your habits. Once formed, having locked into believing the truth about something, the amorphous feeling of having a subjective experience about that something is replaced with a singular, superior sense of having discovered an objective, rock-solid, inarguable truth.

The rush of excitement that surrounds this discovery further emboldens your belief that you've cracked the code and can now discern the difference between fact from fiction. The thrill of understanding something that abolishes prior uncertainty and outmatches previous comprehension of reality is transcendent.

During such elevated moments, the foundation of your new experience, anointed by the upward burst of certitude, is, in fact, nothing more than a revision of your subjective experiences, reconstituted in a fresher version of what you believe to be true. What you've accomplished is the equivalent of having reshuffled the deck of life experiences, some new but most rather aged, that causes you to conclude that you've earned, and deservedly so, your privileged viewpoint and a seat at the distinguished table of absolute truth.

Against this backdrop, the endgame of explaining and predicting everything under the sun appears to have been accomplished. Of course, however, the unearthing of the *final truth* is really an illusion, a well-liked and handpicked version of reality, a concoction of preferences, a musing of the present situation to overcome any anxiety associated with the formidable challenge of not knowing the inevitable.

For all humans, truth is relative. But don't tell the mind. To the mind, after a bit of pushing, shoving, elbowing, and swaggering, truth is a well-earned achievement, a triumph over complexity that disarms possibilities by ascending with intellectual enthusiasm into the sphere of providence. Having reached a state of confirmed knowing, the mind then relaxes, as it no longer needs to concern itself with the constant prodding and poking of imponderables that is linked to the walk of everyday life.

As a side benefit, having relaxed, the mind dissociates itself from considering whether its conclusions are refutable. Amidst such resoluteness, the mind is disinclined to contemplate whether it has run amok. To the mind, the possibility of having been hoodwinked by an ecstatic communion with like-minded thinkers and believers is remote and, consequently, unworthy of consideration.

Mind Rule Life Lesson
The Mind Never Lies, but It Doesn't Always Tell The Truth

Of course, the mind is on your side—always and forever. Plainly, you only hold onto information that is useful presently or in the future. But just because you have a passing thought or an established belief, does that mental activity convey wisdom or merely an admixture of your past experiences?

Is it possible that your excited merger with a convenient truth has triggered a carnal instinct within that compels you to move away from the haze of information and turn instead toward a unifying and coherent, albeit contestable, perspective?

The mind's deeply entrenched faculty of keeping you moving toward a positive result and away from a negative outcome is praiseworthy, even virtuous. Yet, knowing that the mind, at times, is giving you its best guess based on what you've been through and have accepted as being truthful is key to knowing that sometimes you need to get out of your mind, challenge your assumptions, struggle with the scope and character of complexity, and, once again, think for yourself.

As an example, curiously, the forces of common sense and common decency are not universally accepted as reflecting the common good. The mind's tendency to cherry-pick reality based on frames through what you see is viewed as being what everyone else should perceive can reduce the complex world into bite-size chunks of conversation and gestures that proffer to you a sense of possessing objective truth.

Consequently, your version of the common good is whittled down to playing the cards of what you consider to be most important and then, driven by ego, furiously reshuffled when your reasoning breaks down or the subjective nature of your belief system is threatened.

At the end of the day, the mind determines everything you do based on what you've already done. In this way, instead of focusing on newly established proofs, your mind takes its lead from what has transpired. Thereby, your mind absorbs everything that has happened and distills it down into three categories—good, bad, and ugly.

Obviously, and quite thankfully, your mind guides you toward the good and decisively away from the bad and puts up a barrier, whenever possible, so you don't experience the ugly. The ugly represents pieces and parts of the worst days of your life repeating unexpectedly.

Here's the catch. Since the mind is recognized as being a reliable guide, you trust it completely. But should you? On one hand, the mind does not lie. But wait, it's also true that the mind doesn't always tell the truth. What is meant by this paradox?

While the pursuit of truth is applause worthy, the workings of your mind struggle to operate within a parallel universe. Enlightened by self-interest, the mind attaches itself to facts that are self-serving and reasonable, even if only supported by swollen clichés and self-congratulatory glory.

Concurrently, facts that go against the grain of the mind's preferred reality can be detached from and efficiently rendered pointless, even if motivated solely by intellectual dishonesty and misguided verbal blundering.

Consequently, this mind rule challenges you to review and challenge your opinions and beliefs, especially those held onto by white-knuckled, self-serving conviction. What is needed is a triad of capacities—a willingness to place increased emphasis on watchful and critical self-awareness, a greater openness to thorny or threatening feedback, and a suspension of critical judgment, which is equivalent to the readiness to open a closed mind. This is so much easier said than done.

CHAPTER 28

The Mind Struggles with Facial Recognition

When Faced with Adversity, the Mind Often Misremembers What It Sees

You might be thinking that since you respond swiftly and automatically to knowing what you like and don't like, your mind has mastered facial recognition. At times, your mind really struggles with recognizing what it perceives.

What happens when the *Mona Lisa* gets mentioned? What about when the name Marilyn Monroe comes up in conversation? What comes to mind? If someone shares with you that their favorite animal is an elephant, does an image of an oversized animal with a long trunk, skinny tail, and floppy ears show up? One more example. What mental image comes to mind when you think of the word *candy*?

The answer to these questions is directly related to a unique neural pathway in your brain. While there are obvious differences between *Mona Lisa* and Marilyn Monroe, and, of course, both have seemingly nothing in common with an elephant or a piece of candy, all four referents involve activation of your fusiform gyrus. This oddly sounding, spindle-shaped brain region is located along the bottom rim of your temporal lobe, tucked behind the upper portion of both of your ears. This part of your brain, especially in the right hemisphere, is intimately involved in recognizing objects, including faces.

Without even trying, when you're asked about the *Mona Lisa*,

Marilyn Monroe, and even an elephant, your fusiform gyrus lights up. What's distinctive about how your brain processes faces and objects is that it searches for patterns. This part of the brain keys into the human facial shapes, absorbing features and the distance between them.

When, for instance, you are shown a picture of the *Mona Lisa*, visual information about the masterpiece is converted into electrical signals and routed from your eyes to your primary visual cortex, which is located at the back of the brain. Then, the loosely formed sensory information is dispatched to your fusiform gyrus, where facial expression information is extracted and forwarded to relevant brain areas.

When a face matches a memory, the visual data is sent to the frontal cortex, your thinking brain, for further processing and action potential. The connection among your primary visual cortex, the fusiform gyrus, and your frontal cortex comprises the visual *what* pathway that allows you to consciously detect images and consciously perceive an object. Knowing *what* an object is, is critical to rapidly processing your world.

Let's talk further about what happens when you come across a highly meaningful face in your life, such as when you are cleaning out a closet and come across a picture of your mother. This image of the most essential person in your life is imprinted deeply within your brain.

When your mother's picture is shown, not only do you instantly detect this one-of-a-kind face, but you also recall a myriad of entangled emotional memories. The combination of your mother's indelible face and the meaningfulness you've attached to her image creates a vision that seems unforgettable. But is it?

There is a medical condition called prosopagnosia, also called face blindness. Such people are referred to as prosopagnosic, and they cannot recognize people's faces, even highly familiar ones. Under normal conditions, your brain has an amazing capacity for recognizing and distinguishing faces.

Facial recognition happens almost magically by pinpointing the shape of the face and zeroing in on unique features while judging the distance between them. People with prosopagnosia are unable to spot these crucial differences. This condition can be developmental, called congenital prosopagnosia, or can be acquired following a stroke or head injury. Either way, the inability to recognize faces can cause extreme social anxiety and interfere with forming lasting relationships.

Although prosopagnosia is uncommon, it is estimated to affect about 2 percent of the general population. For most of us who do not suffer from this disabling medical condition, we struggle in other ways.

Unforgettable Images

A fresh face, one you've never seen before, grabs your attention in unexpected ways because of its specific features that catch your eye, even if you don't promptly know why. "That person seems so familiar," you might whisper to yourself. The combination of your upbringing, relationship history, and let's not forget your unrelenting exposure to social media has introduced you to countless faces.

Such experiences across time have created a type of facial template that you subconsciously rely upon to discern whether to smile or remain unmoved, to approach or avoid, to turn on the charm or run for the hills. The snap decision you make when you meet a person for the first time is informed by what you see and, like a child's jigsaw puzzle, how rapidly you put the simple pieces together.

Before we explore how your mind handles and mishandles facial recognition, let's talk numbers. Extensive research has shown that humans are extremely visually oriented creatures. About 90 percent of the information that is transmitted to your brain is in the form of visual data, and visuals are handled about sixty thousand times faster in the brain compared to its much slower competition, text. Perhaps even more instructive, research estimates that 85 percent of your interaction with the world, your perception, cognition, learning, and activities, are mediated through vision. It's no wonder why the phrase *a picture is worth a thousand words* rings with such resoluteness.

The main point is that your first impression of something is heavily inked by visual input. In fact, you've probably heard the term WYSIWYG; pronounced wizzy-wig, the acronym stands for *what you see is what you get*. While this phrase is common in the computer world, to your mind, WYSIWYG offers an unbelievable rush of excitement. Because your mind hurries to make sense of situations that don't readily make sense, visual information is pleasing to the mind, as it provides a rich source of stimulus that doesn't appear to be ambiguous. But there's a catch.

Seeing is believing, right? Not so fast. In the visual world, the mind can be tricked into believing something that's not really there. Welcome to the world of optical illusions. Consider the image below. What do you see?

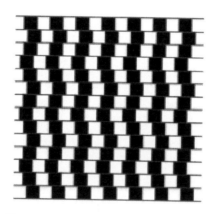

OPTICAL ILLUSION, CAFÉ WALL ILLUSION

This illustration is called the café wall illusion. At first glance, the lines extending from left to right appear to be angled up and down. A second glance shows the lines are parallel. Need proof? Take a piece of paper and cover up everything but the top two lines. You should now see what you didn't see just a moment ago: the slanted lines aren't anywhere to be found. This illusion is evidence that what you see is not always what you get.

Keeping your experience of the above optical illusion in mind that things are not always what they appear, let's consider how your transactions with people in your everyday world may involve similar deceptions.

Let's face it, you tend to be drawn to a particular look or type of person. Without contemplating the reason behind your preferential treatment, you make a snap judgment, up or down, about the person in your immediate gaze. Why does this happen? Essentially, your mind makes fast and frugal judgments when selecting, or deselecting, people by using a mental shortcut known as the recognition heuristic. It's amazing how a simple mental strategy involving subjective recognition sways you one way instead of another without engaging in deliberate thinking.

For example, imagine you are asked by a stranger on the street which city has a larger population: San Diego or San Antonio? What is your response? Without knowing the right answer, there is something in your thinking process that directs you to choose one city over the other.

In a study exploring the mechanics behind the recognition heuristic, approximately two-thirds of Americans surveyed responded correctly. However, 100 percent of Germans polled answered the question correctly. This surprising result explains that while the Germans had less knowledge about US cities, because the majority recognized San Diego, they inferred (or guessed) that San Diego was larger because of the familiarity factor.

Without knowing it, what you recognize gets valued at a higher level over something that's less well known. Simply put, your mind is seduced by familiarity, which persuades you in ways outside of your conscious awareness. Because of this phenomenon, you must remain alert to when your mind is controlling you as opposed to you being in control of your mind.

Recognition heuristic largely explains why so many humans have a strong tendency to take the beaten path, the one most traveled. What happens when the above lesson is applied to the topic at hand, facial recognition? When you experience a newly encountered face, particular features grab your attention because they convey a type of visual charm.

Based on your interactions with untold thousands of people, these life experiences left behind distinct impressions and memories. From a visual perspective, you frequently learn without knowing you've been taught what types of faces are trustworthy, honorable, friendly, agreeable, approachable, and, in a word, attractive.

Let's take a walk down a busy downtown street. As you move forward, step by step, minding your own business, most of the people who pass by, you look right through, barely noting their presence. But, now and again, certain people catch your attention, and still others cause you to do a double take. The attraction you have for such people is undeniable. Like magic, it just appears out of nowhere.

Not so quick. Something else is going on. Scientists have discovered a phenomenon called the *halo effect*. What you find attractive is more readily remembered. The key features of an attractive face are securely stored, easily accessed, and become a mental shortcut you rely upon when discerning whether you've seen that face before. In turn, your kinship with liking familiar things causes you to identify similar things as being familiar. So the answer to the question "Have we met before?" is yes—and no.

Falling on the other side of the attraction scale, there are those faces that give you pause, put you on edge, create a bad feeling in your belly, and may even leave you feeling creeped out. At first glance, you immediately don't trust such people. There's something not quite right about them. You can't put your finger on what it is, but it's there.

Your gut reaction is to ignore or walk away from them, sometimes quickly. Lightning fast, your mind detects certain facial features, compares them against composite sketches collected from your life experiences that have assembled a rough catalog of good, bad, and ugly people, then tells you what to think, feel, and how to act.

This sketchbook in your mind is a master filter that colors your perception, sways your judgment, biases your narrative, and controls your actions. This is why what you see (how you perceive something) is what you get, but what you get may not be what others see. Stated succinctly, your past is always present. You filter the world through lenses created by past experiences that bend to accommodate your preferences and beliefs.

So beware of the impact and ubiquitousness of the recognition heuristic. How you see something and what you believe to be true may be an illusion, a shadowy figure from your past.

A final way your mind's struggles with facial recognition involves the now-and-again experience of when a person's face vividly reminds you of someone from your past. "Don't I know you?" This is something we've all said or thought to ourselves. "Have we met before?" you might query. "I know you from somewhere, but I can't remember where, and it's driving me crazy." So say your lingering thoughts.

While faces are unique, some faces seem oddly familiar. They ring a bell. In the neuropsychiatric world, there is a condition called hyper-familiarity—a disorder in which unfamiliar people or faces appear familiar. This rare condition is apparent when, walking down the street again, every person looks familiar. While the rest of us do not suffer from this cerebral pathology occurring extensively in the left temporal lobe, there is that quizzical feeling when you sense you know someone already, even though you've never met them before.

It turns out that your ability to recognize a familiar face with speed and reliability is due to your mind being hardwired to find and remember patterns while using one basic tool: your intuition. Since intuition is what you've learned without realizing you've learned it (otherwise known as implicit learning), your quick intuitive judgments about whether a face is familiar relies upon your brain's capacity for a type of fuzzy logic.

Often discussed within the field of artificial intelligence, fuzzy logic is based on the observation that human decision-making relies upon imprecise and nonnumerical information. Instead of using the approach to computing that relies upon the conventional *true or false* logic associated with modern computers, fuzzy logic computes based on degrees of truth. This approach has proven quite effective in real-world applications where probability determinations are needed and when something is valid only to a certain degree.

Do you see how fuzzy logic and your ability for facial recognition are related? They're both based on putting forth a best guess and being correct more often than not while doing so with extreme velocity.

Mind Rule Life Lesson
The Mind Struggles with Facial Recognition

All human faces have eyes, nose, and mouth. Moreover, these features are placed in the same configuration, the eyes above the nose, the mouth below the nose. With so much uniformity, it seems utterly fantastic that you can easily, quickly, and almost faultlessly tell one face from another. How this is accomplished is based on the sophistication of your brain anatomy and its impossibly interconnected neural pathways.

When you look at someone, really look, something amazing is happening. Outside of your awareness, your brain, the ultimate supercomputer, is spotting uniqueness, detecting differences, snapshotting outlines and contours, making connections, assembling a three-dimensional or holistic model, and consolidating a memory of this rapid experience called facial detection. And this highly complex neural processing is done without you thinking about it.

Once completed, the image created and stored allows you to retrieve what you stockpiled and distinguish similar faces through an experience called facial recognition. This is a gift that keeps on giving, but you need to be wary that sometimes what is given is not what is needed. At times, how you perceive an individual, read their face, and untangle their emotional expressions can be wrong. In short, you can be fooled by what you see in another person's face.

While people come and go out of your life, your ability to recall their face remains. This astonishing skill not only serves you greatly from a survival perspective but provides you with an inestimable edge in social situations. Just don't think that what you see is always what is going on.

CHAPTER 29

The Last Thing on the Mind Is to Be Vulnerable

Programmed to Protect, the Mind Dodges Moments of Being Socially Knocked around, Which Is Exactly What Vulnerability May Bring

A dominant message emphasized repeatedly has been that the mind's main job is to keep you safe. It doesn't want you to get hurt or to allow you to let any part of your unfavorable past resurface. So it counsels you to be wary of entanglements that may elicit intense feelings of inadequacy, inferiority, and insignificance. Your mind is highly sensitive to destructive patterns and repetitive signs of conflict that are deeply rooted in your upbringing, reinforced by your relationship history, and underscored by your mind's tendency to gather facts that support certain conclusions but disregard other facts that support different conclusions.

Since those experiences can quickly be translated into an inner dialogue that is oppressive and counterproductive, even self-destructive, your mind runs in the background like psychological radar, constantly surveying your surroundings for hints of personal insults, reputational danger, or character assassination.

Moments like these that evoke the possibility of personal harm tend to coincide with the state of vulnerability. After all, when you have put yourself out there and chosen to be vulnerable, you are at the greatest risk for being judged harshly and treated inexcusably.

211

When others put you down, bring you down, or otherwise let you down, that relational dynamic can cause you to deeply doubt yourself and mistrust your personal value, leaving you upended by uncertainty or overtaken by self-contempt. Subsequently, the truth of who you are can become drowned out by a chorus of hectoring, negative feedback of what you've been told—or at least heard. Amidst such despair, you are left alone to fight off fundamental doubts about the core of your true self, and feelings of defectiveness, unworthiness, and hounding shame may emerge as a result.

The sting from such social repudiation can easily degrade your self-portrait with such disfavor that you begin to believe that you're no longer good enough, that you're instinctively unlovable, and, therefore, forbidden from being treated with the type of honesty, fairness, and integrity that is afforded to others who may be more deserving of love and respect.

Despite this tormenting downfall, vulnerability has an impressive, life-affirming, and self-aspiring upside. When you choose to be vulnerable, opportunities for deeper connections become available. What's more, since vulnerability does not occur unless you are being authentic, your self-worth is bolstered and self-image affirmatively reshaped when others receive, embrace, and affirm your genuineness. More to the point, when your vulnerability is met with validation by others, life is good.

The Binary World of Vulnerability

Whether the act of being open with others puts a smile on your face or leaves you psychologically adrift, the outcome of being vulnerable is directly dependent upon the behavior of others. It is this duality and lack of immediate personal control that makes vulnerability an intractable dilemma. On one hand, it can be viewed as something to be avoided rather than embraced, which keeps you safe. Conversely, there's value in confronting it rather than sidestepping the issue, which can replenish your sense of worth and spark your motivation to be increasingly authentic.

It is vital to keep in mind that the precariousness of vulnerability is based on how others respond to you, and how they respond to you may cause you to be acknowledged, affirmed, and applauded, or get laughed at, chastised, and jilted. Consequently, it is indispensable to thoroughly understand two critical aspects associated with the act of vulnerability—when and with whom to be vulnerable.

Let's start off by addressing the second part of that equation. There are two types of people in your world: up people and down people. As you go through your life, now and again, you need and depend on people to bring you up, build you up, and pull you up. When this happens, your spirit is elevated. Bolstered by reassurance, you beam with a sense of fulfillment and affirmation. In essence, you are being rewarded for being you and only you. Being uplifted by others permeates and produces a feeling of genuineness that frees you from any compulsion to deceive or persuade others of your uniqueness and value. These are known as *good days*.

Your sense of self yearns for moments when others experience you in the way you hope to be witnessed. When this happens, you are experiencing a psychological phenomenon known as *synchronicity*. This term was coined in the early 1900s by Carl Jung, the revered psychoanalyst and influential thinker who referred to synchronicity as "meaningful coincidences."

To be synchronized with another person at a time you are being vulnerable is to feel seen and felt, to be understood, to be authenticated. When you are simply being you, the true version of yourself that resonates with somebody else, you experience validation, which empowers a steadier version of the person you want to be to become even more pronounced. Accordingly, this is how vulnerability becomes your superpower.

Then there are those times when you will run into people who bring you down, pull you down, or let you down. When this happens, you experience disappointment, discouragement, and disillusionment and are reminded how rough life can be. These are known as *bad days*.

Navigating this binary world of up and down people can be

challenging. At one time, it may seem as though nothing but up people are heading your direction. But then something happens, and people start to turn on you, leaving you feeling the type of regret and distress that only comes from being in the relational world. While people who barely know you can disappoint and anger you, it is when your up people let you down that life becomes harder than it needs to be.

Since people are unpredictable and it seems only a matter of time before the next person turns on you, of course, your mind becomes highly skeptical of moments of vulnerability. Remember, it is during moments of vulnerability that you are at great risk for being knocked down, torn down, beaten down, or shot down. Is it any wonder, then, that the last thing on the mind is for you to be vulnerable?

Determining with whom you should allow yourself to be vulnerable can be dicey. Typically, it's a relational dynamic afforded to those people who have earned your trust over time across various situations. Yet even when trust is earned, some people can and will eventually let you down. Knowing how to deal with up people who have let you down is key to being relationally intelligent.

While we'll unpack this matter more extensively in the following passages, let's deal with the former part of the equation before we proceed: knowing when you should be vulnerable. Essentially, there are two scenarios to consider. Foremost, when dealing with a person you don't know (or at least not well), if they immediately leave you with an uncomfortable feeling, trust your intuition and step away.

Seriously, walk away. You should not be vulnerable with this type of person. You should not disclose personal information to them. You should not trust them with your inner thoughts or private feelings. You should not even gossip with them or discuss anything of any personal relevance. To do so would be naive and make you extremely susceptible to feeling misused and, eventually, abused and victimized.

The next scenario is more commonplace. There are those people with whom you have an established relationship, who also seem quite adept at upsetting your applecart every now and then. The predicament of such people comes from their capacity and willingness to throw you a curveball by saying or doing something that upsets what you were expecting or hoping they would respond.

People get to know each other one conversation at a time. However, people really get to know you each time you share with them a secret or something about you that isn't readily known. As an ordinary example, when you divulge the side of the fence you stand on related to a hot topic—whether it's pro-choice or life, gun control, or national politics—you are putting yourself at risk for having your opinion misquoted, misinterpreted, misrepresented, or distorted.

In either case, once that person spreads their version of your truth to others, you have lost immediate control of your narrative, your opinion, and your point of view. What was once an important personal truth takes a subjective turn for the worse and becomes less recognizable and further outside of your immediate grasp, all due to the indulgent whim of another person and their willingness to publicize a private matter.

When the matter is much deeper than merely your stance on a particular political subject but involves your most cherished thoughts and deeply held secrets, and such information is leaked by another person to others without your consent, the wounding of such exchanges is violating of your privacy and tremendously disorienting to your relationship with the process of vulnerability.

When such a person reveals a pattern of breaching your trust, it's time to learn a valuable life lesson. When you choose to share an intimate and important truth about a topic close to your heart and the other person does not sufficiently respect your way of thinking, since behavior does not lie, it may be wise for you to rethink how trustworthy this person is and how important they are to you.

Stated another way, since intimacy can bring people closer together, if the other person is not able or willing to honor your vulnerability, then it would appear the time has come for you to take a step back and reassess how important this person is to your sense of happiness. Keeping people close to you who can't be fully trusted is a fool's game and reflective of a desperate person.

Lastly, let's talk about the people in your life who are vitally important to you, even essential, yet occasionally let you down or bring you down by what they say and do—or don't say and don't seem willing to do nearly enough. We'll refer to these people as your *keepers*.

This group of people is likely composed of your family members, good friends, or people with whom you've grown quite close to at work, church, or some other gathering place. Such people are important enough to you that you are meaningfully attached to them. Simply put, there is a good reason or two why you keep them in your life. Now it's time to learn how to manage their misbehaviors.

Your keepers are people who have your back, folks you trust unconditionally. Such people build you up when you're torn down and pull you back up when you've been dragged under. These keepers know you well but not always well enough. There are those times when your keepers let you down. When this happens, practicing a few life skills may come in handy.

First, there is the skill of knowing how to *stand up for yourself without putting the other person down*. This practice entails learning the power of self-advocacy. Too often, in the modern society of extremes and snap judgments, people are green-lighted to put others down, belittle their opinion, laugh at their unknowingness, and, in any fashion so desired, champion their own needs, wants, and desires at the expense of those who oppose them.

Overcoming the impulse to reflexively harm others demands substituting judgment with a mindset for learning and teaching. The skill of giving voice to what you stand for, what you represent, and what is most important to you is a function of self-advocacy. Years ago, this type of thinking was popularly called *activism*. The function of self-advocacy is to promote and not demote, influence rather than impede, and to direct as opposed to indirectly impinging upon the beliefs of others.

A second life skill that facilitates dealing effectively with up people when they let you down involves knowing how to *deal with the problem without making it bigger than it already is*. This skill involves understanding the importance of perspective taking and emotional regulation. Likely, you've heard the saying *don't make a mountain out of a molehill*. This is sage advice, especially when dealing with matters of an interpersonal nature. By keeping things in perspective, you can more readily monitor your actions and, by doing so, give yourself a much better chance to decide whether what you're doing should be continued, modified, or scrapped.

When interacting with another person, it is good to know that there is a human line that divides the details of what is going on from the big picture. Relational conflict emerges from competing ways in which different people are taking in information. When one person looks at specific pieces and parts while the other is looking for patterns and relationships, disagreements show up. Likewise, when one person is living in the present and enjoying what's there while the other person is focusing on the future and anticipating what might be, quarrels erupt. At the same time, when one person prefers things that are definite and measurable while the other person enjoys opportunities for being inventive, strife occurs.

The way you perceive what's going on and emphasize either specifics ("I can't stand it when you roll your eyes") or the grand scheme of things ("I've noticed whenever you're really stressed, you have a shorter fuse, and that's when you tend to roll your eyes") can make things worse or defuse tense moments. When perspective is lost, whatever is happening in the here and now becomes intensely salient.

This is great when you're trying to hit a baseball coming at you at ninety miles per hour or peering through a microscope and looking for a gene mutation that may lead to a medical miracle. But narrowing your focus on the foreground and disregarding the background is not so great when you're operating a snowmobile in the backcountry following a record amount of snowfall. While the bumper crop of snow makes for miles of high-speed thrill seeking, without keeping in mind the big picture—that vast accumulation of snow increases the avalanche danger—the intoxicating elixir of freedom and fun can be deadly.

Similarly, when emotions are running high (hitting the throttle of a five-hundred-pound snow machine that responds instantly and vigorously when there is not a cloud in the sky and snow conditions have never been better), thinking retracts, and attention takes aim at the present moment. Maintaining perspective is a multidimensional process that connects your viewpoint and your understanding about a particular occurrence to your beliefs, convictions that guide your future and determine your options.

At the beginning phase of your learning curve, perspective is broad. You focus on collecting as much information about a topic as possible to ably understand what's going on. Once a conclusion is reached, your perspective shrinks because you now know what you know, and you believe you don't need to know anything more.

The problem with shrinkage is that you stop asking critical questions because your mind's made up its mind and the brain circuits associated with reasoning shut down. Interestingly, in this state of mind, you become susceptible to the all-too-human tendency to remember events that confirm your beliefs and ignore contradictory evidence; welcome to the world of confirmation bias and your mind's blindness to credible alternatives.

This same phenomenon occurs when conflict emerges between people. Once triggered, emotions rise, and thinking retreats to the background. In such situations, perspective taking tapers or stops entirely. Because your mind believes it knows what's going on and who's the source of the problem, it remains unaware that it may be looking at the situation from a misinformed, incorrect, or jaded perspective. Consequently, critical thinking is disengaged, and you may end up paying a psychological price for your mind's smugness.

A third life skill entails discerning, in real time, how your behavior impacts others. The key to improving your impact sensitivity and knowing how your behavior is affecting another person in real time is to practice conscious awareness. To explain this concept, it is important to understand there is a marked difference between knowing and being aware something is happening.

In the context of relational awareness, to *know* is to have a casual sensibility about what is occurring in the room. When conflict develops, it's a piece of cake to feel the tension and to know something's not right. It's something else entirely to be *aware* of how you and the other person are being impacted differently by the turmoil. The gap between knowing and being aware is the difference between reading the room and being able to read another person's mind. While the latter is often presumed to be impossible, you do it all the time.

Each time you interact with someone, to some extent, you're thinking what the other must be thinking. The reason you put your best foot forward during an interview or put on a special outfit in preparation for a first date is to make a positive impression. When things go well in the interview or date, it is the effort you placed in impression management that helped set the stage for a preferred outcome.

During such interactions, you are quite likely under the impression that the other person must be thinking that you are well prepared or take good care of yourself. In both cases, when you are thinking about what the other person is thinking or feeling what the other person may be feeling, you are reading their mind.

What makes conflict so tricky is that you stop being aware of what the other person is thinking or feeling, and, instead, your focus turns toward defending yourself and making sure that you don't get hurt. When your mind is defending itself, it's no longer aware of how your behavior is impacting the other person.

Fortunately, what is hidden is not gone. Although during times of heated exchange between you and another person, your relational awareness may be concealed from your immediate attention, it is within your power to shift your awareness back to the relational dynamics and give voice to what is happening.

When you find the willpower to overcome the seductive force behind the phrase *out of sight, out of mind* by saying something like "Boy, things are heating up between us; let's take a break," you are actively practicing the life skill of being more aware of how your behavior is impacting the other person. With enough practice, your efforts will become more organic, and you will experience yourself increasing your relationship intelligence by knowing how to turn conflict into connection.

The Upside of Taking a Chance

Your everyday walk of life is filled with situations that require you to make judgments and decide what's in your best interest. Some decisions are life changing, such as contemplating whether you should quit your job or, like Rachel, choosing whether to get pregnant.

Fortunately, most decisions in daily life are much less dramatic, like deciding whether to cross the street at the intersection or simply skip across in the middle of the block or debating what color to paint your living room walls. Something that comes up quite regularly are times in which you need to choose whether being vulnerable is in your best interests.

Do you share with the person you have feelings for how much they mean to you? Do you talk with your boss about the undercurrent of discomfort you have been experiencing working alongside one of your workmates? Do you talk with your adult child about your frustrations as to how they are not moving toward their future with enough focused energy? Do you open a dialogue with your life partner concerning your pet peeve related to their lack of tidiness and cleanliness?

The fact that such situations are common reflects something uniquely important about the basic psychology of vulnerability. The experience of being yourself, your true self, while in the company of another person as you share your private thoughts, a past memory, or an emotional outpouring is a growth-inspiring moment if—and this is a big if—the person responds in a compassionate and respectful fashion.

Such moments of vulnerability can enhance your search for a better understanding of yourself in the reflected experience of the other person. When you are heard and feel felt, and what you share privately with another person is met with empathic resonance and heartfelt kindness, an indispensable occurrence happens; your experience of yourself, your view of the world, and how you make sense of life's uncertainties is validated.

In the face of the unbearable possibility that the other person may diminish your reality, when you're not disappointed, and, instead, your intimate truth is witnessed and confirmed, vulnerability illuminates the inner landscape of the depth of your personhood.

By contrast, when vulnerability is mishandled by someone who fails to honor their end of the public contract of decency and secrecy, the sense of betrayal becomes your new predicament. Another name for this life experience is being double-crossed, which leaves you lingering with a sense of dread and loss of control of the private version of self. Exposed by someone's brashness and indifference, in a strange way, you become dislodged from the propriety of your selfhood. In your eyes, to others, you have been exposed and reduced to your darkest secret.

In a nutshell, the human experience of being vulnerable lends itself to rapid fluctuations in self-calculation based on the nature and intensity of feedback received. When favorable, a restorative and energizing reassurance washes over you. The supportive and affirming words, gestures, moments of welcoming silence, and other acts attesting to your vulnerability bolster your confidence and corroborate your preferred sense of self.

On the other hand, when vulnerability is met with intemperance and psychic strain, such unexpectedness separates you from your preferred self and introduces self-doubt and anxiety, both of which distance you from being the person you've always wanted to be.

Mind Rule Life Lesson
The Last Thing on the Mind Is to Be Vulnerable

Nothing in your future is inevitable. This statement evokes two highly different thought processes. On the one hand, it supports the notion that since life going forward is not predetermined, you have an active part in becoming the person you've always wanted to be. That is, you have some say in your fate and, to some extent, control of your destiny. This sounds both invigorating and exciting.

On the other hand, the stark reality that your future is uncertain also provokes a level of discomfort and worry that can be hard to tolerate, let alone manage. Hence, you may experience degrees of anxiety, if not panic, over being responsible for your future and taking the next step. On occasion, you might even forecast doom and, as such, fail to risk doing something that could improve your life, or not.

Vulnerability is an early warning system that signals something quite remarkable or devastating may happen next. The inexactness of this warning system, your felt experience of being vulnerable, creates doubt. Should I go over and ask the person to dance and risk getting rejected? Or should I assume that rejection is likely and, therefore, not take the chance?

The good news is that vulnerability, while being the last thing on the mind, can be your choice and your choice alone. Choosing to be vulnerable is, in essence, the equivalence of deciding to be alive. When you choose to act when feeling vulnerable, the door opens for transcendence, allowing you to move beyond your habits and seize on possibilities.

Remember, whether your life expands or constricts is based on the chances you're willing to take and the choices you make. Think of vulnerability as being your inner Geiger counter that detects such opportunities. Your willingness to be vulnerable involves taking chances and putting yourself on the line. When you do so, you're inviting yourself to experience the opportunity to learn something new and to gain something you hope will be incredibly valuable.

Does he like me? You will only know the answer to this query if you choose to be vulnerable and take the risk of asking the person out on a date. *Am I smart enough?* You will only know if you test the waters by applying for the college of your choice. *Am I worthy of a promotion?* You will only know if you take advantage of the opportunities available to you to show others your skills, talents, and ambition.

The upside for you in taking a leap is enormous. But it's also fraught with the possibility of rejection, being exposed, and being told you're not quite good enough, smart enough, or deserving enough.

Consequently, your willingness to be vulnerable is directly and persuasively linked to your desire to be more in control of your life satisfaction and state of general happiness. When you choose to avoid being vulnerable, you will stay safe and protected. But you will also remain frozen in place, and your satisfaction and unhappiness remain unchanged.

Summing up, vulnerability is a choice, an important choice, a mind-altering choice, and your choice. Choose wisely.

CHAPTER 30

Becoming a Mastermind
Who's in Control – You or Your Mind?

By now you've learned and likely overlearned that your mind has a mind of its own.

If there is one takeaway from reading this book, it's that your mind is brimming with life experiences. Warmed by your mother's embrace, there were days when you were snuggled tightly and assuredly as an infant. Filled with boundless joy, there were days when the school bell rang one last time, introducing summer vacation and all the freedom that came from having nothing but time ahead of you. Then there were those amazing days when you had your first show-and-tell, first best friend, first crush, first sleepover, first kiss, first time you realized you had an exceptional talent, and all that and more. Some of those experiences you might remember vividly and refreshingly, while others are more fleeting, and still others seem to have vanished into thin air.

In truth, much of what you've learned took place during times when you weren't aware that you were being taught. This supposition is the bedrock of your private world, what you rely upon to transmute uncertainty to confidence, ambition to triumph, complacency to zest.

Your thoughts, beliefs, passions, desires, impulses, sensitivities, vulnerabilities, temperaments, aptitudes, and expectations—everything that belongs to you and you only—are the clay from which, through modeling, you are sculpted.

Here's what's strange, though: if much of who you are is based on things that happened to you outside of your immediate awareness, then your past, although it can hold you back, also provides the key to understanding who you've become. Who you've become, meanwhile, is reflected crisply by what you do and how you do it.

This is why the way you behave depicts your character and the dimensions of your personhood, particularly during moments of friction. More so than at any other time, these situations reveal the *you* that you've become. Is this the *you* that you have chosen, or have you become a version of the person scripted by the feedback you received from voices in your past?

During times of discovery and growth, such as in therapy, less focus should be devoted to exhaustively exploring your past. Alternatively, there is more value in being shrewd enough to know, in the moment, when your past becomes present and beckons to be embraced and surveyed. In this way, the journey of personal development hinges on being present, steadfastly in the here and now, when your past barges into the room and tries its best to take over.

Remember, your mind is a composite of your past life experiences and designed primarily to protect you from your most unfavorable days repeating. Yet, since your mind cannot tell the difference between what's happening now from what happened to you long ago, your mind shifts blindly from guiding you wisely to leading you down the proverbial blind alley. To put it more bluntly, your mind is a single-minded control freak.

Consequently, to grow beyond your present state of being requires mind control. To establish control of your mind, as opposed to your mind controlling you, requires effort. And you need to be unafraid of effort, the kind of strong-minded, stop-at-nothing effort that breaks down barriers and bends the light reflecting on your sense of self.

Never Mindedness

The opposite of effort is avoidance. Distracting yourself and delaying what needs to get done is an incredibly seductive way to reduce worry and emotional turbulence in the moment. Procrastination is so pervasive in our culture that the sentiment "Why do today what you can put off until tomorrow?" is so salient it has almost become a sentient being. There's a reason that procrastination has become so popular—it works.

Putting off something you don't want to do is effective in alleviating short-term discomfort. Unfortunately, though, procrastination is like a pain pill: although it downgrades your immediate discomfort, it doesn't uproot the underlying problem.

An industrial psychologist, Piers Steel, and author of the insanely helpful book *The Procrastination Equation,* cleverly assembled a mathematical equation that reveals what's going on in your mind when you're choosing either to get something done or to put it off. The equation reads as follows:

$$M = E \times V / I \times D$$

Where M stands for motivation and the desire to complete the task; E, the expectation of success, which is tightly connected to the level of intense trust you have in yourself; V, the value of completion and the perceived meaning you attach to the endeavor; divided by the I, the immediacy of task or impulsiveness, the extent to which the project dovetails with satisfying your craving for immediate gratification, or not; and D, your personal sensitivity to delay and how far out in the future the finish line is, how long you must wait to be rewarded.

As a helpful reminder taken from our beloved algebra classes, to achieve maximum motivation, everything in the numerator and what lies above the dividing line needs to be boosted or increased, while everything below the line needs to be decreased or governed. In short, as you intentionally amplify your expectancy and enhance value while lowering your impulsiveness and control the distractions around you, you optimize your motivation, and your success rate in whatever you're doing skyrockets.

While the equation, at face value, is rather simple, as you know, during times when you need to do something you'd rather not, the experience can be quite convoluted inside your mind. When you defer doing something, you are prioritizing your feelings at the moment, doing something that makes you feel better, rather than doing something that makes you feel anxious or uncomfortable. Turning on your computer and playing a videogame is much more tantalizing than opening up your math book. Think about which activity offers you immediate gratification and no delay in being rewarded, while providing a high expectation for enjoyment and doing something you value. For most of us, it's no contest. Gaming wins hands down. This explains why parents need to routinely monitor their children and place limits on how many hours they spend on their computer, even when doing such surveillance is met with vehement protests of unfairness and various other forms of rebellion.

What you are essentially saying to yourself when procrastination becomes your go-to coping skill and preferred course of action is "never mind." It's your mind's way of rapidly reducing discomfort and making you feel better. Like painkillers, however, procrastination has an addictive quality that can consume the quality of your life.

Your mind is on your side and working for you when you postpone, stall, or just keep kicking that same old can down the same old road. When pain or discomfort is involved, your mind looks for the quickest escape route. This ingenious reflex illustrates the internal challenge associated with mind control, or lack thereof.

Navigating Relational Waters

What makes navigating daily life so complex and puzzling, especially from a relational perspective, is the push and pull between the compelling desire for connection and the menacing fear of detachment, being disconnected, and left alone to deal with the predicament of feeling psychologically insecure. Without realizing or even articulating it, you crave connection, and connecting with someone requires a relationship of some kind. This is where things get complicated.

At their best, relationships bring you joy and inspiration, expanding your life and making you feel better than ever before. At their worst, relationships bring you shame, guilt, resentment, and disappointment, contracting your life and leaving you feeling inadequate, detached, and puzzled. This is why so many people strive to circumvent conflict, real or imagined, sometimes at all costs. This is also why turning conflict into connection seems daunting and dubious. Yet turning the tide on conflict draws you in the direction of authenticity and actuality, creating the type of genuine connections that make life worth living.

While any type of connection is better than none, the greatest form of connection is intimacy. This unique state of privacy occurs when you lower your defenses, relax your public persona, and make the choice to be yourself, your true self, unguarded with another person in the hope they will respond with trust and confidentiality in return. At the heart of intimacy is the courage to be vulnerable. Being vulnerable is much easier said than done. On paper, being open with another person and sharing your deepest secrets and greatest fantasies sounds amazing. It's romantic, the idea of being completely honest with your innermost truth.

When someone gets to know you with your shield down, without any pretense of being anyone but yourself, the idea is captivating. Every romantic movie, comedy or drama, is based on some version of the leading character eventually choosing to be vulnerable. What the other person does with this information decides if the movie ends with hearts broken or everyone living happily ever after.

The choice to be vulnerable is counterintuitive to your mind's instincts. Since things do not always go according to plan after you disclose something about you that is highly privileged, your mind seems to be a step or two ahead of your romantic impulse. Remember, your mind does not want you to get hurt, and when someone breaks your trust, there isn't a deeper wound to be felt.

Vulnerability is a choice. Choose wisely. In real time, consider the upside and downside to being vulnerable. Don't get lost in computing some complicated relational math problem. Instead, ask yourself if the person is a reliable source. Can they be trusted? What is their track record? How well do you know them? I mean, really know them?

If they pass this screening, test the waters. Give the person a small taste of what you're serving. Then see what happens. Trust, in this case, is measured by the person's capacity to keep your private information, your secret, to themselves. No leaks. No gossip. If they breach your trust, choose someone else with discretion who deserves your confidence.

Blind Obedience

You may place considerable faith in knowing you are fully in control of your thoughts, how your beliefs formulate, how your emotions surge, and every little step you take in your day-to-day life. Once your mind has made up its mind, however, you've abdicated a great deal of control. After you've decided, be it small or significant, your mind shuts down, smug with conviction, and returns to a baseline comfort. In such a scenario, your mind has effectively closed.

In a state of closed-mindedness, your mind is no longer motivated to actively search for additional evidence. In fact, unless such pleadings present themselves and prove what your mind was thinking to be right all along, additional data is absorbed as noise and easily ignored. If alternative information shows up, your mind brushes aside anything that doesn't fit or sound right and readily returns to a comforting illusion of correctness.

In developmental psychology, this way of reasoning is called *magical thinking*. It's common for children between the ages of two and seven to believe that unrelated events are causally connected, no matter how fallaciously obvious it is to adults. A father claps his hands and sneezes at the same time. The child is amazed. "Do it again," they urge. Clap, clap, clap … sneeze, sneeze, sneeze. Magical thinking is so much fun, until it isn't.

When adults engage in reasoning that is methodologically messy, flawed by credulity or carelessness, muddled by plausibility, and shaped by preference, the distance between truth and falsehoods becomes irrelevant. Once your mind secures itself to something that *sounds* right, it then looks for similar tidbits of truth, and when enough stories have been heard, feeling convinced, your mind transforms what it's thinking into a belief.

The formulation of a belief becomes foundational to the core of who you are and what's important. Think about what God, money, and the Green Bay Packers all have in common—they all have superfans. And such people are passionate and obsessive beyond measure, fanatical, about their beliefs. They are the true believers.

When thoughts turn to beliefs, the space between knowing and not knowing vanishes. A key component to successfully adapting to life's ups and downs and twists and turns is learning how to discern between being approximately correct versus having a blind obedience toward needing to be absolutely right. Why is this so challenging? Because your mind's approach of choosing a side is attached to your identity. Once connected—and this can't be said with enough gravity—your mind actively ignores or dismisses alternative realities; it is not squeamish about being a know-it-all.

Now, knowing that your mind operates based on a set of rules and after studying the interplay among such rules, you are placed in a unique position to examine, inside out, the extent to which you're currently in control of your mind or your mind (a.k.a. your past) is controlling you. Over the course of reading *Mind Rules* and identifying specific rules that cause you consternation, this experience places you in a better position to regain control over your mind. By doing so, you are taking steps toward mastering the practice of mind control (i.e., being present when your past returns).

On balance, your mind knows what it knows; it places confidence in what it knows and is not nitpicky about how it came about its knowledge. Your mind also doesn't see any obvious reason to place value in knowing much more. Once you've come to believe something is true, nothing else needs to be learned. There is an upside and downside to this reality, and both sides are critical to recognize and acknowledge.

Having gained insight into how *the* mind operates based on a constellation of interwoven rules that work behind the scenes, you can now turn your attention to better understanding how *your* mind works. There are certain keys to understanding how to unlock the inner workings of your mind so that you can be more in control of what's happening, as opposed to your life events, hurdles, challenges, and predicaments controlling you.

You have learned that the mind is essentially a closed system. Namely, once information comes into the mind that proves to be valuable, the mind stores this knowledge securely and proceeds to show little interest in considering any type of competing or discrepant data. Ultimately, the story being told by your mind is satisfying because of a sense of completeness. Because the narrative is completed, which gives order and meaning to your life and circumstances, your perspective narrows, and the natural state of wondering ceases. You own your truth. But do you really? Or does your truth own you?

This tendency for your mind to be disinterested in entertaining additional information after forging a response, resolving a matter, or landing on a conclusion is a rather ingenious method for your mind to achieve and maintain a sense of relative balance. Conversely, if your mind remained continuously open to all types of alternative assertions, your understanding of reality would remain muddled, and your capacity to distinguish between fact and utter fiction would be highly fallible.

At the same time, if you were perpetually at the mercy of a swirling, mixing, and merging of ideas, thoughts, views, and opinions, then your critical reasoning capacity essentially would become nothing more than a hit-and-miss affair. You would become psychologically overwhelmed, and your mind would be eternally puzzled over how to discern fact from fiction, truth from deceit, sincerity from hypocrisy.

Consequently, it's essential for your general well-being, if not your sanity, that your mind makes up its mind. But you should also have some say in how your mind goes about its business, which requires a capacity and willingness to be open-minded.

Open-Mindedness

Although your mind operates mostly as a closed system, that's not to say you are incapable of learning or expanding your wealth of preferred knowledge after you have formulated a strong opinion, reached a conclusive conviction, or adopted a heartfelt belief. But to do so, to unlock your shuttered mindset and expand your mind, requires a willingness to examine your stance, review your attitude, challenge your belief system, and embolden your capacity to implement different and yet-to-be-proven strategies.

Being open-minded is a sign of impressive mental health, sturdy and self-rising confidence, and an unswerving drive to become a better version of yourself. Yet being open-minded is also counterintuitive in that it implies a willingness to actively search for information that may go against the grain of your highly treasured beliefs, preferred lifestyle, and long-term life goals.

Think about this paradox: If your mind makes up its mind based on information that it believes to be true, then why would you ever question or jeopardize the integrity of such valuable and revered information? By doing so, aren't you begging to be left feeling dazed and confused?

Remembering that the process of learning involves not only deciding about something, but once an initial verdict is rendered, your mind then works extra hard to fortify that decision and be prepared to defend the position at all costs. This two-step process of identifying and fortifying hardens your position, rendering you more resistant to adjusting your views or having a second thought. Your mind essentially resists the notion of changing its mind, preferring instead to be routinely single-minded.

Because of these dynamic forces in play, the process of being open-minded is easier said than done. To be open-minded is a choice, and each choice exists on three separate spectrums, with each spectrum represented by a concept called *mindsets*. A mindset is what your mind is doing, whether being actively navigated by you or working on its own. (These three essential mindsets will be examined and tinkered around with in detail in the final portion of this final chapter.)

When all is said and done, beyond your incredible human biology, you are primarily a collection of mental habits. What you do when you don't know what to do is typically answered by doing what you have always done. To do otherwise invites uncertainty, randomness, and doubt into your life.

Because you are a creature of habit, like most of us, you don't readily and recklessly jump at new opportunities or leap into situations without some degree of testing the waters or otherwise discerning the probability of success versus failure. On the other hand, there are some of us whose minds are wider open than others—those of us, for instance, who believe in ghosts, fairies, reincarnation, even UFOs.

Naturally, when minds are wide open, anyone can become vulnerable to such forces as religious cults or other fanaticism and be preoccupied with an unusual or aberrant belief system. Just the same, these folks, who may often be told their heads are in the clouds, may also be presumed to be a step ahead of the more small-minded humans.

There are others, meanwhile, who substantially lack any obvious interest in fantasy or daydreams. Preferring to keep their feet firmly always planted on the ground, they love routine, find comfort in a predictable and linear lifestyle, and tend to perform at a high level when dealing with straightforward matters and seeking concrete solutions. While these folks may be seen as old-fashioned or behind the times, they prefer to see themselves as being secure, solid, and dependable. In short, they get things done that they believe are worth doing.

Whether you are the type of person who prefers to have your head in the clouds or your feet on the ground (or somewhere in the middle), knowing how to open your mind to new experiences can lead to an elevation of trust, an expansion of self-confidence, and a vast improvement to your overall quality of life. Before the discussion turns to unfolding the three mindsets, it's essential to understand the obstacles preventing your mind from being more open.

Mind Traps

Now that you know your mind is a closed system and appreciate the importance of having new experiences now and again, it's vital to understand what hinders your mind from opening under its own power.

Your mind works rapidly and, in turn, views the world through a partially obscured or biased lens, which causes you to be highly selective with incoming information and cherry-pick what best suits your worldview. This tidbit is highly informative yet substantially insufficient. You also need to know more about how to navigate and mitigate your habits of mind.

Because your mind naturally follows its internal rules, quite often, you find yourself doing the same thing over and again, even when doing so doesn't make sense, doesn't produce great results, doesn't meet your deepest needs, and doesn't make you any happier in the long run.

Welcome to one of the most unique experiences of being human. Sometimes you adapt to your circumstances in a way that makes things worse, not better. When your mind takes over and controls you, rather than you being in control of your mind, you end up behaving in a way that does not provide lasting benefit. These experiences are called *mind traps*. You know that you've stepped into a mind trap when, afterward, you say to yourself something like "What was I thinking?" or "I know it was wrong, but it's like I couldn't control myself," or "I wish I could stop doing that."

Perhaps the most obvious example of a mind trap is addiction. Under conditions of persistent stress, your mind and body band together to seek relief. Since your mind is self-protective, it steers you quickly toward stress reduction by reminding you of what has worked in the past.

If, for instance, you've learned that alcohol provides an immediate escape from such unwanted private experiences as negative thoughts, dark emotions, and bodily tension, then it makes absolute sense that you would turn to alcohol whenever you begin to experience mounting distress. After all, if alcohol turns off negativity, reduces pain, and provides relief, then it's like a miracle drug.

Unfortunately, what goes up must come down, as the saying goes. In the real world of addiction, the up is experienced as a type of high (euphoria) followed by a sense of relief. However, since drinking only makes your trouble go away temporarily, the down in the addiction cycle is two-sided.

First, whatever was triggering you to start drinking in the first place eventually reappears. Secondly, since you've learned that alcohol turns off discomfort for only a short time, you have an added problem—because you need to keep doing what you did to keep the pain away, you become addicted. Instead of dealing with the underlying cause of your discomfort, you are seduced by the magical qualities of an elixir, in this case, alcohol.

Of course, addiction comes in many forms, some extremely obvious, like alcohol and painkillers, while others are much more discrete, like shopping and eating. Whatever provides you relief from unwanted personal discomfort has addiction potential. This explains why you can be addicted to a wide variety of distractions, such as video gaming, food, gambling, strip clubs, pornography, sex, work, sports, exercise, plastic surgery, and, well, you get the picture.

Another example of a mind trap is when your mind makes up its mind about the opposite sex based on past experiences. For instance, consider a young woman who has had a series of traumatic experiences with men beginning early in life. Her father, while mostly available and caring, taught her it was "normal" to take showers together.

During her middle school years, her uncle was "friendly" in ways that made her feel uncomfortable and dirty. In high school, she went on an adventure with a group of girlfriends and, with alcohol guiding their decisions, she ended up with a person she barely knew who "went too far," while her friends were close by but preoccupied by their drinking haze. Then, in her early adult years, she fell deeply in love with a young man who ended up being controlling and abusive.

When this young woman's traumatic experiences are tied together, she has learned to not easily trust men. Her mind has also been trained to protect her by keeping her distant from opportunities for intimate connections. While her past experiences are vital for her to remember, the life lesson she carries forward hinders her from having new experiences that may prove to be healing. In this way, she has fallen into a mind trap without even knowing it.

Other examples of mind traps include trying to please everyone except yourself; hiding from others when you feel excluded; being unable to say no for fear of negative judgment; avoiding rejection by not joining in on group activities; remaining committed to your shyness and reserved nature to offset the possibility of feeling even lonelier than you already do, standing out in ways that assure you'll never fit in; placing exceptionally high and rigid standards on your behavior in the service of being ahead of any perception of not being good enough.

Three Pivotal Mindsets

A mindset is a way of thinking as well as an attitude. It is what your mind sets on when the going gets tough. Each mindset plays a critical role in learning how to turn conflict into connection, setting the stage so that your needs can get met. Each mindset is powerful on its own. Together, they become highly effective in resolving unsolvable problems, the ones that keep repeating.

To better manage your mind traps and regain control of your life requires understanding how the three mindsets each provide you with opportunity for improved mastery and enhanced autonomy, while, in combination, they give you the capacity to become more relationally intelligent.

The process of opening your mind involves three uniquely different but interlocking mindsets: *intentionality, curiosity,* and *flexibility.* Like many ideas in psychology, each mindset is described rather than executed, meaning it's more demanding to carry out each mindset in real time than merely explaining them and advocating for their use. Let's explore each of these three mindsets one by one.

First Mindset—Intentionality

The leading mindset focuses on intentionality. Defined succinctly, intentionality is moving forward with design and connection in mind. As reflected by the illustration below, when you are not being deliberate or steadily conscious of your actions, you'll tend to either be avoidant or preoccupied with your thoughts and behavior.

INTENTIONALITY

Being *avoidant* rests at one end of the intentionality spectrum, reflecting your preference to keep your private experience at an arm's length from yourself and others. If you lean in this direction, your capacity for sidestepping unwanted or undesired situations is likely well practiced. When you avoid something, although only temporary, you put off having to deal with it. And not having to deal with it is uniquely rewarding and, therefore, highly likely to be repeated and become an overlearned habit. What's the reward? If you don't have to engage in something unpleasant or undesired, then you experience a type of freedom, freedom from those moments when you're assailed by doubts and worries and a host of other disquieting private experiences.

Most of us practice avoidance, to some extent, during times of tension and conflict. Avoidance comes in many shapes and forms. Some of us avoid quietly, so others don't notice we're skirting around, wriggling out of, or steering clear of what's bothersome. Avoidance is perfected when you act as if everything is fine, when underneath the veneer lie degrees of vulnerability and human suffering.

Others of us are more assertive with avoidance. In such cases, we use sarcasm or passive-aggressive strategies to make people aware of what we can't say directly to them. When you disguise hostility as humor or subtly sabotage others, such behaviors are reflections of your insecurity and inability to deal effectively with conflict.

Let's figure out how prone you are to being actively avoidant by taking the following quiz. For each question, rate how true the statement is by circling a number between one and three. The higher the score, the greater your inclination for avoiding stressful life circumstances.

Avoidant Quiz	Slightly	Somewhat	A Lot
I usually don't bother to gather more information than I think is needed, preferring to calm things down	1	2	3
I often feel that it's useless to keep talking while in conflict, thinking that "we're going nowhere"	1	2	3
Once conflict hits a certain level, I pull back to prevent things from getting worse	1	2	3
At a certain point, I either shut down or "unplug" from the other person because I dont' like things getting out of control	1	2	3
I typically avoid conflict because "in my life" conflict has never resulted in making things better	1	2	3

AVOIDANT QUIZ

On the other end of the intentionality spectrum is *preoccupation*. You are prone to being preoccupied when your mind stays overly focused on a particular subject or concern and you cannot easily let things go. While you excessively seek answers to questions, ultimately your pursuit leads to little lasting satisfaction. Further, while your power of concentration and attention to details involves a sharp focus, your style of focus requires intense effort, which can shrink your life and cause you to pivot your private experience around a highly specific event or topic, and you lose perspective of what matters most.

At times, your preoccupation motivates you to seek perfection based on your strong dislike for making mistakes. During conflict, you become embroiled in catastrophic thinking or believing things are worse than they are. Your preoccupation drives you to constantly search to confirm what you believe in your mind is true or the best thing to do.

Let's test out how prone you are to being preoccupied by taking the following quiz. Again, for each question, rate how true the statement is by circling a number between one and three. The higher the score, the greater your inclination for becoming overly concerned and wrapped up in stressful life circumstances.

Preoccupied Quiz	Slightly	Somewhat	A Lot
I constantly search for new information, always thinking "maybe I don't know everything"	1	2	3
I often feel that if I can just do or say one more thing maybe things will be different and we can reconnect	1	2	3
Once conflict hits a certain level, I can't stop thinking about it and stay preoccupied about it until things get settled	1	2	3
I push and push at the other person until things get better or everything just blows up	1	2	3
I am constantly trying to stay on top of potential problems so they do not sneak up on me unexpectedly	1	2	3

PREOCCUPIED QUIZ

Now that you know that avoidance and preoccupation are polar ends of intentionality and you have determined whether you gravitate toward being avoidant or preoccupied, you need to learn how to find the middle ground where insightfulness thrives.

Being insightful means being deliberately perceptive or astutely aware of what's happening both within and around you. When you bring conscious acknowledgment to your present state of mind and transfer awareness to your primary focus, you are staged to break the automatic cycle that allows you to respond rather than react. Without insight, you'll go back to your old behavior and act in accordance with your overlearned habits.

Beyond awareness, insight also involves realizing you have a choice. When you make a conscious decision to be present, you choose to stay out of your old habits and permit new experiences to expand your mind. Being insightful is the first step toward being in control of your mind as opposed to your mind controlling you.

The practice of intentionality will help you be grounded, feel balanced, and increasingly capable of being engaged in what's going on as opposed to becoming lost in what's going on in your mind.

Second Mindset—Curiosity

The next mindset involves curiosity. Defined briefly, curiosity is keeping an open mind and filling it with the unknown. Curiosity involves an active imagination, a thirst for knowledge, and a willingness to not always be right. An inquisitive state of mind motivates you to seek answers to all types of questions, even those that are unknown and unknowable.

You possess a curious mindset when you're not overly bothered during those times you find yourself being a bit lost. Uncertainty and mystery are dear friends, and navigating the unforeseen brightens your energy. Where others may experience suspense or crisis, you see opportunity. Exposing yourself to different ideas and perspectives is welcoming rather than threatening, and spending time with people who challenge your thinking is something you find compelling, not vexing.

Curiosity increases when you make a daily habit of stimulating your brain. Reading, podcasting, TikToking, or engaging in any reliable source that diversifies your thinking are ways to exercise your sense of wonder. Spending time with smarter people reflects your willingness to embrace your ignorance while corroborating a self-awareness of where your knowledge runs short. In this way, the act of curiosity is evinced by keeping an open mind and filling it with the unknown.

As reflected by the image below, when you refrain from being curious, you move in the direction of either being convinced in or confused by your thoughts, feelings, and surroundings. Both extremes are equivalent to having a closed mind or one that keeps recycling old learning. In either case, without developing a curious state of mind, you remain content with what you've already learned, and nothing changes.

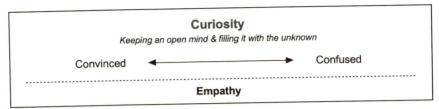

CURIOSITY

Akin to the discussion about the mindset of intentionality, there exists a spectrum related to the mindset of curiosity in which each pole is represented by a distinct tendency of mind and opposing attitude. At one end of the spectrum, a *convinced* mind believes that when past experiences are repeating themselves, people should just "get over it."

If you are of this type of mindset, you are confident in your worldview and lack a willingness or desire to seek new information. You don't frequently doubt or question your interpretation of the other person's opinion or behavior. Instead, what you think and perceive satisfies your mind, so you end up being content with your mode of thinking and ways of perceiving the world around you. As such, you may be seen by others as being closed-minded and possessing a rather inflated sense of worth.

But while others may view you as consumed with self-assuredness and self-satisfaction—in a word, smug—under ordinary circumstances, you are optimistic, resilient, and unperturbed by details. For the most part, you do not consider alternative explanations for situations since what you believe to be true is taken as being accurate. Holding your convictions tightly to your chest, your capacity for and interest in receiving feedback is limited.

Let's measure your proneness to being convinced by taking the following quiz. For each question, rate how true the statement is by circling a number between one and three. The higher the score, the greater your inclination for possessing strong convictions and not being easily persuaded otherwise.

Convinced Quiz	Slightly	Somewhat	A Lot
I make up my mind quickly and feel certain of where a problem is coming from	1	2	3
I'm opinionated and come up with strong explanations for why the other person is doing what they are doing	1	2	3
I typically react with a sense of "I know exactly what is going on here!"	1	2	3
I focus on getting the other person to understand that what I am think is correct and the best way to solve a problem	1	2	3
When conflict arises, I get frustrated by the familiar feeling of "here we go again!"	1	2	3

CONVINCED QUIZ

Night-and-day different from being convinced, the other pole on the curiosity spectrum is *confusion*. If you tend to possess a confused mindset, you are constantly milling over possibilities and actively refraining from having an opinion. Set betwixt and between two worlds, one you prefer and one you know, what you know you'll never trust, and what you trust you'll never really know. Hence, confusion reigns supreme in your mind.

Generally, you don't organize information into themes or patterns but rather continue updating your viewpoint and contemplating possibilities. You struggle with confidently predicting or understanding problems, or you grapple with conceptualizing people as having any sort of patterned behavior. You are constantly questioning and using the input of others to confirm what is happening. Welcome to the club; being uncertain is a common life experience.

Your proneness for being confused can be tested by taking the following quiz. For each question, rate how true the statement is by circling a number between one and three. The higher the score, the greater your inclination for having difficulty making up our mind, formulating a clear and convincing opinion, and sharing your worldview with others.

Confused Quiz	Slightly	Somewhat	A Lot
I have a hard time understanding what the real problem is and tend to contemplate or "overthink" things	1	2	3
I search long and hard for reasons for the conflict, but seem to never land on an answer and become frustrated	1	2	3
Typically, things happen very quickly and I react with a sense of "what the hell is going on!"	1	2	3
I'm easily jumbled and have a hard time following the argument and frequently get "beat down"	1	2	3
When conflict arises, a common feeling I have is "why does this keep happening over and over again?"	1	2	3

CONFUSED QUIZ

Having taken the two previous quizzes, you have determined where you stand on the curiosity spectrum. Knowing your relative position on this spectrum gives you guidance as to the direction you need to go to access a more inquiring mind.

The process for developing a curious mind requires finding the middle ground. What's between a convinced and confused mindset? Believe it or not, the key to becoming naturally curious is empathy. Empathy provides you the opportunity to get out of your mind and penchant for self-importance and step into the imagined life space of another person.

Your capacity for empathy is intimately connected with your ability to understand the thoughts and feelings of other people. Experiencing care or concern for others is a version of being able to read another person's mind. The field of psychology has created a term called *theory of mind* (ToM) that is closely connected to this process and refers to your ability to understand the mental states of others. Both empathy and ToM are associated with your ability to recognize social cues and appropriately respond in social situations in a mutually satisfying fashion.

While most of us know that empathy is the ability to understand and share the feelings of another person, for purposes of this section, the definition of empathy is stretched to include your capacity to teach others how to care for you. This version of empathy, called reciprocal empathy, also invites you to look inside for purposes of experiencing care and concern for yourself.

When another person responds compassionately to your life situation, you feel like they *get you*, which serves as a touchstone, one of the most important forms of validation. During moments of empathic connection, it's as if the other person is joining your inner world and helping you to hold a vital aspect of your secret world. At once, you feel grounded and connected with the person you were always meant to be.

So how does empathy connect with curiosity? Without knowing it, a basic requirement for empathy involves developing and harvesting a curious state of mind. Without curiosity, it is argued, empathy is not possible. Without empathy, no curiosity takes place. Consequently, the two psychological constructs are highly interrelated.

When conflict arises either within an individual or between people, there is a disconnection that is felt. This disengagement is experienced as a type of psychological vacuum or an empty space devoid of understanding. An empathic response during such conflict involves the deliberate willingness to leave the vacuum unfilled so the other person can fill it. It is the filling of the vacuum that constitutes the exact nature of empathy.

The mind becomes extremely active in times of conflict. In accordance with its design, the mind relies upon its learning history to understand the tension or paradox of the moment. From the perspective of an empathic mindset, we actively restrict the past from filling the vacuum. Instead, by maintaining a stance of openness, we stay present and are better able to deal with the challenging situation that is in front of us.

Beyond remaining open to new experiences, which is indispensable for a curious mind, you also need to be actively willing to learn. This process is referred to as teachability. The ability and willingness to learn is a highly creative endeavor. By changing your mind and being willing to change your perspective, you grow into your relationships and sense of self.

Third Mindset—Flexibility

Let's now turn our attention to the final mindset of flexibility, which is defined as having options and bending to avoid breaking. Psychological flexibility has long been recognized as a benchmark for optimal mental health. When the concept of psychological flexibility is mulled over, what is being circulated is your capacity for mental agility and adaptability, which both contribute to resilience. The reason flexibility is so key to sound mental health is that it provides you with options, so you spend less time regretting your actions, getting stalemated by your choices, or finding yourself cornered by your habits of mind.

The image below reflects the opposing aspects associated with the flexibility spectrum, including your tendency to be either rigid (too little flexibility) or permissive (too much).

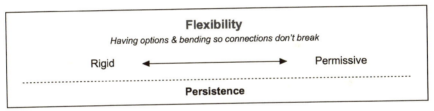

FLEXIBILITY

When asked, it's quite likely that most of us would say that *rigidity* is the opposite of flexibility. In the context of the flexible mindset, being rigid is reflected when you decisively predict and interpret events based on your own preferences, ignoring the input or counsel of others. If your estimation is that you tend to be a bit rigid, you struggle to shift your manner of thinking and do not easily make room for additional information.

Inconsistencies, loose ends, and vague details manifest discomfort and are readily discarded by your mind. In fact, most often, you only consider possibilities based on what has occurred in the past that fits squarely into your highly regarded and tightly secured core beliefs. To do otherwise, to entertain alternative facts and opinions, would be equivalent to letting your guard down and admitting to the possibility of defeat. The upside of being continuously deliberate and on top of things is you luxuriate in a sense of personal control, a style of self-management that doesn't let the complexity of the outside world infiltrate into your organized frame of mind. You maintain, therefore, a relative peace of mind.

The downside of rigidity is that even when you're mostly right or approximately correct, other people often see you as being stubbornly disposed and having overly determined convictions that don't easily blend with opportunities for relational connection. While being tenacious and self-disciplined is great for getting things done, being viewed by others as stubborn and unbending makes for one-sided relationships. A simple rule of thumb is that if you find yourself being overly rigid, your relationships likely lack depth and breadth and likely have limited staying power.

At the end of the day, rigidity is a sign that control is a critical component to your sense of self and connection with the world. Since rigidity is essentially remaining anchored to the status quo, being rigid is highly effective when you are interested in controlling, altering, or avoiding your most private experiences. Weighing the upside against the downside of your controlling nature would likely produce some interesting dialogue.

Your capacity for being rigid can be tested by taking the following quiz. For each question, rate how true the statement is by circling a number between one and three. The higher the score, the greater your inclination for being reluctant in switching your mental mindset, letting go of the familiar, and changing how you think about things.

Rigid Quiz	Slightly	Somewhat	A Lot
I can be set in my ways, doing things without consulting or considering others	1	2	3
I tend to have great confidence in how I understand the world around me, and will insist on doing things my way	1	2	3
Being stubborn, I tend to hold my ground and not easily give in to the other person	1	2	3
I tend to hold onto my views and not examine the viewpoint of others, even when it causes problems	1	2	3
I prefer to explain rather than apologize for any mistake or wrongdoing I may have done	1	2	3

RIGID QUIZ

Next, let's shift to the other extreme on the flexibility spectrum and discuss the implications of being *permissive*. While a permissive mind might infer a broad-minded and easygoing type of person, in the context of mind rules, the notion of being permissive is less effective and more problematic.

If you believe yourself to be permissive, when conflict arises, you tend to be overly engaged in the discord and cannot easily let things go. You excessively seek answers to questions without getting much satisfaction. Often, you are described by others as being perfectionistic, someone who dislikes making mistakes.

Permissiveness causes you to become embroiled in catastrophic thinking or thinking things are worse than they are. Your permissive mindset leads you to be constantly searching to confirm what you believe in your mind is true or what's the best thing to do. In the end, your extreme form of open-mindedness and live-and-let-live attitude may appear stress reducing, but you rapidly internalize your stress, and your deep truth is not easily shared with others.

Your knack for being permissive can be tested by taking the following quiz. For each question, rate how true the statement is by circling a number between one and three. The higher the score, the greater your inclination for agreeableness with tendencies toward being highly selfless, somewhat gullible, and having difficulty standing up to others and fighting back.

Permissive Quiz	Slightly	Somewhat	A Lot
I feel more comfortable doing things the way others want me to	1	2	3
I am often unsure of myself, and typically mold myself to the expectations of others even without realizing it	1	2	3
Being guided by generalized worry and fear, I tend to give in easily	1	2	3
I tend to surrender my opinion to the other person to calm things down and restore peace	1	2	3
I am hesitant to disagree or challenge others out of fear of disapproval or loss of support	1	2	3

PERMISSIVE QUIZ

Finding middle ground as related to flexibility requires persistence. In fact, the saying *if at first you don't succeed, try again* is quite apropos and really sends home the message of how being flexible is more of a process than an event or outcome. Stated another way, being flexible is best suited when you adopt flexibility as a behavioral habit rather than something to do now and again.

The process of becoming more flexible involves two strategies. First, by learning how to be more adaptive, you improve your ability to respond to changing or unexpected conditions. The development of an adaptive mindset is necessary; if you do not bend, you break. If you are unwilling to bend, nothing changes, and your past repeats. Stated simply, the expression *nothing changes if nothing changes* reflects the problem if you resist becoming more flexible.

The second strategy that enhances flexibility is creativity, defined as willingness to devise new approaches that haven't been done before. The process of putting deliberate energy into creating a new present and future allows you to unmake and distance yourself from past injuries and create opportunities to meet your basic needs that require your interaction with others: attention, affection, acknowledgment, approval, and applause.

Wrapping Things Up

In this concluding chapter, the challenge of mind traps has been discussed within the dynamic and interwoven nature of three powerful mindsets, which include deliberate insightfulness, inquiring empathy, and persistent flexibility. The accompanying quizzes provided you an opportunity to examine your relative strength and weakness as related to each mindset. Knowing where you stand along each mindset spectrum guides you in the direction of becoming more in control of your mind as opposed to your mind controlling you.

The main point of introducing mindsets defined along a spectrum is to demonstrate how your mind operates based on a set of unspoken yet extremely persuasive internalized rules. Reflected by your upbringing and relationship history, your past has informed your mind as to what is most important, most historically relevant, and most unforgettable. Filled with invaluable knowledge drawn from such experiences across time, your mind becomes *set* by welding together what it has learned and what it believes to be true. Fortified by a wealth of rarely contested imperious knowledge, your mind works hard to protect you from your worst days happening again, while attempting to replicate your best days.

Because of the persuasive influence of mind rules on how you see the world and make sense of what's happening, especially during your more difficult moments, those encounters with obstacles and resistance, you are continually challenged to be a step ahead of how your mind is connecting the dots and what your mind is telling you to do. This behind-the-scenes habit of your mind often functions to diminish or deny the complexity of the world around you. Knowing how mind rules operate individually and intertwine is meant to help you tap down your proneness for self-deception while bolstering self-observation, self-knowledge, and self-trust. Being successful in this way allows you to become increasingly self-aware and self-directed, a dynamic duo that moves you toward becoming the person you were always meant to be.

Since your mind is so great at following its internal rules, too often, you may find yourself doing the same thing over and over, even when doing so doesn't make immediate sense, doesn't produce great results, doesn't meet your needs or satisfy your desires, and doesn't make you any happier. As previously emphasized, when your mind controls you, rather than you being in control of your mind, this deeply private and covert experience is called a mind trap.

To begin navigating your mind traps, the following exercise is provided to help you put your knowledge about mind rules into action and regain mastery over your life. Instead of continuing to conceal your ambitions, bury your head from realizing your potential, oversimplify your life experience, hoodwink yourself into believing that current-day circumstances are good enough, and avert your gaze away from what you really prefer to be doing and who you choose to be, by putting mind rules into motion, you are investing wisely and learning how to mastermind your life. In the fullness of time, learning mind control in a complex world provides you an edge so things stop taking you by surprise and maybe, just maybe, your dreams then come true.

Mind Trap Exercise

Now that mind rules have been identified, defined, and untangled, let's get busy putting this knowledge to work.

Life becomes difficult and unexpectedly cumbersome during times when you experience your limits or are confronted by hindrances unforeseen. The way your mind activates in accordance with a constellation of interconnected mind rules nudges you to do what you've been taught. Remember, a prime mechanism of your mind is to keep you safe and to reduce the odds of your most unpleasant life experiences repeating. So your mind guides you toward doing the same thing over and over.

During times when your habits of mind are benevolent and mutually rewarding, it is a very good thing to duplicate your efforts. But far too often, your repetitive ways tend to move the ball in the wrong direction, leaving you stalemated or making things go from bad to worse. To offset this inclination to stall or slide backward, a *mental map* can be used to move more confidently and predictably in the direction you really intended.

The following exercise represents an example of a mental map. This five-phase model describes a blueprint that guides you toward mastering the process of being more in control of your mind, as opposed to your mind controlling you. This mental map includes 1) selecting an essential mind rule; 2) increasing your awareness of when this mind rule is active and being activated by your surroundings; 3) acknowledging the reality and familiarity of the predicament you find yourself in; 4) asking yourself the types of questions that keep you out of judgment; and 5) gaining insight into the importance of stepping up and into your private experience in a new way.

Phase One—Select

Think about the ups and downs in your life and identify a small handful of mind rules that deeply resonate with you. Then, from this small group, *pick one mind rule* that uniquely strikes a chord and feels like it explains a lot of what you've been going through in your life and what has kept you from performing at the top of your game.

Ask yourself, "What roadblocks me from becoming the best version of myself?" Trust your instincts when reviewing the mind rules. Then, when ready, pull the ripcord by selecting a specific mind rule that your intuition has guided you toward.

For purposes of this exercise, this becomes your top-priority mind rule.

Top-Priority Mind Rule #_____

Phase Two—Awareness

Next, commit to bringing *focused awareness* to those times in your daily life when this mind rule shows up and hinders you from getting your needs met. During times when you become unexpectedly confused and distressed by what is happening, or not happening, in your outside world, this is the time to bring this mind rule to your attention. This is the time to pause, quiet your mind, distance yourself from the distractions around you, and bring attention to only what's happening inside of you.

Down below, we'll see how your top-priority mind rule helps explain what you are experiencing inside and what to do about this unlikable and unwanted situation.

Phase Three—Acknowledge

Throughout the day, start the habit of deliberately *acknowledging* the moments when you fall into this mind trap, when you feel disconnected, experience unwanted emotions and thoughts, and sense that your mind is controlling you.

Importantly, there is a difference between awareness and acknowledgment. Awareness involves narrowing your perception and deciphering signals from noise in your everyday walk of life. Becoming intentionally aware of something is like putting this in-the-moment life experience in the crosshairs of your perceptual gaze. By doing so, for the moment, everything else is pushed to the side, and you focus intensely on this single moment.

Acknowledgment, by comparison, is the process of taking this felt experience and bringing it into the executive branch of your brain. This is accomplished by labeling your experience and muttering to yourself something like "I'm in a mind trap right now. I need to make a note of this." Or "Mind rule number seven just showed up again—wow, again!"

By acknowledging the reality of what you're experiencing, you're making cognitive space for this situation when you activate your thinking brain. Currently, we still do not want you to do anything about what's going on; simply bring it to your conscious mind and make a note of it.

It's a great idea to start a *tracking system* that lets you easily jot down an entry every time you're feeling off-balance or otherwise disconnected from your preferred life stance. These are the times when you're not feeling quite like yourself, when you think you need to be a version of yourself, or when the world is providing unfriendly feedback about the person they experience you as being.

By tracking your mind traps, you'll end up being surprised how often this disquieting private experience shows up in your walk of life.

Phase Four—Ask

Now, let's start processing what you're experiencing. By breaking down what's happening, you're setting the stage to experience a breakthrough from your defensiveness. By becoming versed in how your unswerving worldview, your insecurities, and your subjective experience take over, you have started to flip the coin and become a master of your mind.

When you've stepped into a mind trap, pause, be curious, and ask yourself,

1. What just happened?
2. What triggered my sense of feeling off-balance?
3. If I wasn't in pause mode, how would I be acting? How do I typically react in these moments?
4. What else can I do?
5. Is doing nothing an option?
6. What prevents me from breaking the pattern?

Note to self: this is a wonderful time to be empathically curious. It's important to remember that being curious opens your mind, which is the opposite of a closed mind. You'll know that your mind is closed if you find yourself in a place of judgment or otherwise mentally cooking the books. Some classic examples of a closed mind include those times when you put yourself down, blame others, feel like giving up or giving into the situation, feeling misunderstood, not providing space for the other person to say what they need to say, shutting down or turning off, using a tone that doesn't sound like you, or feeling like you just became the target of someone's indignation.

When the above list is contemplated, isn't it amazing how often we have a closed mind? Unrestricted by conventional rules of evidence, even if something is fantastically unlikely, your mind can expand the boundaries of knowledge so that what you believe must be true. Therefore, practicing focused awareness and deliberate acknowledgment lays the groundwork for thoughtful exploration of what makes you tick.

Phase Five—Step Up!

When you fall into a mind trap and sense that you're in one of those fuzzy periods or hard places, it's time to take decisive and habit-changing action. This can be accomplished by following a step-by-step process. Let's explore four steps designed to help you improve your mind control in a complex world.

Step 1
The first step is doing what is needed, nothing more.

This step involves practicing being flexible by *stepping in* and doing what is needed rather than doing what you have always done. This is a time to consider your options. Stepping into a situation requires taking deliberate action and having an intentional mindset. When you purposefully step in, by design, you are doing something that demonstrates a relational awareness as to how your behavior impacts other people.

Step 2
The second step is not *doing something.*

This step focuses on *stepping out* and consciously not doing something. This choice is called restraint, which is much harder than it sounds. When you restrain, you are holding back the energy that is surging through you. Instead of giving into the energy source, you are unplugging from the current and electing to be observational rather than speculative, descriptive rather than judgmental, and curious rather than critical.

When the world around us gets loud, we tend to get louder. As an analogy, when you think of how a car operates with the use of two pedals, one for speeding up and the other for slowing down, when you face intense competition associated with challenging discourse, the internal volume of your insecurities increases, much like pressing the accelerator pedal. Restraint, as you've already guessed, involves taking your foot off the gas pedal and tapping the brakes.

What makes doing nothing unusually tricky is that it requires a willingness to delay your mind's intrigue with instant gratification. The postponing of getting what you need, want, desire, and deserve goes against the grain of your mind's grand design. When you encounter an obstacle or run into resistance, your mind instantaneously gets busy trying to figure out how to get through the hindrance. This is accomplished by deciding what direction to move to resolve the tension, restoring your sense of security and well-being and, if possible, transforming frustration into a sense of felt satisfaction, perhaps even joy.

The point being emphasized in this second step toward improved mind control is realizing how your mind is driven, when stimulated, toward rapid stabilization without consideration of how its predisposition may make things worse for you in the long run. Consequently, the option of doing nothing provides a useful strategy for you to find equilibrium between stabilization and stimulation.

Step Three
The third step is compassionate disengagement.

The act of *stepping down* reflects an awareness that disengaging from what's going on in the moment may be incredibly helpful and may coincide with the perfect thing to do. However, and of critical importance, the way you disengage makes all the difference in the world. That is why the word *compassionate* is placed before the act of disengaging.

Of interest, when you place compassion ahead of any behavior, the result is quite often positive and mutually beneficial. For instance, giving yourself permission to have a compassionate confrontation implies a willingness to have a difficult conversation but doing so in a manner that is kindhearted, often executed by a kind, friendly presence and giving voice to what you've experienced rather than being swamped by your emotions or throttled by judgment.

The act of compassionately disengaging functions to slow things down and stop things from going from bad to worse, and worse to ugly. An example of compassionate disengagement might sound like "My emotions are starting to rev up. Let's stop what we're doing and get back to it later. Does that sound right to you?"

Step Four
The fourth step is going above and beyond.

This step is captured by the phrase *stepping up*. When asked to imagine a person stepping up, what comes to your mind? Like the picture below, do you see a person lifting their leg and starting the process of walking upstairs?

PHOTO, WALKING UPSTAIRS
PHOTO BY BRUNO NASCIMENTO ON UNSPLASH

No one walks up a flight of stairs without knowing it. In fact, the process of physically stepping up requires intentional effort, and sometimes more than expected. Consider how many times after climbing a flight of stairs, you've said to yourself or heard others saying, "That was a lot harder than I thought it would be!"

Just like in the physical world, stepping up in the psychological world is an undertaking. The relational equivalence of climbing stairs is the willingness to go above and beyond—the state of mind of knowingly taking your interpersonal effort to another level, of doing more or better than you usually do.

To put things into stark perspective, the longer expression of *going above and beyond the call of duty* described soldiers who gave their lives in combat. While most of us are not putting our lives on the line, going *above and beyond* can have life-altering effects.

During times of distress and disarray, remember, your mind is self-protective and not in a relational state. So going above and beyond necessitates a capacity and willingness to get out of your mind's way of responding and become an active agent of your life situation. You can make a difference by doing something different. And if you're going to make a difference, why not go above and beyond?

EPILOGUE

The Story Arc
Putting Mind Rules into Action

Throughout this book, we introduced you to several characters and shared their stories. The remainder of this closing chapter closely examines each of these characters and shows how their understanding of mind rules helps them to understand and better anticipate the complexity of life. In the process, through the rise and fall of everyday life, you'll see how gaining improved mind control gives them greater emotional stability during times of upheaval when inevitable twists and turns take place in their lives.

Rachel's Dilemma
Let's first examine Rachel's situation. As you may recall, Rachel found herself suddenly wanting to have a child, after having mutually agreed with her husband, Todd, that they weren't interested in being parents. Upon this recent realization, Rachel wrestled with whether she should bring Todd into her quandary.

What makes Rachel's dilemma harder than it needs to be is that she is doing all the hard work by herself here, internalizing her maternal desire and dealing with the subsequent deliberation and consternation on her own. Rachel is relying upon a one-person psychology in a two-person world. The perfect flaw with this one-person strategy is that Rachel's processing is caught up in an unproductive and unending feedback loop. No matter how long she contemplates or how thoroughly she assesses the pros and cons, by keeping Todd out of the loop, Rachel is set to struggle.

Consider how Rachel's mind has taken over. Let's go through a mind rule mental checklist:

The mind is not relational. Rachel is not sharing her perplexing thoughts with Todd and is playing her cards close to her chest—check.

The mind is self-serving. Not wanting to get hurt, Rachel is preserving the status quo in her relationship with Todd by remaining silent—check.

Avoidance is the mind's natural reflex. If Rachel is doing nothing else, she's actively avoiding having *the* conversation with Todd—check.

The mind's favorite color is black. Imagining the worst, Rachel is overthinking how Todd might respond and believing he might end the relationship—check.

The mind is directly connected to the past. Rachel remains overfocused on the beginning phase of her relationship with Todd when they decided not to have children—check.

The last thing on the mind is to be vulnerable. While she is maintaining her public appearance of being fine on the outside, internally, because she's avoiding being vulnerable with Todd, Rachel is feeling increasingly trapped, isolated, deprived, and empty—check.

Like the strings of a puppet, Rachel's sense of self comes to life during moments of affirmation, acknowledgment, and validation. Conversely, her selfhood deflates and becomes increasingly lifeless when subjected to conditions of being ignored, rejected, disapproved, and treated with indifference.

By refraining from starting the conversation with Todd, Rachel's mind is controlling her actions, ensuring things don't get worse. At the same time, not knowing how Todd might respond has left her feeling exasperated, hampering her ability to deal with this dilemma by herself. So, finally, after weeks and weeks of hand wringing, the time has come for Rachel to do the last thing that's on her mind, which is to be vulnerable.

"Todd, I was thinking a crazy thought," Rachel says to her husband, opting to be playful with her underlying serious truth. "Do you have a minute to talk tonight? There's something I want to bounce off of you."

Todd responds as he always does, "Sounds great. What time do you have in mind?"

What happens next is between Rachel and Todd. Knowing them, given their mutual capacity to mirror and magnify each other's private worlds with respect, curiosity, and flexibility, they're going to be just fine. From Rachel's perspective, she's learned an important lesson: to take her time, fear less, dare more, trust her relational instincts, and be more in control of her mind rather than allowing her mind to control her.

Charlotte's Life Decision
Next, let's revisit Charlotte, who's trying to find a life worth living after having suffered from a chronic medical condition that has kept her from enjoying an engaging existence. The severity of her condition kept her from having a normal childhood. As she became increasingly bedridden and gradually housebound, she was substantially sequestered from the support and feedback of others who, most assuredly, would have been part of her life if not for her great misfortune.

Although doctor after doctor attempted to identify the root cause of her affliction, with no clear medical pathway to navigate, eventually, the consensus opinion became that Charlotte suffered from a medically unexplained illness. Naturally, it seems, when the medical model fails, clinicians turn to psychogenic mechanisms to explain the unexplainable, which tend to be viewed as less legitimate than conditions that are organically based.

Suffice to say, it didn't take long for Charlotte's medical chart to become peppered with a variety of pejorative phrases and labels. "It's all in your head." That was the general message Charlotte received time and again. But she knew better—she always knew better. The chronicity and severity of her symptoms, coupled with the unrelenting suffering and resultant disability, told her that something was wrong, very wrong.

To the medical community, Charlotte became an anomaly. In Charlotte's family, she became the source for disbelief, sarcasm, cruelty, and eventual desertion. Ultimately, Charlotte was betrayed by both her practitioners and her kinfolk, everyone except for her father. Abandoned and left to fend for herself, Charlotte felt as though she had essentially been kicked to the curb by the unfairness twisted into life's diabolical ways.

"Except for my father" was a phrase Charlotte repeated when coming out of a phase of darkness, after her melancholy loosened its defeatist grip and her suicidal ideation paused. This phrase would also be cited when she felt markedly dispirited and begged to talk about whether her life was worth living. Charlotte knew deep in her heart that life, in general, was worth living; it was her life that remained shrouded in doubt.

"Except for my father," Charlotte divulged, "there is no reason why I should go on living." Charlotte's father, you see, was always there. His steadfastness, eternal optimism, and terminal loyalty pulled Charlotte out of despair, lightened her despondency, reignited her sense of having purpose, and somehow restored hope when not a speck could be found.

Several mind rules apply to Charlotte's perplexing saga:

For example, *the mind only remembers what it can't forget.* Charlotte is reminded daily that the worst day of her life is the one she just survived.

The mind can't forget what it doesn't want to remember. The experiences of medical trauma when Charlotte was repeatedly treated disrespectfully by top professionals and reminded that her problems were imagined, not real, combined in Charlotte's mind as a type of master trauma, the kind that never goes away, can never be forgotten, and that reduces her existential value. Why live? She had a hard time remembering.

The mind organizes and prioritizes what it knows to be true. Charlotte's deep little secret is that she doesn't matter, that she's disposable, that she's not worthy of being treated with patience, love, and respect; that becomes her number one most trusted truth. A truth that can never be proven yet is never wrong.

The mind is hypersensitive and struggles with empathy. Because of Charlotte's memories of being left behind, easily forgotten, she has stopped caring about herself, and her capacity for self-understanding and desire for self-completion have dried up.

The mind is time blind. To Charlotte, every day is the same; not much more needs to be said. Except, because of her mind's time blindness, she may be persuaded to believe that tomorrow can never be better than yesterday.

The mind believes it is constantly being judged. Charlotte has been judged, severely in fact, by many people in different areas of her life. Her challenge is to remember that although their judgment was shared with her at one time, they all have one thing in common, and that is that they've all moved on. But to Charlotte, the theme of their judgment is stained in her memory bank.

Charlotte's story illuminates the notion that we're all interested in the same thing, and that is to form a strong and unique personal identity. But how this happens is quite surprising. Your beginning is unedited and raw. Then, as the outside world touches you, you observe, contemplate, and begin practicing how to respond.

Gradually, across time and exploits, your sense of self unfolds as you move in the direction of seeking comfort while minimizing distress. Concealed from immediate awareness, what steers you in one direction and not the other is the feedback you receive from the outside world, especially from those who are most trusted by repetition and familiarity. Their esteemed feedback is what captivates your attention and distinctly shapes the person you become.

Because such influences are outside of your immediate control, the paradox about the conception of your most prized possession, your selfhood, is whether you progress in the direction of becoming the person you were meant to be or get diverted in another direction in response to the feedback you receive from others. Although the folks who offer up such input likely mean well, they may not fully appreciate or sufficiently care about the degree of influence they've had on your identity formation.

Sometimes that feedback can be positive and affirming, and when it dovetails with how you see yourself, the net effect is authenticating, particularly if you've inspired such feedback simply being yourself. At a base level, our primal desire is to discover and display our true selves while simultaneously being validated by others.

But life is not always accommodating, corroborating, and affirming. In fact, sometimes it may feel as though the world is against you and outside forces are combining to flatten your sense of self. When you think one way and the world discounts the way you think, this experience is called cognitive dissonance. Such inconsistencies cause restlessness and discomfort in your mind.

When dissonance arises, when feedback from others differs from your private voicing, the result is ambivalence. And within the grasp of bewilderment, when uncertainty surrounds you, the question becomes which voice do you trust more? Do you rely upon your internal instincts, the one formulated in the wake of your lived experiences and inner nature?

The discordance of competing voices causes you to experience confusion and self-doubt. You find yourself calling on strengths, while being inundated by weakness. The struggle inside you causes you to wonder, *who is the real me?* Is there a difference between your public self, the one that others see and have come to recognize, and your private self, the one that may only be recognizable to you, even if only now and again?

Fearing rejection, exclusion, and devaluation, do humans intentionally deceive themselves? If this is true, then why is this so? Why does your innermost identity remain a secret from others? Are you telling yourself about a silent lie by not addressing this personal duplicity? Do you keep your true sense of self to yourself, concealing the truth of who you are from others to prevent being put down, brought down, or pulled down?

Is your habit of refraining from being *real* a form of psychological sleight of hand, by which you stay distanced from the possibility of being crucially injured? Do you deliberately fail to reveal your interior self because if you did so and others were strikingly critical or unabashedly cruel, such injurious truth would gravely unsettle your preferred sense of self and leave you feeling existentially shattered? This backdrop of ambivalence explains what happened to Charlotte.

What Charlotte struggles to remember is that with or without her disability, she already possesses a unique personal identity. Although she's of course had it worse than so many people, her latest surgery provided much-deserved pain relief. Committed to a regime of stretching, she's also experienced an improved range of motion and sense of bodily freedom.

And that, along with the continual support and fanfare from her father, has provided an opportunity to see herself for who she is, to put the past behind her and step into the present. As her body responds productively to physical therapy, her willingness to become versed in mind rules and practice being more in control of her mind will allow her to envision a future life worth living. For Charlotte, the day has come that tomorrow looks better than yesterday. Finally!

Tyler's Cross to Bear
Tyler's a controller. It's a trait he picked up growing up. Having been raised in a family characterized by emotional dishonesty, self-sufficiency, unspoken expectations, lack of trust, and near complete absence of nurturing, he knows that he missed out on something growing up, something important. While he had friends, he never felt as close to them as he observed others being close to one another.

Much of Tyler's upbringing remained focused on those things he had control over. He became obsessed with putting together model cars, airplanes, and battleships during his later elementary school years. He painted every detail before assembling them together. His older brothers routinely teased him for being "in love" with stupid things like models.

In middle school, Tyler's interest shifted to outdoor adventure.

Tyler would spend his free time and much of his summer vacation exploring, sometimes with friends but more often by himself. He became fascinated with insects and reptiles. He caught butterflies, mounted them proudly, and researched each new specimen.

One time, when he asked his father for permission to bring a snake he caught into the house and make it his pet, the response he received was firm and without a trace of kindness. "Those damn things better not get into this house," his father scorned. "If they do, I'll show you who's boss."

His father's intimidation factor was immense. It was rivaled only by Tyler's fearfulness of his father. Tyler would never cross that line by sneaking a "pet" into the house. Instead, Tyler's imagination became extremely active as he pored over one book after another searching for more and more information about snakes, their habitat, their habits, their food supply, and so on. Again, his brothers mocked him for being into "creepy things" and not "having a life."

In high school, things didn't change much for Tyler. He stayed busy with homework, school projects, and hobbies, and he continued to be a lover of the great outdoors. When he went to college, in his second year, Tyler had his first relationship, his first kiss, his first almost everything with a young woman who he eventually married. Together, they produced a beautiful family that was anchored by religion, traditions, and expressions of unconditional love.

As Tyler's daughters developed into young women, they needed more from their father than just knowing he loved them. They wanted him to join them in their world, in their likes and dislikes, in their passions, and much to Tyler's discomfort, in their tears. This is what made Tyler reflect on his background and wonder why he couldn't more naturally connect with his girls.

Following his routine of prayerful connection with God, with the full support of his wife, Tyler sought out therapy. Also, when one of Tyler's daughters told him that he "never had time" for her, he flashed back to his own childhood, when his parents never made time for him. This was Tyler's wake-up call, and three cheers for him, he took it seriously.

Tyler essentially became a controller by default. Saturated by paternal hostility and psychological chaos, Tyler's upbringing shaped him to be compulsively engaged in projects, chores, and work assignments. As an adult, he consciously represses his emotions to *get by*. Too busy to feel, Tyler's life strategy has worked wonderfully for him.

But in his relational world, being married with four teenage daughters, he has begun to realize being a controller leads to loneliness and passive defection by those he loves most. Although he longs to know how to connect with his loved ones, when he's advised that vulnerability is required, Tyler's eyes glaze over, and he looks lost. His attachment style has prepared him to react to intimacy by controlling his surroundings or pulling back. Tyler has reached a crossroad.

Connecting the dots of Tyler's upbringing, relationship history, and victories and valleys throughout his life, Tyler couldn't decide if he's more trapped within or outside of himself. While he began to feel his feelings, perhaps for the first time in the presence of another person, Tyler showed signs of being overpowered by his affect that seemed curiously foreign and familiar at the same time.

Under the pressure of overwhelming emotions, the mind assumes a survival stance and quickly adopts an extrication strategy. What you choose to do, whatever it may be, is motivated by an instinctual urge to offset the moment going from worse to ugly. When you experience an emotion, any kind of feeling, this neurophysiological event has triggered something to enter into your awareness. As this feeling grows in intensity, it gains neurological momentum and persuasively vies for your immediate attention.

For Tyler to gain proper insight into what his emotions are trying to convey, he benefited from completing a mind rules checklist.

The mind is not relational. Because Tyler spent his childhood in a family filled with emotional abuse and neglect, he learned that relationships were unsafe, unpredictable, and something more to avoid than cherish.

The mind is designed to resolve uncertainty. Tyler spent much of his childhood alone and preoccupied in activities that provided him satisfaction as well as escape from the uncertainties of family living.

The mind self-regulates. Tyler tends to express what he's thinking about a situation rather than what emotion he is experiencing. He's motivated to repress emotions and *get by* rather than delving into his interior world and exploring the rest of the story.

The mind is directly connected to the past. Outside of Tyler's awareness for the longest time, over time, he began to act in ways highly reflective of his father.

The mind prefers repetition. "That is what you think; can you share with me what you're feeling?" was a response Tyler's therapist often voiced to gently invite Tyler into his emotional world.

At the end of the day, Tyler is focused on growing by understanding the life lessons he learned during times he wasn't aware he was being taught. He's coming to realize how much his past has shaped the person he's become. Armed with increased curiosity, Tyler is beginning to experience how his emotions from the past have kept him from becoming the person his wife and daughters have been waiting patiently to embrace.

Because of his life experiences, Tyler's mind has protected him from moments of vulnerability, and, as such, he is only now beginning to realize the importance of trust, the power of intimacy, and the way emotions can guide him toward opportunities to connect more meaningfully and authentically with those he loves the most, rather than away from them.

As Tyler's story illustrates, during times of repeated drama, when life gets noisy, or trauma, when life becomes terrifying, your mind gets busy doing what it does best, protecting you so things don't get further out of control.

Whether your experience is real or imagined, minimized, or amplified, threats to your experience of homeostasis and sense of well-being accumulate quickly and trigger unwanted recollections. In this state of heightened awareness and alertness, what you do next reflects the intersection of your nature and nurture.

As you contemplate your course of action, the faster pathway of your limbic system is rapidly activated, and this emotion-driven state begins to hijack your brain functioning. At once, you are on edge, stressed, and perhaps a bit twitchy. In the background, the slower pathway of your brain's cortical region and decision-making hub is trying mightily to decide the *right* thing to do.

Attempting to override your emotional circuitry, your thinking brain struggles and often comes up short. Bottom line, the competing neural activity in your brain gives you the experience of ambivalence. As your mind races, frustrated by a type of cortical push and pull, you may even experience a type of dissociation or distancing from the reality of the moment that serves to reduce the anxiety that comes from feeling trapped in an ambivalent circumstance.

During times of emotional arousal, you become partially detached from your intellect. When discomfort transforms into distress, this emotional experience takes over, and what becomes most salient is what it takes to decrease the internalized upheaval. You are driven to feel less anguish.

How this gets accomplished sometimes creates bigger problems, evinced by things going from bad to worse. Stated differently, while your mind is focused on diminishing pain, at times, the way your mind executes its rescue mission produces its own messiness.

Susan's Crossroad
Finally, we have the story of Susan. Adopted and then abandoned, not once but thrice, Susan adapted to her adversity by acting as if nothing bothered her. She developed world-class resilience, bouncing back from every misfortune. In fact, after every letdown and setback, Susan seemed to rebound higher each time.

To others, the confusion, complexity, and uncertainty that run deep within the journey of life didn't appear to apply to Susan. Her commitment to unselfishness and devoted capacity to be at the side of others when needed obscured the observations of those closest to Susan, making it difficult to see how the uneven topography of her life's journey altered and disrupted the landscape of her interior world.

At her core, she felt incomplete and damaged. While enormously self-disciplined, liked by nearly everyone, and tenacious in her pursuit of countless life goals, Susan was also deeply lonely. At her most private and primitive level, Susan felt unlovable.

The basic blueprint of human psychological functioning involves being driven to enjoy the positive things in life, while minimizing the ones that are less pleasant, more unfavorable, and just plain negative. Some of us are better than others at pulling this off.

We know that truly bad parenting can have a strong negative effect on everything that you rely upon to have a good life, reach your potential, and live happily ever after. Just the same, Susan flourished, despite her birth mother's drug addiction and decision to place her up for adoption; regardless of her adopted mother's mental breakdown and moving out of and far away from the family home—irrespective of the heavy guilt she carries for believing she caused her adopted mother to run away. Just as inexplicable, despite her husband's romantic epiphany, a revelation that broke her heart and shattered their togetherness, Susan emerged undeterred. Or so it seemed.

While bad things happen to everyone, Susan has received more than her fair share. Yet, even though the misfortune she experienced over the course of her life has been distressing and agonizing, Susan never seemed to be openly bothered.

To a weaker person, such life experiences could have been soul crushing. But to Susan, she never lost the spring in her step. From the perspective of her friends and colleagues, she bounced back from everything, every time. This begs the question, what is Susan's secret? How did she ostensibly transcend the existential injuries thrust upon her? Was she born with a bulletproof temperament? Did she learn that since no one can be trusted to only trust herself?

One thing that's remained broadly consistent across Susan's life journey is her positive self-concept. Like everyone, Susan grappled during moments of confusion, upset, and disappointment. But Susan always liked being Susan, and it showed. Not in an over-the-top, pathologically narcissistic, look-at-me fashion but with steadiness and firmness of character.

What's more, she's been fortunate to have people around her throughout her life who have reflected her positivity when she achieved, accomplished, or just beamed naturally. These timely and authentic reflections were keystone for Susan in developing a sense of internalized security and emotional stability. In turn, her healthy self-esteem provided a comforting buffer against setbacks and strengthened her capacity to tolerate distress and prosper from failure.

Amazing as she is, being human, Susan struggles uniquely within the interior of her being. Under the surface, Susan's self-reflections are complex and contradictory. In her head, she knows she's competent, bright, social, and attractive enough. She takes pride in her independence, positive attitude, strength of will, and ability to adjust quickly during challenging times.

At the same time, she also knows what nobody else knows, that the closer people get to her, the more likely they are to walk away and leave her feeling fragmented and flawed. What Susan can't figure out is why she's not allowed to have a connection with a life partner, one that's stable and predictable. One that doesn't end badly. She hungers for a relationship with an intimate partner who is secure and daring enough to walk alongside her during the tough times, to engage in the types of difficult conversations that clear the air and make things better, and to remain committed as things break down so that, together, she can break through her preoccupation with not being good enough.

For Susan, when she examines her upbringing and relationship history, she finds herself feeling curiously detached, as if what happened didn't necessarily happen to her but all around her.

In her half-dreamed and half-remembered thinking, Susan waits to be discovered—not for her attributes or accomplishments that are out there for anyone to see but for who she is and for who she has always craved to become. She needs help. She's ready, willing, and believes herself to be able. It's the waiting that hurts.

Let's walk through a mind rule checklist for Susan and see how the rules apply.

The mind self-regulates. Susan has mastered the perseverance necessary to not give up; she knows the importance of being patient, that, at times, slow is fast enough; and she's highly skilled at coping with life's unsolvable problems.

The mind is a pattern detector. This mind rule more than any other trips Susan up, given her series of interpersonal body blows.

The mind has a low pain threshold. Susan has endured through some of life's most difficult challenges, has answered back gracefully to the twinges of relational discomfort, and views herself to be more responsive than reactive, more curious than confident, but remains immensely cautious and tentative around matters of the heart.

The mind is often approximately correct and absolutely wrong. Susan's deep, little secret is knowing that she must be unlovable, unwanted, and undesirable; this secret has come to dominate her negative thinking that there may not be someone out there just for her.

Susan's okay with being alone. She learned long ago the power of solitude and how such a complete state of privacy keeps her out of harm's way. The composite of being discarded by her biological maker; being swooped up into a ready-made family, only to have her stand-in mother step out; and having her most-trusted intimate partner in her early adult years prove untrustworthy cultivated into Susan a type of high-speed readiness for anything, no matter how unbearable and unexpected.

Susan's not anxious or depressed, and she never has been. But she does, at times, feel strangely detached. When life slows down and she's not finishing a project or trying to set a new personal record of some kind, she sees herself as a misfit. Getting along with everyone but ending up with no one creates confusion for Susan and causes her to ponder her true value.

Although she has grown accustomed to being separate from others, it is the degree to which she feels separated that, at times, causes her to feel unidentified, unnoticed, tentative, and unsteady.

Susan's sense of detachment hinders her in becoming the person she believes she was always meant to be.

Susan will triumph. The bright light within her guides her cleverly. She's resilient, self-disciplined, and tenacious. Her capacity for being unusually driven coupled with her tone for authenticity allows her agency to outmaneuver any trace of victimhood.

As her powers of mind increase with improved clarity about how several mind rules explain and foster her insecurity and have caused seeds of self-doubt to take root, Susan's penchant for carving out her identity will flourish. Her zest for life is too appealing and inviting for her to not find the partnership in life she needs, wants, desires, and deserves.

Susan's default mode, the one that has kept her lifted from moving into darkness, is her penchant for frequently wanting to be the person she really is. We can all benefit by following in the footsteps of someone like Susan. She shines, not effortlessly but with the type of intentional effort needed to remain above and beyond the relational gravity that pulls some of us under and keeps many more of us trapped in the complex and confusing ecosystem of our past.

Becoming a Mind Reader

Something that is well known but rarely considered in daily life is that perception reigns supreme. This means that the way you perceive something determines what you know or believe to be true. In this way, your perception, and your truth meld together and become one. Yet the truth of what you see may be different, sometimes dramatically so, from reality or the way the world really is.

Notwithstanding this curious phenomenon, everything starts with how you perceive something; how you make sense of a perplexing situation, how you judge the accuracy of an overheard comment, and how you choose to respond all hinge on your perception.

The phrase *what you see is what you get* comes to mind. But, in your mind, what you *see* is really a reflection of what you've experienced before. To your mind, the past is always present. In this way, your mind may be playing tricks on you.

The life lesson here is that how you discern the appearance of something, and its actual existence are not necessarily identical. What you see and how you interpret what you've seen, for instance, colors your perception of what's really in front of you. Consequently, existence is dependent upon interpretation, and interpretation is entangled in what you've experienced throughout your life, both consciously and unconsciously. Accordingly, perception is an imaginative and discriminating process that reflects your experiences across time and situations that you determine to be relevant.

When your mind plays tricks on you, you can rest assured that this is at least partially due to the notion of perception and interpretation being inseparable. Further, when combined, the net result is an assignment of meaning to your experience. And once meaning has been attached to a life experience, it becomes anchored in your biology and biography.

Perception, interpretation, and meaning—this is how your beliefs are created. You experience something. You make sense of what you've seen or heard. This interpretation, in turn, serves as the foundation upon which you assign meaning to your experience. If what you've experienced is meaningful enough, it becomes a revered point of view. If asked about your experience, you now have an opinion. If your opinion is important enough, you will state your viewpoint with conviction, which is another way of saying attitude. Your attitude, therefore, reflects the intersection of conviction and resourcefulness.

One last trailing thought. Your mind leaps from theory to practice at lightning speed. A hard truth is that your mind knows what it likes and dislikes and relies heavily on this emotional data, much of the time, outside of your awareness. Since your mind is designed to free itself from the unpleasant impact of what has happened in the past, the strategic role played by your mind is to remain astutely aware when similar events may happen again.

In this way, more often than imagined, your mind may be talking you out of doing things that may bring you joy and happiness, such as raising your hand in class to answer a question, asking a person out on a first date, talking to your boss about a pay increase, or signing up for your first marathon.

The challenge for you is to learn how to be open-minded and not blindly controlled by your dispirited past. Or, stated more directly, the task at hand is to accomplish the art of mind control by improving your mastery of being in control of your mind as opposed to your mind controlling you.

This psychological swap involves being intentional in your actions, curious about your cognitive and emotional back talk, and flexible in the way you approach and dance with life's unexpected twists and turns. The orchestration of these three mindsets, when intertwined with your authentic way of being, provides you the freedom and choice of getting what you need, want, desire, and deserve. Now you've learned what it takes to move in the direction of becoming the person you were always meant to be.

As a final point, bring to your mind as often as possible what Picasso wisely stated, "Learn the rules like a pro, so you can break them like an artist." Thank you, Pablo, for summing up what the spirit of mind rules is all about.